(List continued overleaf)

Further titles are in preparation

Please note that a sister series, *Social History in Perspecti ve*, is now available. It covers the key topics in social, cultural and religious history.

British History in Perspective
Series Standing Order ISBN 0–333–69331–0
You can receive future titles in this series as they are published by placing a standing order. Please contact your bookseller or, in case of difficulty, write to us at the address below with your name and address, the title of the series and the ISBN quoted above.

Customer Services Department, Macmillan Distribution Ltd
Houndmills, Basingstoke, Hampshire RG21 6XS, England

CHARLES I

MICHAEL B. YOUNG

First published 1997 by
MACMILLAN PRESS LTD
Houndmills, Basingstoke, Hampshire RG21 6XS
and London
Companies and representatives
throughout the world

ISBN 0–333–60135–1 hardcover
ISBN 0–333–60136–X paperback

A catalogue record for this book is available
from the British Library.

This book is printed on paper suitable for recycling and
made from fully managed and sustained forest sources.

10   9   8   7   6   5   4   3   2   1
06   05   04   03   02   01   00   99   98   97

Typeset by EXPO Holdings, Malaysia

Printed in Hong Kong

Published in the United States of America 1997 by
ST. MARTIN'S PRESS, INC.,
Scholarly and Reference Division
175 Fifth Avenue, New York, N.Y. 10010

ISBN 0–312–16515–3 cloth
ISBN 0–312–16516–1 paperback

CONTENTS

ACKNOWLEDGEMENTS

I am profoundly grateful to Jeremy Black for the invitation to write this book. It was the perfect project at the perfect time, and I cannot thank him enough for giving me the opportunity. It has been a real pleasure working with Macmillan Press. I especially appreciate the professionalism of Vanessa Graham, Simon Winder and Judy Marshall. As always, I am indebted to Maija Jansson for her many favours and invaluable assistance at the Yale Center for Parliamentary History. I am also grateful to two colleagues who read parts of the manuscript and gave me excellent suggestions. Johann Sommerville commented on chapter 2, and Caroline Hibbard commented on chapters 3 and 4. I have profited greatly from their comments, though of course they are not responsible for what I have ended up saying.

A book of this sort, surveying the current state of scholarship in a field, is especially indebted to all the many authors who have contributed to the field. In my effort to assess this previous work, I hope readers will find that I have been as free with my praise as my criticism. I hope this is particularly true regarding the work of Conrad Russell. Some years ago Professor Russell and J. H. Hexter, an unlikely combination to be sure, gave me critical support and encouragement which I will never forget.

To My Parents

INTRODUCTION

'I do plead for the liberties of the people of England more than you do', King Charles I told his accusers. But there was no dissuading the makeshift court that had been assembled to engineer his execution. It took only a week for the judges to announce their predetermined verdict: 'that he, the said Charles Stuart, as a tyrant, traitor, murderer, and public enemy to the good people of this nation, shall be put to death by the severing of his head from his body'. Thus it was that on a cold January day in 1649, King Charles laid his head on the block, gave the signal to his executioner, and was beheaded with one blow of an axe in full public view. The crowd that had gathered for the spectacle did not burst out in cheers. A young man who stood among them reported only 'such a groan as I never heard before, and desire I may never hear again'.[1]

It has never been easy for King Charles I to get a fair trial, but now is as opportune a time as any. The past two decades have witnessed a veritable deluge of new works about early Stuart politics. While these new works have caused excitement, they have also caused confusion. It has not always been clear how one work relates to another or how, in general, this new scholarship relates to older scholarship. More importantly for our purposes, it has not always been clear what the net effect of all this new scholarship is on the reputation of the king. The present book attempts to dispel this confusion. It guides the reader through recent literature about Charles, clarifies the relationship between one work and another, and assesses the extent to which new scholarship has improved upon old. This analysis is carried out, however, within a narrative framework which should make it more interesting and intelligible. The overall organisation of the book is chronological, and each chapter begins with a brief overview of events. Along the way there is enough background and explanation to meet the needs of readers not already well acquainted with the subject. We thus tell the story of King Charles I's reign while simultaneously assessing the different interpretations

1

which historians have attempted to impose on that story. Our goal – as the title of this series, 'British History in Perspective', suggests – has been to put Charles back into perspective by examining his life in relation to what historians have been saying about that life. A book of this nature cannot have the uninterrupted dramatic drive of a biography, but it can engage the reader at a more advanced level where the subject matter of history and the creative intellect of the historian meet.

The confusion about Charles I is a fairly recent phenomenon. Toward the end of the nineteenth century, the great historian S. R. Gardiner wrote a multi-volume history of Charles's reign that was so detailed and thorough it remained the standard authority for nearly 100 years. Writing in the Victorian era, it was natural for Gardiner to attribute the failures of Charles's reign chiefly to defects in the king's own character. As Gardiner explained, Charles worked hard and paid close attention to the minutest details of business. 'For government in the higher sense', however, 'he had no capacity.' To begin with, Charles did not view the world realistically. He 'looked upon the whole world through a distorting lens'. He 'refused to look facts in the face' or 'to subordinate that which was only desirable to that which was possible'. As a result, Charles was inclined to misread a situation and overestimate what he was capable of achieving. The problem was compounded because, once Charles adopted a plan, he was 'obstinate in refusing to abandon' it. Given these predispositions, Charles naturally encountered plenty of criticism, but he showed no capacity to absorb this criticism or learn from his mistakes. He 'had no power of stepping out of himself to see how his actions looked to other people'. He was 'uncompromising' and 'did not like to be contradicted'. He displayed a 'persistent determination to ignore all opinions divergent from his own'. Instead of adopting a conciliatory stance, Charles's characteristic reaction was 'to relapse into silence, to fall back upon his insulted dignity, and to demand' submission. One of Charles's worst habits was his penchant for dividing people 'into two simple classes – into those who agreed with him, and those who did not'. He combined 'blindness, narrow-mindedness, and obstinacy... with an exaggerated sense of the errors of his opponents'. All of these qualities made it likely that Charles would provoke confrontations and then lack the deftness to escape from those confrontations without making matters worse. There was a final, perhaps fatal, obstacle to any amicable resolution where Charles was concerned: he could not be trusted. Deep down inside,

Charles lacked an 'elemental quality of veracity'. He 'gave and broke his promises'; he made 'promises never intended to be fulfilled'. He practised 'duplicity', used 'deception', and resorted to 'double-dealing'.[2] He was, to put it succinctly, a bad king.

Near the middle of the twentieth century, several historians, more or less inspired by Marxism, tried to replace Gardiner's Victorian emphasis on character with a more modern emphasis on impersonal socio-economic forces. The most famous episode in this effort was the 'gentry controversy', which promised a great deal more than it was able to deliver. Ultimately, it proved impossible to demonstrate that the political events of Charles's reign, particularly the outbreak of the Civil War, were byproducts of deeper socio-economic trans-formations. A prominent founder of this school of interpretation was R. H. Tawney, and its most brilliant exponent was Christopher Hill. Back in 1940 Hill confidently asserted that the English Revolution was 'a class war' and 'a great social movement like the French Revolution of 1789'.[3] Over time, however, Hill modified this crude Marxist formulation and developed greater appreciation for the complexity of history.[4] He attached increasing importance to the role of ideas and religion (particularly Puritanism); and he did not discount the personal role played by King Charles. In his popular textbook, *The Century of Revolution,* Hill listed the character of the king among the causes of the Civil War, and he elaborated: 'the King's high idea of his own station, his rigid inability to compromise in time, and his transparent dishonesty, made it impossible for him ever to have functioned as a constitutional monarch'.[5] Although Hill refined his position over time, he never stopped hoping for 'a new socio-economic interpretation'.[6] In Lawrence Stone, another major exponent of this approach, the disillusionment was more complete. His *Causes of the English Revolution 1529–1642* is sometimes described as a reassertion of the socio-economic interpretation, but a close reading of the book reveals a strong current of doubt running beneath the surface. In the opening chapter of his book Stone sur-veyed several social scientific theories of revolution, but he made very little effort to connect these to the actual revolution in England. In the balance of his book Stone dutifully rehashed the gentry con-troversy and offered numerous other sociological arguments, but he was forced again and again to admit: 'None of the polarities of feudal-bourgeois, employer-employee, rich-poor, rising-declining, county-parish gentry seem to have much relevance to what actually happened in the 1640s.' Stone started with the assumption that 'this is more than a mere rebellion against a particular king', but in fact the closer he got to the actual outbreak of Civil War, the more decisive seemed the 'misguided personal decisions', 'bottomless duplicity', and 'proven untrustworthiness' of King Charles. After the original publication of Stone's book, he came more and more to appreciate the king's personal responsibility. In a postscript added in 1985 Stone admitted that the importance he had attached to 'the folly, obstinacy and duplicity of Charles I in causing the catastrophe was if anything understated'. Charles was, as Stone now described him, 'a man who made every mistake in the book, and in consequence eventually brought disaster on himself and his country'.[7]

One positive effect of the gentry controversy was that it spawned a multitude of local studies. These studies shifted attention away from Charles and the court to the countryside, away from the centre to the localities. The authors of these studies had remarkably little to say about Charles. They traced the lives of numerous provincial gentry whose dominant concerns revolved around county politics instead of national politics. For Alan Everitt, a pioneer in this field, there was practically no national consciousness but only 'the localism of provincial people'. The county community was 'a strange and introverted society', and each county was 'a little self-centred kingdom on its own'.[8] Similarly, Thomas Barnes's early study of *Somerset 1625–1640* was over 300 pages long, but the index listed only fourteen references to King Charles. Where Barnes did refer to Charles, he took an astonishingly original approach. 'Few kings who have sat on England's throne and few ministers who have counselled them', wrote Barnes, 'appear to have been more genuinely desirous of the subjects' good than were Charles I and his principal counsellors.'[9] This line of argument might have led to a wholesale reassessment of Charles, but neither Barnes nor other local historians embarked on such a bold project. In subsequent local studies Charles remained a shadowy figure relegated to the background. Although Charles was a far less prominent figure in these local studies than he had been in earlier histories that emphasised the high politics of Parliament and the court, he still oddly remained the decisive figure: royal policies were repeatedly shown to be the moving force that stirred up local enmities and laid the groundwork for what John Morrill called *The Revolt of the Provinces*.[10]

A thoroughgoing reconsideration of King Charles did not occur until the development of 'revisionism'.[11] This ambiguous term is perhaps best defined by concrete examples, and we shall consider several of these in the following pages. At this point, however, it may help if we provide a general characterisation of two kinds of revisionism in the early Stuart period. The revisionism that had the greatest effect on the reputation of King Charles dealt chiefly with the politics of the 1620s and 1630s. Works of this sort clearly deserved to be called revisionist because they did attempt to 'revise' the longstanding interpretation of S. R. Gardiner (and his successors such as J. R. Tanner, G. M. Trevelyan, and Wallace Notestein). Gardiner and his successors were faulted for writing the history of this period as if events were leading inexorably towards Civil War (a teleological or Whig view) and for making critics of the Crown seem too modern and heroic. Revisionists concerned with the 1620s and 1630s questioned the whole concept of 'opposition' under Charles, and their work generally tended to cast the king himself in a more favourable light. This was truly revisionist.

Recent scholarship on the later years of Charles's reign, especially regarding the outbreak of the Civil War, is also sometimes referred to as 'revisionist', but here the label is less deserved. For people who still believed in the socio-economic interpretation of history (the followers of Tawney, Hill, and Stone), this new scholarship looked revisionist because it stressed short-term causes of the Civil War as opposed to long-term socio-economic causes. There were a surprising number of these diehard disciples still around who presumed their interpretation was being challenged. They labelled new work about the roots of the Civil War as 'revisionist', and the label has stuck. For the most part, however, the so-called revisionists of the Civil War period did not even bother to address the dead issues of the socio-economic school.[12] If one judges these historians against the real standard – that is the classic work of S. R. Gardiner – they appear less revisionist. Indeed they wrote detailed political narratives very similar to Gardiner's. What distinguished their work from Gardiner's was their emphasis on the accidental and unpredictable course of events, as opposed to his dramatic story of escalating conflict reaching its natural climax in the Civil War. They also told a more mundane story. In their version, faction, patronage, and self-interest were more important than high-sounding concepts like liberty and constitutional conflict. Most recently they have stressed the fact that Charles ruled over multiple kingdoms and the Civil War must therefore be viewed as a truly British, not just English, phenomenon. For the most part, however, revisionist work on the period surrounding the outbreak of Civil War has done more to

augment than dispute Gardiner's account. This is particularly true
with respect to King Charles. Recent historians of the Civil War may
be called revisionists for other reasons, but they have not revised the
traditional view of the king. Their portrait of Charles may be more
detailed, more complex, more finely nuanced than Gardiner's; but it
is still recognisably the same man. Consequently, as we shall see, it is
far more difficult to put Charles back into perspective in the 1620s
and 1630s (where differing viewpoints abound) than it is in the
1640s (where, despite other heated controversies, there is general
agreement about Charles).

Turning from this general characterisation of revisionism as a
movement to the specific work of individual historians, we can see
more precisely how King Charles's reputation has been affected.
One of the first historians to call for a revised perspective on early
Stuart politics was G. R. Elton. Although his own great expertise lay
in the Tudor century, Elton began in the 1960s to publish a series of
provocative essays on 'The Stuart Century'. In these pioneering
essays Elton anticipated many of the themes that would be associated with the revisionist approach to early Stuart politics: the Civil
War was not inevitable (in Elton's famous phrase, there was no 'high
road' to Civil War); too much attention had been given to conflict in
early Stuart Parliaments; too little attention had been given to
harmony, shared assumptions, and the routine work of Parliaments;
and the Civil War was more a breakdown of government than a
Puritan or social revolution. On the question *why* the government
broke down, however, Elton's answer was decidedly old-fashioned:
'the failure of Charles's government ... was conditioned by the inability of the king and his ministers to operate any political system'.
The system of government did break down. 'But it did not break
down because it had been unworkable from the first.' Rather: 'It
broke down because the early Stuart governments could not manage
or persuade, because they were incompetent'.[13] Thus Elton called
for a radically altered view of early Stuart politics but not a radically
different view of King Charles.

Conrad Russell took the next logical step and quickly became the
pre-eminent revisionist of the early Stuart period. Russell agreed
with Elton that traditional parliamentary history had exaggerated
constitutional conflict and assumed the inevitability of the Civil War,
but he parted company with Elton on the subject of Charles. In a
pathbreaking article published in 1976, Russell declared, 'it is
impossible to follow Professor Elton in laying all the blame on

incompetent kingship'. Russell was not concerned in this article with Charles's competence or incompetence. The only adjective he attached to Charles was 'poverty-stricken'. The article was not about Charles but about the structures, institutions, processes, and circumstances within which he operated. Russell portrayed the Crown and Parliament as 'two declining institutions, both overtaken by the functional breakdown of English administration'. One major underlying cause of that breakdown was the increasing gap between the cost of government and royal revenue. Another major cause was the 'permanent tension between the centre and the localities'. It was these impersonal, structural problems that undermined parliamentary politics, turning what Elton called the 'point of contact' into what Russell called the 'point of friction'.[14] In 1979 Russell elaborated on these themes in his landmark book entitled *Parliaments and English Politics 1621–1629.* There Russell laid particular emphasis on the role played by war in exacerbating the problems of early Stuart government and driving it to the point of breakdown. Russell's overall conclusion was that the difficulties Charles encountered in these years were 'first and foremost, not the difficulties of a bad King, but the difficulties of a nation reluctantly at war'.[15]

On one front, then, revisionism made Charles look better by emphasising the daunting circumstances he faced: inadequate financial resources, structural weaknesses in the system of government, and an antiquated administration that tottered on the brink of 'functional breakdown', particularly under the strains of war. How could anyone have made this shaky system run smoothly? On yet another front, revisionists made Charles look better by taking a more cynical view of his contemporary antagonists. J. N. Ball, for example, took a more realistic view of Sir John Eliot, transforming the heroic martyr for liberty into an inept tactician who prevented an accommodation from developing between Charles and his Parliaments at the end of the 1620s.[16] Similarly, Anthony Fletcher made John Pym seem the wrecker of a later period. As Fletcher told the story, Pym and a handful of associates who shared his warped fears of a popish plot drove the Long Parliament into 'a war that nobody wanted'.[17] Members of Parliament in general were made to seem less like principled men fighting over lofty constitutional issues and more like petty politicians fighting over money and power.[18] They resented the Duke of Buckingham's monopoly of office.[19] They used Parliaments as opportunities to settle personal grudges and pursue their factional rivalries. They failed to comprehend the financial needs of the

Crown. They were parochial men. Their foremost loyalty was to their counties, and they were paralysed by fear of offending their constituents back home. Far from seeking a larger voice in national affairs, they avoided responsibility.[20] Thus Parliament began to look, not like the seedbed of liberty, but like a hotbed of personal motives, ignorance, and obstructionism. How could Charles be expected to govern effectively when his work was constantly undermined by these factious and irresponsible Parliaments?

Charles did not have to be glorified. He simply looked better by comparison when Parliament and its members were cut down to size. Works published at the end of the 1970s had harsh words for Parliament. Russell insinuated that Parliament was 'a negative, irresponsible, obstructionist, and vindictive body'.[21] Kevin Sharpe was equally contemptuous. 'A disorganized, divided, and undisciplined House of Commons', he charged, 'proved unable to give counsel for the governance of the realm.'[22] However, the prize for Parliament-bashing must go to J. P. Kenyon. In his textbook for the period, Kenyon ridiculed early Stuart Parliaments, describing them as 'frenetically excited' and subject to 'dizzying changes of mood and outbursts of violent emotion'. Kenyon scolded his fellow historians for treating 'Parliament's excesses with the fond indulgence of a psychotherapist towards a schizoid juvenile delinquent'. It was erroneous, wrote Kenyon, to believe 'that the political struggles of the seventeenth century revolved around nineteenth-century notions like personal liberty, freedom of speech or constitutional government'. MPs were not champions of liberty. Sir John Eliot, for one, was 'unbalanced' and his behaviour in Parliament was 'indefensible'.[23] Finally, in a heated exchange with J. H. Hexter in the pages of the *Times Literary Supplement*, Kenyon described Parliament as 'a parcel of self-centred and largely ignorant lawyers and landowners, to whom "liberty" meant little more than the freedom to do what you willed with those below you without interference from those above you'.[24]

It was getting difficult to tell the good guys from the bad guys. Indeed, one of the most salutary effects of revisionism was to destroy the simplistic assumption that there were two mutually exclusive 'sides' in early Stuart politics. This simply was not the way contemporaries viewed politics. It is anachronistic to impose the concept of adversarial politics on a political culture where it did not yet exist.[25] It was erroneous to think in terms of Crown *versus* Parliament. Parliament was not a monolithic bloc, many of its members were dependants of the Crown, and none of its members would have thought of themselves as standing in opposition to the Crown.[26] Likewise, it was erroneous to view early Stuart politics as a contest between 'court' and 'country'.[27] These were not polar opposites; they cannot even be entirely differentiated from one another. Consequently, when a man like Sir Thomas Wentworth who had been a leading critic of royal policies at the end of the 1620s became a leading minister of the Crown in the 1630s, he had not gone over to the other side, least of all from the good 'country' side to the bad 'court' side.[28] Nor were there sharp ideological differences in the politics of early Stuart England. Commenting on the 1620s, Russell observed that 'it is remarkable how little ideological division developed during these years'.[29] If contemporaries did not view politics in adversarial terms, if they did not see themselves as belonging exclusively to either court or country, if they did not belong to one ideological camp or the other, then this necessarily cast Charles in a better light. He was no longer the focus of opposition, the chief protagonist in a battle between competing ideologies, the villain in a moral tale about the struggle for liberty against tyranny.

If there was any one villain in the early years of Charles's reign, one might have thought it was the infamous Duke of Buckingham. However, in 1981 Roger Lockyer produced the most truly revisionist work of the decade: *Buckingham: The Life and Political Career of George Villiers, First Duke of Buckingham 1592–1628*. In this densely documented book, Lockyer completely altered the traditional view of Buckingham. Instead of being a political lightweight who ruined the early years of Charles's reign, Buckingham was apparently a conscientious administrator, courageous leader, and visionary statesman who happily forgave his enemies and struggled valiantly to prevent the Habsburgs from overrunning all of Europe. In Lockyer's view, 'there was not a great deal wrong with Buckingham's policies other than the money with which to carry them into effect', and Parliament turned against him merely because he was 'the personification of their own neuroses'.[30] Lockyer's only concern was to exonerate Buckingham, but his work tended to vindicate Charles as well. The two men were inseparable political allies united in a common policy until the Duke was felled by an assassin's knife. If Lockyer could succeed in improving Buckingham's reputation, therefore, it would necessarily improve Charles's reputation too.

While most of the work during the last two decades that enhanced Charles's reputation did so only implicitly, a few did so explicitly.

Stephen Orgel, Roy Strong, and R. Malcolm Smuts, for example, explored Charles's contributions to the formation of a court culture that embodied the highest ideals of art and politics.[31] Martin J. Havran found 'ample reason to amend to some degree the heavily negative interpretation of his life and reign'. Havran praised Charles for his broad-mindedness towards Roman Catholicism. He described Charles as 'a gentle, humble, shy, compassionate, and scholarly man' who won the respect of his contemporaries through his 'deep spirituality, quiet strength of character, and equanimity under stress'.[32] By far the most extensive defence of Charles, however, came from Kevin Sharpe. In two early articles that anticipated his later book on the subject, Sharpe took a distinctly sympathetic view of Charles, portraying him first as the victim of bad counsel in the 1620s and then as an earnest reformer in the 1630s who worked hard to foster order and virtue.[33]

As a result of all the foregoing works, by the early 1980s it looked as if Charles's reputation might take a permanent turn for the better. But then came another wave of new works that gravitated back towards Gardiner's negative estimation. Local studies by William Hunt and Ann Hughes were less parochial than their predecessors; Charles figured more prominently in their exploration of an alienated countryside.[34] Richard Cust's study of *The Forced Loan and English Politics* uncovered the darker side of Charles who turned out to be a vindictive and suspicious king obsessed with loyalty.[35] L. J. Reeve's *Charles I and the Road to Personal Rule* depicted an even more sinister and autocratic king.[36] Both authors suggested that Charles was paranoid. An anthology edited by Richard Cust and Ann Hughes rediscovered *Conflict in Early Stuart England*.[37] One chapter in that anthology by Christopher Thompson strongly argued for the 'orthodox rather than revisionist interpretation' of the king's dealings with Parliament.[38] On another front, Caroline Hibbard, Nicholas Tyacke, and Julian Davies rewrote the religious history of the period; and though they disagreed in other important respects, they all heaped blame on Charles for fanning the fires of religious controversy.[39] Other authors exposed Charles's mismanagement of Scotland. In *Charles I and the Making of the Covenanting Movement 1625–1641*, Allan I. Macinnes portrayed Charles as a dogmatic, self-righteous, and inept absentee monarch who displayed 'crass insensitivity to Scottish sensibilities'.[40] Similarly, Peter Donald's *An Uncounselled King: Charles I and the Scottish Troubles, 1637–41* placed much of the blame for the Scottish crisis on Charles, who 'showed a staggering unwillingness to listen to moderate judgement'.[41] On a much more sweeping scale, J. P. Sommerville's book about *Politics and Ideology in England 1603–1640* attempted to re-establish the importance of competing political visions and the reality of opposition in early Stuart politics. As Sommerville saw it, 'ideological conflict is a blindingly obvious feature of early Stuart history', and Charles played the central role in precipitating that conflict.[42] Finally, when it came to the Civil War, the prodigious work of John Morrill interpreted that event as an explosive combination of religious zeal and a king who was not only incompetent but 'inaccessible, glacial, self-righteous, deceitful'.[43]

Meanwhile, Conrad Russell did not stand still. He continued to downplay the role of constitutional or ideological conflict, but his opinion of King Charles proved more susceptible to change. As Russell turned his attention from the 1620s to the events surrounding the outbreak of the Civil War, he took an increasingly critical view of Charles. This negative view first appeared in a series of articles Russell published during the 1980s. Russell still sympathised with Charles in so far as he was handicapped by inadequate revenue and the difficulty of governing three disparate kingdoms, but the king's faults now came to the foreground. Charles was a ruler who practically invited resistance. He failed to see political reality, refused to recognise the limits of the possible, compromised only under duress, broke his promises, and habitually resorted to force.[44] How far Russell had moved back toward S. R. Gardiner's opinion of Charles was finally evident when he published his two major books on the outbreak of the Civil War: *The Causes of the English Civil War* in 1990 and *The Fall of the British Monarchies* in 1991.[45] To be sure, Russell's approach to these years was far from reductionist. He explored an immensely complex web of circumstances, but the trail kept leading inexorably back to Charles. In one place, for example, Russell argued that Civil War resulted from the conjunction of seven key 'events and non-events', yet he observed that 'nothing except perhaps Charles I can be likely to have been a cause of all seven of these'. Obviously Charles was not 'the sole cause of the Civil War', but he did appear to be the *sine qua non*. In the end, Russell concluded, 'I find civil war without him almost impossible to imagine'.[46]

The tide appeared to be turning completely against Charles, but then Kevin Sharpe's massive study of *The Personal Rule of Charles I* appeared. Sharpe's book was a throwback to the revisionism of the 1970s. Unrepentant and unpersuaded by more recent studies, Sharpe persisted in the themes that dominated his earlier articles. As

Sharpe represented him, Charles was driven into the personal rule of the 1630s by the failings of Parliament, and he thereupon undertook an ambitious programme to reform church and state that was far more successful and generated far less resentment than previous historians allowed. If Charles lacked the aptitude of a politician, Sharpe argued, so much the better. Unlike most politicians, Charles was a man 'of profound conscience and deep principle' who steadfastly adhered to his convictions.[47] One cannot help but admire the magnitude and audacity of Sharpe's defence of Charles, amounting to nearly 1000 pages and appearing almost simultaneously alongside Russell's two more orthodox books. Both historians displayed an awesome command of the sources. Both wrote enormously detailed and compelling narratives. Where the character of Charles I was concerned, however, they could not both be right.

Where are we left, then, with respect to Charles? Despite the flurry of monographs or perhaps because of them, no one has yet attempted the daunting task of writing a whole new biography of the king.[48] That leaves us with a series of scholarly but piecemeal studies produced over the last two decades, each of which focuses on only an isolated period or aspect of his reign. Furthermore, many of these studies make little reference to one another or to previous secondary literature. This mode of operation makes it difficult for readers, even knowledgeable readers, to see how one work relates to another and to judge which is superior. A trend back toward Gardiner's low opinion of Charles is evident in recent literature, culminating in Russell's two formidable books. But how is this trend to be reconciled with earlier revisionist work on the 1620s, including Russell's own, that portrayed Charles in a more positive light, and with Sharpe's tenaciously favourable portrait of the 1630s? Clearly this is an opportune time – indeed an urgent time – to evaluate recent literature, weigh the relative merits of competing views, and put Charles back into historical perspective. Among the questions we will have to ask are the following. Did Charles create the circumstances of his own ruin, or was he a victim of circumstance? Did Charles change from one decade to the next, or can we find enduring qualities in his character throughout his reign? In the 1620s did he blunder into war and then mismanage the war effort, or was he urged into war by a Parliament whose subsequent lack of support sabotaged any hope of success? In the 1630s did he foster virtue, honour, and efficiency; or did he alienate sizeable numbers of his subjects through his domineering religious and fiscal policies? Was

Charles chiefly to blame for the outbreak of the Civil War? Was he overwhelmed by the inherent difficulty of ruling multiple kingdoms, or did his own actions transform a difficult situation into an impossible one? Did his religious policies provoke the last of Europe's religious wars, or was he the victim of zealous Puritanism, rabid anti-Catholicism, or a handful of desperate politicians like Pym who demonised the king in order to save themselves? How well did he acquit himself during the Civil War? Why did he fail to come to terms with the victors? And in the end, to put it bluntly, did Charles get what he deserved?

1

PRIOR COMMITMENTS

King Charles I did not begin his reign with a clean slate. When he ascended to the throne in 1625, he was already saddled with two huge liabilities – the Duke of Buckingham and war – and these liabilities bedevilled him for the next four years. The first step toward putting Charles into perspective is to understand how he had acquired these liabilities, and more especially to consider how far they were liabilities of his own making.

Buckingham

It was improbable, to say the least, that Charles would befriend Buckingham, who was the notorious favourite of his father, King James VI and I. Every indication we have is that Charles abhorred his father's lifestyle and was determined to be as unlike his father as possible. Kevin Sharpe observed that Charles 'was in many respects a complete contrast to his father'; and Thomas Cogswell called him a 'mirror opposite' of his father.[1] Whereas James presided over a raucous, disorderly court, Charles would make his court a model of decorum and order. Whereas James was a coarse man who drank to excess, Charles would prove to be an abstemious man of refined tastes and one of the greatest connoisseurs of art in his day. Whereas James was sociable and ebullient, Charles would be taciturn and private. Whereas James was alienated from his wife and engaged in a series of intimate relationships with male favourites, Charles and his wife would have an ideal marriage. Historians have not sufficiently appreciated the degree to which Charles intentionally defined himself as the opposite of his father. It was not just that Charles happened to be the opposite of his father; he consciously set out to make himself the opposite of his father.

If Charles so abhorred his father's ways, why did he befriend his father's most famous favourite? To answer that question, we have to know more about the emotional tenor of his early life. Charles was born in Scotland in 1600, three years before his father succeeded to the English throne. Charles began life as a lonely and sick child who had difficulty learning to talk and walk. His mother, Anne of Denmark, has been reduced to a misogynist's caricature by historians. Maurice Ashley actually called her a 'dumb blond'.[2] In reality, though, Anne was an intelligent woman who wanted to take a more personal role in the raising of her children than she was allowed to. Anne fought fiercely to keep her children by her side, but James insisted that Charles be removed from his immediate family and raised by guardians.[3] When James inherited the English throne in 1603, the whole family moved to England except Charles who was left behind for another year to improve his health before undertaking the arduous journey southward. He was nearly four years old when he rejoined his family in England. What made Charles's childhood even worse was that he grew up in the shadow of his far more glamorous older brother, Prince Henry. Henry was widely admired except by King James who kept a jealous eye on his popular heir. Many people hoped that Henry would resume the Elizabethan war against Catholic Spain. As Roy Strong observed, the youthful prince became 'the focus of a major popular cult ... the epitome of militant Protestant chivalry'. Henry was enthusiastically grooming himself to play this heroic role when he died unexpectedly in 1612.[4] Despite his public image, Henry appears to have been a nasty older brother for Charles, lording his superior position over the younger boy and taunting him. What all this adds up to quite simply is a precarious and unhappy childhood; one need not agree with all the tenets of psychoanalysis to believe that it explains a great deal about Charles's later behaviour, including his tell-tale stutter.

Charles was desperate for a friend. Coincidentally, as the health of King James deteriorated, Buckingham became more conscious of his own need to befriend Charles or face the prospect of losing everything when his royal benefactor died. Understandably, there was tension between Charles and Buckingham at first, since they were both in a way rival suitors for the king's affection. On one occasion

Charles was reported to have sprayed water on Buckingham. Judging from his later repudiation of James's sexual mores, Charles must have had at least some inkling of the relationship between his father and Buckingham. But it is likely that the physical side of that relationship diminished over time (accelerated perhaps by the king's declining health and Buckingham's marriage in 1620); and that would help explain why Charles became less hostile toward Buckingham. James also took an active hand in this reconciliation; he very much wanted his son and his favourite to like each other. In a letter that he wrote to James several years later, Buckingham referred to 'Baby Charles, whom you likewise by your good offices made my friend', and he said that James 'first planted me in your Baby Charles's good opinion'.[5] It was certainly in Buckingham's best interests to get along well with the heir to the throne. As Buckingham himself said, 'I am suspected to look more to the rising sun, than my Maker'.[6] Charles found, too, that if he wanted to stay on the good side of his father, Buckingham could be a useful ally.

Most historians characterise the friendship between Charles and Buckingham as brotherly. Charles Carlton, who has done most by far to explore the psychology of Charles's childhood, described Buckingham as 'a surrogate elder brother', a 'substitute for the elder brother he had lost six years before'.[7] Kevin Sharpe agreed that Buckingham played 'the role of the charismatic elder sibling Charles had lost after the death of his radiant brother Henry'.[8] Roger Lockyer concurred that Charles found in Buckingham 'not only the company he had hitherto lacked but also a replacement for his lost elder brother'.[9] Anyone who has lived unhappily in the shadow of an older sibling may well question the plausibility of this interpretation. Charles may have missed Prince Henry, but there is no reason to believe he was eager to rush out and replace him. Charles needed somebody who would make him feel better about himself and build up his self-esteem, not tear it down, as Henry had. This is the emotional need that Buckingham filled. He helped Charles to pass through his youthful identity crisis. He gave the young prince the necessary confidence to stand up to his father, even eventually to prevail over his father on the question of war. Buckingham became Charles's alter ego. Together they were stronger than either one alone could have been. That is how Charles entered early adulthood thinking and acting in concert with Buckingham, and only the great favourite's violent death would force Charles to go it alone.

Rex Bellicosus

Charles came to the throne already allied to the death with Buckingham. He also came to the throne joined with Buckingham in a fierce determination to wage war. Why? There was pressure on Charles to take up the cause of militant international Protestantism after the death of Prince Henry, and this role might naturally have appealed to a young man. Judging from his coolness toward this crusade later in his life, however, it is doubtful that he would have embraced it at this point had it not been for other influences. Dearer to Charles's heart was the plight of his sister Elizabeth, whose marriage to Frederick, the Elector of the Palatinate, placed her at the perilous centre of the Thirty Years War when it broke out in 1618. War also appealed to Charles as a way of declaring his independence and difference from his father. King James was a pacifist who abhorred violence in general and war in particular. One of his first accomplishments as king had been to end the protracted Elizabethan war with Spain. He had no interest in reviving that war, even after the outbreak of the Thirty Years War, even after his daughter and her husband were driven from their homeland. For his devotion to peace, James was styled *Rex Pacificus*. In this respect, too, Charles was determined to be different from his father. Finally, there was Charles's own emotional make-up. As we will have ample opportunity to observe, he was quick to take offence, particularly when his will was thwarted or his honour questioned. His style of politics was confrontational. He was reported to have said early in life, 'I cannot defend a bad nor yield in a good cause'.[10] While the sense of integrity implied by that statement is commendable, it also betrays an 'unctuous rectitude', to use L. J. Reeve's phrase.[11] Charles tended to assume the righteousness of his own position and to be unyielding in its defence. All these qualities combined to make Charles a combative personality. It is a sobering fact to remember that he spent nearly half his reign at war – with Spain, with France, with his own subjects. As Bishop Goodman observed, 'Never man did desire wars more than King Charles'.[12] He was *Rex Bellicosus*.

When Charles made his first major appearance on the public scene in the Parliament of 1621, his belligerent nature was not yet in full evidence. It was later said of Charles that he had 'been bred in parliaments'.[13] The MP who made this statement (Sir Benjamin Rudyerd) meant it to imply that Charles could be expected to establish a good working relationship with Parliament. Charles's behaviour in 1621 gave some reason to be optimistic on this score. His manner in the House of Lords appeared to be circumspect, but the attitude he expressed in private toward the lower House of Commons revealed a more spiteful and pugnacious side of his personality. From his vantage point in the Lords, Charles disapproved of the 'unruly' Commons, and he confided in Buckingham that he wished King James would issue orders that 'such seditious fellows might be made an example to others'. He had spoken to members of the Privy Council on this matter, and they had agreed with him in general, 'only the sending of authority to set seditious fellows fast is of my adding'.[14] It was, unfortunately, all too typical of Charles to brand MPs with sedition and try to suppress them by force. It was also typical of Charles to assume that Parliament should provide money as a matter of course. When the Commons approved a grant of two subsidies in 1621, he judged it 'not so great a matter that the King need to be indulgent over them for it'.[15]

In 1621 it was not yet unambiguously clear where Charles and Buckingham stood on the subject of war. Whatever their true sentiments, they had to defer to King James. Under the influence of the Spanish ambassador Gondomar, James had been led to believe that he could regain the Palatinate for his daughter and son-in-law through mere diplomacy without having to fight. As his part of the bargain, however, James would have to agree to a marriage between Prince Charles and a Spanish (Catholic) princess. The Parliament of 1621 had tried to avert this horrible prospect by petitioning the king to marry Charles to a Protestant, but James and Charles were both irate at this attempted intrusion into the affairs of the royal family, and negotiations over the projected Spanish Match continued.

In 1623 Charles and Buckingham determined to bring negotiations to a conclusion by going to Spain in person. This was a terribly risky, even reckless, stratagem. King James desperately pleaded with his son and favourite not to go, but they refused to be dissuaded and, in effect, overruled the king. This event marked the beginning of the end for James. He had lost the initiative to Charles and Buckingham, and he had become too weak and emotionally dependent to stop them. What Charles and Buckingham did with their newfound power hardly inspired confidence. Rather than sailing to Spain in a fleet that would have afforded them sufficient supplies and protection, they set off secretly on horseback, sailed across the Channel, and then continued overland to Madrid by way of Paris. They travelled practically alone with false beards and false names

(Tom and John Smith). It must have been an exhilarating adventure for the two young men, but it was also a testimony to their immaturity and a near miracle that they arrived in Spain without having been robbed, captured and held for ransom, or worse. What they discovered upon their arrival, of course, was that the Spanish had no intention of concluding the marriage without obtaining major concessions from Charles, particularly regarding his religion. In negotiations that lasted several months, Charles and Buckingham came perilously close to making these concessions, although Charles appears to have thought he could later evade or stretch the meaning of some of these promises – a habit of mind that he would unfortunately carry to the grave. Both men were under considerable pressure to strike a deal lest they return to England empty-handed. Charles was further motivated by his personal desire for the Infanta. He embarrassed himself on more than one occasion by being too eager toward her, and the fact that she showed no reciprocal interest in him could only have deepened his sense of rejection. Gradually, it dawned upon Charles and Buckingham that they had exposed themselves to considerable danger and generally made fools of themselves with no real prospect of success. When they left Spain in September of 1623, they were filled with a new determination – to embark upon a war of revenge.

It is important to understand that Charles and Buckingham had decided upon war before they met the Parliament of 1624. When they returned from Spain, their objective was not to seek the advice and counsel of anyone but, rather, to manoeuvre King James and Parliament into embracing the course of action they had already decided upon. A few historians have found lofty justifications for this decision. Roger Lockyer, for example, alleged that Buckingham wanted war because in Spain 'he had been made forcibly aware of the very real dangers that the expansion of Habsburg power offered to the western world'. Through his experience in Spain, Buckingham had also come to the realisation that 'the best way in which to win concessions from a powerful, unscrupulous and arrogant enemy was by the sword'.[16] In a similar vein, Thomas Cogswell emphasised that Buckingham and Charles were motivated by their understanding of conditions on the continent where a series of stunning triumphs by Catholic Habsburg forces threatened to overwhelm the Protestant cause. In Cogswell's opinion, 'Charles and Buckingham's urgent press for intervention had much more to do with the radically altered balance of power than it did with their shabby treatment in Madrid'. It was only after their shabby treatment in Madrid, however, that Charles and Buckingham were sufficiently motivated to concoct a war plan; and even Cogswell conceded that 'the vindication of sullied honor figured prominently' in that plan.[17] Furthermore, although Buckingham eagerly assumed the role of international statesman, he was spurred on by domestic considerations. Concern for the future of the western world, no matter how sincere, was mingled with concern about his own personal future. The trip to Spain had not diminished Buckingham's favour with the king, who had elevated him from a marquis to a duke during the interval, and it had served as an intense bonding experience with Prince Charles. But it was also a foolhardy escapade that ended in ignominious failure and raised suspicions about Buckingham's loyalties. To avoid negative political repercussions, he had to show that, despite the protracted negotiations in Madrid, he was no friend of Catholicism or Spain. Leading the charge for war was his best hope of vindicating himself and turning the tables on his domestic enemies.[18]

Granted that political and diplomatic considerations strengthened the desire of Charles and Buckingham for war and enlarged the scope of the actual plans they made afterward, contemporary testimony still supports the impression that the wellspring of that desire was injured male pride and a simple determination to even the score. Lord Kensington reported that when Charles boarded his ship to leave Spain, one of the first things he heard the prince say was that he considered it 'weakness and folly ... in that after they [the Spaniards] had used him so ill, they would suffer him to depart'.[19] Charles's physician provided a similar description of his state of mind at this time.[20] King James likewise confided in a Spanish agent that the first thing Charles said upon his return was that he was ready to conquer Spain. (James also was reported to have said that Buckingham 'had he knew not how many devils within him since that journey'.[21]) Furthermore, Charles's sister Elizabeth received letters from him written in Spain which left no doubt in her mind, as she told the Venetian ambassador, 'that the marriage treaty will certainly be broken off and that her brother writes in such a manner as clearly to show his disgust and his desire for revenge'.[22] What principally drove Charles and Buckingham into war was not Parliament or a perceptive understanding of continental politics but the simple desire for revenge. S. R. Gardiner got this right a century ago. He wrote: 'Both Charles and Buckingham had come back with the full persuasion that they had been duped by the Spaniards, and with a full determination to take their revenge.'[23] Robert E. Ruigh got it right in his study of the Parliament of 1624, writing that the prince and the Duke had returned from Madrid 'with a burning desire for revenge against Spain'.[24] And more recently, Simon Adams got it right when he, too, concluded that 'Buckingham and Charles were moved by their experiences in Madrid to seek a war of revenge'.[25]

No matter what motives one attributes to Charles and Buckingham, the decision to embroil England in war was their decision, and it was made well before the Parliament of 1624. It is important to bear this point in mind because it contradicts a line of argument that has been popular in recent years to the effect that Charles and Buckingham were pressured into war by the Parliament of 1624 and then left in the lurch by subsequent Parliaments that failed to honour the commitment allegedly made by their predecessor. Kevin Sharpe, for example, made Parliament seem the initiator of war. Sharpe wrote that Charles was 'engaged, at the entreaty of parliament, in three wars', and he described Buckingham as 'the architect of the foreign policy advocated by parliament'.[26] Howard Tomlinson placed the blame squarely on Parliament for its 'reluctance to finance a war which it had advocated'.[27] John Morrill enshrined this view in *The Oxford History of Britain* in one pithy sentence: 'Parliament brayed for war but failed to provide the supply to make the campaigns a success.'[28] Readers should beware of this argument. It is the perennial stab-in-the-back argument which explains away military defeat by blaming it on the politicians (in this case, the MPs of the 1620s). The stab-in-the-back argument does not do justice to those MPs who resisted or opposed the war. It is true, of course, that MPs had called (not brayed) for war back in 1621 when they were faced with the dreaded alternative of the Spanish Match. The situation was dramatically different in 1624, however. In 1624 it was Charles and Buckingham, not Parliament, who initiated the cry for war.

The Parliament of 1624

Of course Charles and Buckingham could not go about waging war by themselves. They had to persuade King James to seek war, and they had to manipulate Parliament into backing their enterprise. So the next question becomes: how successful were Charles and Buckingham in these efforts? Granted that they had already made the decision to embark on war before Parliament met, if they managed to obtain the unequivocal backing of Parliament in 1624, and then subsequent Parliaments reneged on this promise, there would still be some basis for the stab-in-the-back interpretation. But it did not happen that way either.

The Parliament of 1624 has been subjected to two major interpretations in recent literature. Conrad Russell argued that Parliament's commitment to war was lukewarm at best. Although the House of Lords was eager for war, the House of Commons displayed no such urgency.[29] Russell detected a distinct change in mood as he turned his attention away from the bellicose Lords to the cautious Commons: 'It is precisely this note of practical belligerence, of a sense of impending conflict between the forces of light and the forces of darkness, which is almost entirely lacking in the Commons' debates of 1624.' Russell found 'very little in the Commons of the practical readiness to prepare for war' that was evident in the Lords. Charles and Buckingham had conspired with several leading spokesmen in the Commons prior to Parliament's meeting, and these men tried to rouse the House to action. Russell's conclusion, however, was that this effort met with only limited success. MPs were worried about the high cost of war and hesitant to impose that cost on their tax-paying constituents. At best, under pressure from Charles, Buckingham, and the House of Lords, the Commons became 'reluctant partners in the enterprise'. For all intents and purposes, then, 'war had been forced on the House of Commons', not the other way around. Since 'the demand for war originated from Buckingham, rather than from members of Parliament', it would be most accurate to consider these 'Buckingham's and Charles's wars, and not Parliament's wars'.[30]

The alternative interpretation of the Parliament of 1624 came from Thomas Cogswell. As Cogswell told the story, Charles and Buckingham organised 'one of the most effective lobbying groups in the history of early modern Parliaments'. This 'Patriot' party acted as 'a formidable phalanx in the Commons'. In the critical debates of 19 and 20 March, a 'rising tide of pro-war speakers' overwhelmed the faint-hearted. If at times MPs appeared to be lukewarm about war, this was more appearance than reality. Proponents of the war had to keep cutting off discussion of the war's details both to protect the delicate foreign alliances that were being negotiated and to prevent Parliament from learning too much about the exact kind of war that was being planned. Consequently, there never was a clear-cut vote on war in the Parliament of 1624, but this did not result from any lack of enthusiasm for war. As Cogswell saw it, there was more latent enthusiasm for war among MPs than Russell was able to detect. Cogswell concluded that Russell's judgement was 'surely too harsh', and he cautioned his fellow historians to 'react warily to the proposition that a majority of contemporaries and their parliamentary representatives were only marginally interested in the war'. Quite the contrary: 'Englishmen by and large did not have to be dragged into the middle of a continental war; rather they seemed to want to be there.'[31]

How we judge Charles's later actions depends very much on who is right about the Parliament of 1624, Russell or Cogswell. Russell is right.[32] Charles and Buckingham subsequently acted as if the Parliament of 1624 had given them an unqualified mandate to embark on war, but no such mandate in fact existed. Outside Parliament, one can find enthusiasm for war expressed in poetry, sermons, and polemical tracts. However, these sources are by their very nature biased, and it is impossible to say whether they represented the opinion of anywhere near a majority of MPs or the nation at large. The polemicist Thomas Scott certainly clamoured for war, but when it became a real possibility instead of a literary posture, the question is how many people who would have to take responsibility for the war were actually prepared to put their money where their mouth was? That is what MPs were being asked to do. If we look at the actual records of parliamentary debates in 1624 rather than polemical literature, there is admittedly room for interpretation. Nevertheless, one of the most impressive features of these debates is the way in which a handful of sceptics were able to slow down the headlong rush towards war. Among these sceptics were Edward Alford, William Mallory, Sir George More, Sir John Savile, and Sir Francis Seymour. What one historian said of Alford could be said of all these men: they 'fought a rearguard action against the powerful interests propelling the country toward war with Spain'.[33] This was a dangerous business, not only because the war party was allied with the court but also because it could appeal to the potent forces of nationalism and religion. Anyone who dragged his feet on the subject of war could be smeared with accusations of disloyalty and Catholic sympathies. Sir Humphrey May subtly suggested that MPs who resisted war were giving comfort to the enemy. May warned, do not 'give them [the Spanish] occasion to rejoice at our dissenting'.[34]

There were strong emotions and deep suspicions running through the House of Commons in 1624. John Chamberlain described MPs as 'so warie and cautious on all sides as yf they were to treat with enemies and in daunger to be overreacht'. Whereas anyone who resisted war ran the risk of having his patriotism and religion questioned, an MP who zealously advocated war ran the alternative risk of appearing to have made a bargain with the court, surrendering his independent judgement in return for the prospect of personal advancement. Chamberlain knew who these people were. He named Sir Edwin Sandys, Sir Dudley Digges, and Sir Robert Phelips (he could have added Sir Edward Coke). And he observed that these men 'have so litle credit among them [other MPs] that though they speake well and to the purpose sometimes, yet yt is not so well taken at their hands for still they suspect them to prevaricate, and hold them for undertakers'.[35] It was perhaps to avoid this stigma that Sandys defected from the war party.[36] Historians can cite speeches from a handful of MPs who cautiously resisted war and speeches from a larger handful who eagerly advocated war. But we must remember that there were roughly 500 men sitting in the House of Commons, and for the overwhelming majority of these, we have no recorded speeches either in favour of war or against it. This does not leave us in the dark, however, about the degree to which MPs supported war. We have only to look at the measures they ultimately agreed upon.

Nothing passed by Parliament in 1624 called for war. What MPs did endorse with unadulterated enthusiasm was breaking off the treaties with Spain regarding a royal marriage and the restitution of the Palatinate. If these treaties could be terminated without war ensuing, that would have suited a great many MPs. Much of the debate in 1624 was therefore over this question of whether or not war would somehow automatically, unavoidably result upon the termination of the treaties. Unswerving advocates of war like Sir Edward Coke passionately argued that war was inevitable after breaking off the treaties, but this was a conjecture that simply could not be proved. Sir Edwin Sandys (after his defection from the war party) urged his colleagues 'not presently to rush into a War' because it was 'Not a necessary immediate Consequence'. As Sandys now understood, the job of Parliament at this point was 'not particularly to determine a war but to be prepared for it'.[37] Breaking the treaties might provoke Spain into war, so it was sensible to strengthen the nation's defences while waiting to see what happened. However, as John Glanville said, 'to provide for war before it be propounded is to christen a child before it was born'.[38] The text of the message both Houses gave to James outlining their position followed this line of argument. In return for dissolving the treaties, Parliament would supply James with money not toward a definite war but, rather, 'towards the Support of the War which is likely to ensue'. It is true that the Commons voted an unprecedented sum (three subsidies and three fifteenths to be collected in one year), but this was roughly half the amount James had told them was necessary for war. More money would be forthcoming only 'if You shall be engaged in a real War'.[39]

Next, of course, there is the Subsidy Act. Cogswell asserted that this Act was proof that 'the House in the end plumped for the war'.[40] Actually, it is the best proof that the House of Commons was not suckered into blindly supporting war. The Subsidy Act very carefully spelled out the specific uses for which the subsidy money was intended, what were commonly known as the four points: '[1] for the defence of this your realm of England, [2] the securing of this your kingdom of Ireland, [3] the assistance of your neighbours the States of the United Provinces and other your Majesty's friends and allies, and [4] for the setting forth of your Royal Navy.' Although the latter two points could conceivably be construed as a mandate for war, none of the points necessarily implied direct offensive military operations. What they did amount to was defensive preparations, a prudent shoring up of the nation's defences and assistance to the Dutch, so that the nation would not be open to invasion if war did develop. (When the four points were paraphrased in subsequent royal commissions to the Council of War, they were expressed in even more unambiguously defensive terms – for example, 'setting forth' the navy became 'putting our navy in readiness and safety'.[41]) Sir Heneage Finch succinctly stated the Commons' understanding that war was not inevitable and that the four points were essentially defensive in nature: 'We find not that war is absolutely determined, only it is inferred as possible, which is to be provided for, as far as is fitting for to make us secure against it.'[42] The words of the Subsidy Act itself, like the words of the joint message that preceded it, clearly stated that this money was being provided in case the termination of the treaties with Spain caused England to 'be engaged in a sudden war' or, as the Act said elsewhere, the 'war that may hereupon ensue'.[43]

Furthermore, MPs tried to guarantee that the money they provided would be spent on nothing more than the four specific purposes they had agreed upon. The subsidy money of 1624 was allocated to the four points, and parliamentary treasurers were appointed to ensure that it was spent on just those four points. This process of allocation was a major concession of constitutional significance that Charles and Buckingham forced James to accept in order to get the money.[44] Finally, MPs knew that they were only providing for a possible eventuality. If war did actually ensue, the understanding they had was that they would be resummoned later in the year around Michaelmas to deal with this real war. In this next session, James told them, they would be allowed to consider 'what is next to be done'.[45] Many MPs explicitly stated their assumption that the outbreak of real war would necessitate their meeting again in the fall, but William Mallory put it most colourfully. 'If I were not in expectation to meet here again', said Mallory, 'I would not give a farthing.'[46]

It has become fashionable to describe Parliament in the 1620s as irresponsible, but the Parliament of 1624 could hardly have behaved more responsibly to their nation or their constituents. Under enormous pressure from Charles, Buckingham, and their allies in the Commons, the balance of MPs nevertheless refused to issue a blank cheque or an unqualified mandate for war. They did not naïvely allow themselves to be manipulated into 'the open-ended financial commitment the duke had desired'.[47] What they produced instead was as close as they could come to an airtight contract, providing for the defence of the kingdom, allocating the subsidy money only to the immediate needs that had been identified, and ensuring that Parliament would be consulted again if those needs enlarged. MPs thought that the money they had voted would be spent exclusively on the four points for precautionary defensive preparations. They thought that if a real war ensued, Parliament would be called back into session to discuss its scope. Furthermore, many MPs thought that if war did develop, they could limit it to a relatively inexpensive naval war against Spain (what was called the 'blue water' strategy or a 'diversionary' war). In every one of these respects they were mistaken. Of course one reason these expectations did not come to pass was the death of King James, which could not have been anticipated. Another reason was that Charles and Buckingham wanted to complete difficult negotiations with potential allies, particularly France, before facing another Parliament. Yet another reason was the simple fact that no war ensued. The treaties with Spain were terminated, and no Spanish armada appeared off the coast of England. If the English wanted peace, they could have it. But of course Charles and Buckingham did not want peace, and that was the major reason the contract of 1624 collapsed.

The War Plan

The contract was made on false pretences to begin with. Unbeknown to Parliament, plans were already under way for a vast war on several fronts that would go forward no matter how Spain reacted to the termination of the treaties. This plan included naval assaults on Spain, but it also included land operations against Spanish and Imperial forces aimed more directly at the recovery of the Palatinate and carried out in concert with several Protestant and Catholic allies – France, Denmark, Sweden, the United Provinces, Venice, and Savoy. This was the plan that had to be kept secret from Parliament. This was the plan that entailed a costly subsidy of £30,000 per month to Christian IV of Denmark, who was Charles's uncle, and £20,000 per month to the mercenary soldier, Count Mansfeld. These obligations alone came to £600,000 per year, a staggering amount which could hardly have been intended by most MPs when they voted for 'the assistance of your neighbours the States of the United Provinces and other your Majesty's friends and allies'. Indeed, this was the plan, as subsequent Parliaments discovered, that came with a total annual price tag of £1 million. It is hard to imagine any MP in 1624 knowingly authorising expenditures on that scale. This was also the plan that forced Charles to marry a French Catholic princess (who was not much better than a Spanish Catholic princess in most people's eyes) as the price of a French alliance. Whose plan was it?

King James lived long enough to be implicated in the plan. When he spoke about war, he envisioned it as a crusade to recover the Palatinate, a prospect which sent shivers through the Commons. Sir Francis Seymour best expressed the apprehension of the Commons: 'His Majesty speaks of a war in the Palatinate, which is a thing of infinite charge and to us impossible.'[48] Throughout this Parliament, Charles, Buckingham, and all the supporters they could muster had to act like political 'spin doctors', reassuring MPs that no matter what James said, what he actually meant was a naval war against Spain. One of Buckingham's clients, for example, assured the House that 'the general aim and the necessity is apparent to be a war with Spain'.[49] Nevertheless, James persisted in thinking about a war in and for the Palatinate. In his declaration accepting Parliament's offer of supply, James said that if he did not recover the Palatinate, 'I could wish never to have been born', and he vowed, 'no Means shall be unused for the Recovery of it'.[50] Worse still, James tried to intervene in the Commons to get the four points of the Subsidy Act revised to include the recovery of the Palatinate as a fifth point. Sir Walter Earle recorded that this effort 'was utterly disliked by the House' because, among other things, 'that which was proposed was clean contrary to the intent of the House ... it being otherwise resolved upon debate before, viz. that the Palatinate should not be named'.[51] At the close of Parliament, James was still insisting that his goal was the recovery of the Palatinate, and he even threatened to amend the Subsidy Act to this effect with his own hand.[52] No wonder that Edward Nicholas described the members of Parliament departing 'with much more discontent and fear of the success of this Parliament than when we came together'.[53]

King James contributed to the early shape of the war plan, but the driving force was provided by Buckingham. In his biography of Buckingham, Roger Lockyer, far from foisting this plan off on James, gave full credit to the Duke, representing it as a masterful scheme to counter Habsburg aggression.[54] Simon Adams agreed that this was Buckingham's foreign policy, but he took a dimmer view of it. The plan turned out to be a far cry from what Parliament had in mind because Buckingham 'had no intention of making foreign policy in parliament, or even of taking parliamentary opinion into account'. James and Parliament may have been talking past each other, but James at least was being relatively honest. Buckingham was more deceptive. To get the money he needed, Buckingham led Parliament to believe that they had an understanding spelled out in the terms of the Subsidy Act. Afterward, however, he had no intention of waiting to see if war ensued or limiting his actions to the four points. More than £60,000 of subsidy money was soon spent on a disastrous expedition to the continent led by Mansfeld, which Adams considered a 'direct violation of the terms of the Subsidy Act'. Perhaps the Duke simply made the gross assumption that whatever the detailed language of the Act, he had in effect been given *carte blanche* to conduct the war as he pleased. Or perhaps, as Adams wrote, Buckingham's 'cavalier attitude towards the Subsidy Act can only suggest that he never had any real interest in its terms'.[55]

Was it Charles's plan? Charles and Buckingham certainly worked in concert. Interestingly, though, no one would say that Charles was the mastermind behind the plan (as one could say of Buckingham) or that he was the key person whose preferences had to be taken into account (as one could say of King James). One reason it is impossible to assign individual responsibility for the war plan is because it was designed to satisfy several constituencies. Charles was hell-bent on war with Spain, but he also apparently felt a genuine duty to help his sister Elizabeth and her husband Frederick regain the Palatinate. Buckingham, like Charles, was eager to retaliate against Spain, but he also relished the role of international statesman, conducting ambitious diplomatic efforts to put together a grand alliance. No plan could go forward if it did not suit James, who was reluctant to attack Spain, objected to a purely religious war, promoted the alliance with France, and pushed for direct military operations aimed at recovering the Palatinate. Yet no plan was likely to win parliamentary approval which did not feature a revived naval war against Spain, preferably in alliance with the Dutch. Cogswell treated the war plan as a joint product of the prince and the Duke, and he praised its 'adroit resolution' of all these differing strategic preferences. 'Charles and Buckingham', wrote Cogswell, 'had taken great pains to draft a plan to overcome James's objections and to attract the broadest possible support.'[56] That puts the best possible face on a plan that looks like it was put together by a committee with something in it for everybody. In private Charles and Buckingham could keep James's support by emphasising the campaign for the Palatinate, while in public they could win Parliament's support by emphasising the naval campaign against Spain. Everyone who wanted war could find some piece of this package to like. But few people had any idea what the full package looked like; if they had known its full dimensions, they would have had grave misgivings. Whether it was because of the need to placate all these constituencies, the megalomania of Buckingham, or the sheer lack of realism on the part of both the prince and the Duke, the plan that resulted was wildly ambitious and expensive. Whether the fault was more Charles's or Buckingham's it is impossible to say; the two men were now partners in war.

First Impressions

All in all, then, what impression do we have of Charles before he actually succeeded to the throne? Charles was eager to take centre
stage. As Conrad Russell described him, 'Charles, unlike James, suffered from energy'. (Students may wish to note that Russell added,
'both the energetic Stuarts lost their thrones, while both the lazy ones
died in their beds'.[57])In the last two years of James's life, Charles
played an increasingly prominent role, surprisingly prominent in
fact. Perhaps James was simply declining too much in his physical and
mental capacities to rein in 'baby Charles', as he still called him, but
it seems more evident that it was Charles's alliance with Buckingham
that made him irrepressible. What Charles did in these two years
reflects both favourably and unfavourably on him. There is nothing
favourable to be found in the trip to Spain. It was impetuous and
foolhardy. The best construction that could be put upon it would be
to claim that Charles understood the insincerity of the Spanish and
was only attempting to call their bluff. If Charles had understood this
much, however, he would also have realised that the trip was too dangerous to undertake. Besides, the letters that Charles and
Buckingham sent back from Spain clearly indicate that they had no
such understanding.[58] They went to Spain with the full expectation
that they could complete the Match, and it took them an appallingly
long time to figure out the real situation. These letters also reveal
James's pitiable emotional dependence on his 'sweet boys' and something of their own political instincts. For example, Charles urged his
father: 'I beseech your Majesty advise as little with your Council in
these businesses as you can.'[59] Under the circumstances, this may
have been a prudent precaution, or it could have been a premonition
of Charles's penchant for secrecy and double-dealing. The latter interpretation is supported by a letter in which Buckingham and
Charles instructed James how to handle the Spanish demand that
'you promise that the Parliament shall revoke all the penal laws
against the Papists within three years'. This was a preposterous
promise on which James could not possiby have delivered. It presented no difficulty for Charles and Buckingham, however, because
'if you think you may do it in that time (which we think you may), if
you do your best, although it take not effect, you have not broken
your word, for this promise is only as a security that you will do your
best'.[60] Here we find an early expression not only of Charles's lack of
political realism but also of his elastic view of promises.

What reflected most favourably on Charles in this period immediately before he came to the throne was his performance in the Parliament of 1624.[61] He played the heroic role of the youthful prince whose eyes had been opened by Spanish perfidy. Through his journey to Spain, Sir Benjamin Rudyerd told the Commons, Charles had 'expressed unto the world his courage in undertaking it, his wisdom in managing it, and the experience thereof hath actuated and produced those excellent parts which are naturally in him and enabled him for great counsels and resolutions'.[62] Another contemporary observer, John Chamberlain, was impressed by Charles's transformation. At the opening of Parliament, Chamberlain found the prince a changed man: 'I went especially to see the prince, who indeed is grown a fine gentleman, and beyond all expectation I had of him when I saw him last ... and, indeed, I think he never looked nor became himself better in all his life.' A month later Chamberlain was still impressed. He remarked that the young prince 'never misses a day at the parliament', and he praised Charles's 'virtuous disposition, as being noted free from any vicious or scandalous inclination; which makes him every day more gracious, and his actions to seem more graceful than was at first expected'. Notice that on both these occasions Chamberlain expressed surprise that Charles had turned out so well, contrary to the expectations that had previously been formed of him. The trip to Spain 'hath improved him so much', Chamberlain explained, 'that it is a received opinion he concealed himself before'.[63]

Charles worked hard to cultivate his new image and to get what he wanted out of Parliament. He participated in person in the deliberations of the House of Lords, and he did all that he could indirectly to influence the House of Commons. For example, MPs thrilled to Charles's story that when he was in Spain, he had sent back word that if he was taken prisoner there, then James should 'forget you have a son, & look after your daughter'.[64] On another opportunity Charles exhorted Parliament not just to show their teeth 'but bite also'. If they should fail to act, the heir to the throne pointedly reminded his listeners, 'it would be dishonourable unto yourselves as well as unto me who am now first entering into the world'.[65] Charles's intervention was especially crucial when it came to clarifying or interpreting the king's position. James was the loose cannon in the Parliament of 1624. Sometimes he spoke as if he was still wedded to peace. Other times he spoke alarmingly about the Palatinate or about the true cost of war. Charles and Buckingham

worked frantically to keep James committed to war and to persuade
MPs that, no matter what the old king seemed to say, what he had in
mind was a naval war against Spain.

   Overall Charles's behaviour was widely applauded. He was the
hero of the day. This impression had only been sustained, however,
by silencing two major critics. Charles and Buckingham inadvertently furthered the development of parliamentary impeachment
when they used this procedure to remove the Lord Treasurer
(Lionel Cranfield, Earl of Middlesex) because he had conspired
against Buckingham and opposed war on grounds of economy.
Likewise, they contrived to keep the Earl of Bristol away from
Parliament because, as special ambassador to Spain, he threatened
to relate a less flattering version of what had occurred in Madrid.
The ruin of Cranfield was total, but Bristol would prove to be a more
tenacious critic. With remarkable prescience, King James tried to
warn his son and favourite that they would live to regret the way they
had empowered Parliament by involving it in questions of war and
using it to destroy a royal minister, but the two young men were
happily riding the tide of popularity.[66] Another older voice, the Earl
of Kellie, understood the price of that popularity. He observed that
Charles had been 'a little too popular' or 'a little more popular than
was fitting for him', and he too predicted that the concessions
Charles had made to garner popularity in 1624 would catch up with
him in the future.[67]

   As these forebodings suggested, Charles's popularity in 1624 was
built on sand. Roger Lockyer asserted that Buckingham (and presumably Charles too) were 'extraordinarily successful in bringing
King and Parliament together in a commitment to war'.[68] But
Parliament was not truly committed to war yet, least of all the war
that was being planned. And in the interim before another
Parliament met, those plans started going badly awry. In the hope of
obtaining a French alliance, Charles married Henrietta Maria, the
sister of Louis XIII, but the military alliance failed to materialise.
Meanwhile the debt to Denmark kept piling up, and the army that
was improperly financed by subsidy money under the command of
Count Mansfeld literally disintegrated on the continent as a result
of harsh weather, desertion, and disease. John Chamberlain was one
of the contemporary observers mystified by this turn of events.
Regarding the 'talk of a league, offensive and defensive, against
whomsoever', he remarked: 'If this be true, it is much otherwise than
was given out at first.' In Chamberlain's opinion, 'if we may live

quietly at home, we shall not greatly care how the world goes abroad'.[69] Of course the English were not destined to live quietly at home. In March of 1625 *Rex Pacificus* died, and *Rex Bellicosus* took charge.

2

A BAD START, 1625–1629

Charles I's reign got off to a terribly bad start. At first peace broke out, which was not what Charles wanted. Since Spain failed to attack England, Charles tried to attack Spain. This sputtering war with Spain then unexpectedly expanded to include war with France, which was supposed to have been Charles's chief ally, and one ignominious military defeat followed another. Defeat abroad was paralleled by defeat at home, where Charles was unable to enlist the support he needed to prosecute the war successfully. A series of quarrelsome Parliaments refused to finance the war, assailed royal policies across the board, and turned with special animus against the Duke of Buckingham. To protect Buckingham from impeachment, Charles dissolved the Parliament of 1626. To pay for the war, he resorted to extraparliamentary measures. He levied a forced loan, imprisoned people who refused to pay it, billeted troops in private homes, and imposed martial law to maintain order among the mutinous troops. None the less in 1628 lack of money again forced Charles back into the arms of Parliament, which proceeded to condemn all his extraordinary expedients in the Petition of Right, a document which Charles accepted but only under duress and with characteristic evasiveness. Shortly thereafter Charles received a much more personal blow when Buckingham was stabbed to death by a lone assassin. After the Duke's assassination, one might have expected the parliamentary session of 1629 to make a fresh start, but it was no more cooperative than its predecessors had been. When Charles commanded the Commons to adjourn, disgruntled MPs held the Speaker in his chair long enough to conduct a confused vote on three resolutions declaring that anyone who encouraged certain policies they found objectionable would be considered 'a capital enemy to the Kingdom and Commonwealth'. Government at all levels had been strained to the breaking point by the effort to conduct a war without the necessary means, and the Crown was virtually bankrupt. Fed up, Charles resolved to govern without Parliament, reluctantly made peace, and turned for consolation to his French Catholic wife. Who was responsible for this mess?

Exoneration

There is a widespread misconception that, whatever else they disagree about, so-called 'revisionists' agree that King Charles was largely to blame for his own problems. One reviewer, for example, wrote that revisionists see 'the early years of Charles I's reign as troubled less by structural weaknesses of the monarchy than by the failings of the king'.[1] This is a gross misunderstanding of revisionist work on the 1620s. It would hardly have been revisionist to claim that Charles bungled the first years of his reign; that was the standard view established by S. R. Gardiner over 100 years ago. The only way to revise the standard history of the period 1625–29 was to direct attention away from Charles, to focus on structural weaknesses, to speak broadly of a functional breakdown of government under the strain of war, and not to raise the awkward question of how far Charles himself was personally responsible for straining the system where it was weakest and driving it to the point of breakdown. If there was any identifiably revisionist approach to these early years of Charles's reign, therefore, it was not to blame Charles but to exonerate him. In the words of G. A. Harrison, revisionists were 'intent on absolving Charles and Buckingham from much of the blame that historians have customarily placed on their actions'.[2]

Kevin Sharpe and Conrad Russell made the strongest efforts to rehabilitate Charles's reputation. In his pioneering introduction to *Faction and Parliament*, Sharpe blamed Buckingham, the Privy Council, and Parliament for what went wrong. Buckingham factionalised the Council, which was not an especially talented body of men to begin with. The king was forced to turn for advice to Parliaments, but they too were 'ill equipped to offer sound counsel'. The problem lay not with the king but with his counsellors. 'The King needed able counsellors in order to govern well', Sharpe explained, 'and the

parliaments of the 1620s had been unable to provide good advice.'
'On nearly all counts', wrote Sharpe, 'they failed.'[3] In a later article,
Sharpe related the problem of counsel to a communication
problem. The court, the Privy Council, and the aristocracy in
general 'needed to maintain open communications' with the king.
'This in the 1620s they failed to do.'[4] In Sharpe's view, therefore, the
turmoil that occurred in the early years of Charles's reign resulted
from a failure of counsel or a failure of communication, not the failings of the king.

Russell's defence of Charles in the 1620s was not as blunt or
direct, but it was much more extensive. As we noted in the introduc-
ton, Russell's seminal article on early Stuart parliamentary history
shifted attention away from the person of the king toward the impersonal structural problems that plagued early Stuart government. In
Parliaments and English Politics, 1621–1629, Russell elaborated on
these structural handicaps and crippling circumstances. Above all,
Russell emphasised the role of war. If there is any one idea associated with Russell's interpretation of the later 1620s, it is the idea that
war is the key. The political difficulties of this period, wrote Russell,
were 'first and foremost, not the difficulties of a bad King, but the
difficulties of a nation reluctantly at war'. Or, as he wrote in another
place: 'It was this burden of war, imposed on an administration
already in a state of functional breakdown by a Duke of Buckingham
whose purposes, and even whose enemy, appeared unidentifiable,
that brought relations between central and local government, and
hence between King and Parliament, to the point of collapse.'[5]

The further Russell proceeded through the war years, the more
sympathy he developed for Charles. At the outset he got the story
right. In 1625 the actions of the House of Commons demonstrated
that it was opposed to the war. 'It was Charles and Buckingham's
failure to face this central fact', Russell observed, 'which produced
most of the troubles of the next three years.' By the end of his book,
however, Russell shifted his position, making it seem as if Charles
had been stabbed in the back by Parliaments which first demanded
war then shamefully refused to support it. 'The depth of incomprehension which grew up between Charles and his early Parliaments',
Russell now claimed, 'arose from Charles's pardonable belief that if
they said they wanted him to fight a war, they would assist him to
finance it.' In this new version of the story, Charles made a 'remarkable' effort to reach an understanding with his Parliaments. And he
made this effort because he truly believed in the institution of

Parliament, not just because he was desperate for cash. 'Only a principled belief in Parliamentary institutions', wrote Russell, 'can explain the effort Charles made to work them between 1625 and 1628.' Of course Charles kept running into a brick wall, but that was not his fault. He actually deserved more recognition for 'the patience he showed with the negativism and obstructionism of the Parliaments of 1626 and 1628'. He 'wanted to be known as a King who could get on with his Parliaments, and devoted a surprising amount of time and patience to attempting to succeed'.[6]

Russell's most extreme case for Charles appeared in an article published in 1982.[7] Here Russell argued that 'Charles had an attachment to the rule of law, yet he believed that the law must be compatible with his obligation to defend his kingdom'. Early modern monarchs like Charles 'had no great objection to law, and strongly preferred to do things legally if possible'. On the other hand, 'when a legal right came into conflict with an urgent necessity of defence, they gave priority to the urgent necessity'.[8] The trouble in the early modern period was that the representative assemblies which were called upon to finance war had no comprehension of the cost of war. Their ignorance and refusal to fund royal military enterprises put their nations in jeopardy. Of course the critical question was whether these military enterprises were truly necessary in the first place. To this question Russell had a plain answer: 'The king could be presumed to know about military necessities.'[9]

Thus the revisionist interpretation of Charles in the early years of his reign represented him as a beleaguered king. His counsellors failed to give him good advice. His Parliaments failed to give him money. He was trapped in a war which others had wanted him to fight, yet deprived of the necessary means to succeed. He struggled valiantly to work through the ordinary parliamentary avenues, but he was at last forced to resort to extraparliamentary measures through no fault of his own. How well has this revisionist interpretation held up? Not very well at all.

The Parliament of 1625

To say that the difficulties of this period were 'first and foremost, not the difficulties of a bad King, but the difficulties of a nation reluctantly at war' begs the question. How was it that the nation came to be reluctantly engaged in war? As we saw in the previous chapter, it was Charles and Buckingham who made the decision to embark on war, and they orchestrated proceedings in the Parliament of 1624 toward that end. Russell is his own worst enemy on this point because it was his signal contribution to the historiography of the 1624 Parliament to note its lack of enthusiasm for war. Russell thought it was 'becoming clear that the demand for war originated from Buckingham, rather than from members of Parliament'. He portrayed the House of Commons as 'reluctant partners' who had war 'forced' upon them by 'Buckingham and his team' or 'the Duke, the Prince, and the House of Lords'.[10] Russell deserves credit for this major re-evaluation of the mood in the Commons in 1624, but it hardly squares with his interpretation of subsequent events.

The argument among historians today about the level of commitment to war is a mirror reflection of the argument that took place in the first year of Charles's own reign. In 1625 the key issue was whether the previous Parliament had made a commitment which was now binding on the new Parliament to provide whatever money was necessary for war.[11] Did such an 'engagement' exist? Charles and Buckingham certainly thought so.[12] In his opening speech to Parliament, Charles bore down heavily on this point. He described himself as a man who was not free to act as he pleased but solemnly engaged to fight a war for the recovery of the Palatinate. And who had engaged him in this course of action? 'It is you that engaged me', said Charles. Representing himself as the agent of their will, Charles told Parliament that his actions were undertaken 'by your entreaties, your engagements'. Elaborating on the king's speech, the Lord Keeper drew particular attention to the word 'engagement'.[13] In a later speech, Buckingham posed the question rhetorically, 'by what counsel this great enterprise has been undertaken and pursued hitherto?' 'I answer', the Duke declared, 'First by the parliament.'[14] Charles and Buckingham never wavered in their conviction that Parliament had authorised and should finance their undertakings. Today's historians who make it seem as if Charles was left in the lurch by a mercurial Parliament are essentially taking the king's own argument at face value. Roger Lockyer, for example, wrote that Charles felt betrayed by Parliament in 1625 when they would not support him in the prosecution of 'the policy which both Houses had urged on the crown in 1624'.[15] Kevin Sharpe similarly wrote that Charles was 'engaged, at the entreaty of parliament, in three wars

for which it had voted insufficient revenue', and he described
Buckingham as 'the architect of the foreign policy advocated by
parliament'.[16]

Why is this sympathy for Charles and Buckingham unwarranted?
First, as we saw in the previous chapter, they were not the pawns of
Parliament in 1624. It was the other way around. Secondly, their
effort to manipulate Parliament to their own ends had not entirely
succeeded. MPs advised the Crown to break the treaties with Spain;
they did not advise war. This is the distinction that Charles glossed
over when he lectured Parliament in 1625: 'I hope in God that you
will go on to maintain it as freely as you were willing to advise my
father to it.'[17] What was 'it'? If Charles had been referring merely to
breaking the treaties with Spain, he would have received no argument. But he was instead referring to an ambitious war on land and
sea to regain the Palatinate – an interpretation of the 1624 mandate
that was bound to provoke plenty of argument. Thirdly, Parliament
had promised to provide further aid only if breaking the treaties led
the Crown to become 'engaged in a real War'.[18] MPs had suffered
more from a war scare than a war fever in 1624. They were led to
expect 'a sudden war ... that may hereupon ensue'.[19] Amid this atmosphere of apprehension, they made provisional decisions to put
the nation's defences in order. This was never intended as anything
more than an interim policy; only time would tell whether 'a real
war' was necessary. They expected to face that decision when they
met again. When they did meet again, not in the Michaelmas session
they had expected to occur in the fall of 1624 but in a new
Parliament of a new reign in the summer of 1625, the war that was
thought likely to ensue had not ensued. Except for the subsidies
promised to Denmark and the army sent to the continent under
Count Mansfeld, which was disintegrating as Parliament met,
England was not yet actually engaged in a real war. The issue in the
Parliament of 1625, therefore, was not whether MPs wanted to
support an ongoing war but whether they wanted to *start* a war. No
defensive war had been forced upon them. No Spanish armada had
descended on England. As Sir Edward Coke expressed it, 'none
invades – we have no "88"'.[20] Relieved of having to fight a defensive
war, it was an open question now whether there was any compelling
reason to initiate an offensive war. In any case, there seemed no
urgent need to give money to Charles in the absence of an enemy.
Fourthly, those MPs who were inclined to start a war wanted a naval
war against Spain, not the kind of war that Charles and Buckingham

appeared to be planning, involving expensive alliances and land-based operations directly aimed at recovering the Palatinate. As Robert Ruigh explained, 'what they had wanted was a diversionary naval campaign against Spain; what they got was the endless prospect of subsidizing continental mercenaries to attempt the recovery of the Palatinate'.[21] In this connection, there was a strong body of opinion that Mansfeld's expedition was not only inconsistent with the strategy Parliament had been led to expect but an actual violation of the Subsidy Act.[22] MPs were even more mystified by the strenuous efforts of Charles and Buckingham to ally with the Catholic nation of France. One price of that alliance, the new queen, arrived in London just before Parliament met. To make matters worse, the Duke of Chevreuse and other French dignitaries who had accompanied her could be seen on the opening day of Parliament sitting as spectators in the House of Lords.[23]

The expectations of 1624 simply did not square with the realities of 1625. Some MPs, especially royal officials who had worked alongside Charles and Buckingham in the interval between Parliaments, thought that what they were now proposing was perfectly consonant with what the previous Parliament had pledged to support. But other MPs who had not been party to the evolution of policy were more impressed by the differences. Sir Robert Phelips best summed up this viewpoint: 'There is no engagement; the promises and declarations of the last parliament were in respect of a war. We know yet of no war nor of any enemy.'[24] Charles and Buckingham knew what questions were being raised in Parliament. To allay this particular question, the Duke actually told MPs, 'my master gave me commandment to bid you name the enemy yourselves'.[25] It was slightly ludicrous to put this question to Parliament. If no enemy loomed on the horizon, why name one? If forced to name an enemy, the bulk of MPs would presumably have chosen Spain. There was no engagement to wage war against the Holy Roman Empire for the recovery of the Palatinate. Edward Alford left no doubt on that point: 'He holds we are not engaged to give for the recovery of the Palatinate; for when it was in the act of parliament [the Subsidy Act of 1624], as it was first penned, it was struck out by the order of the House.'[26]

Just as there was disagreement over the engagement Charles presumed to exist, so was there disagreement over the financial necessity he alleged. Nearly all of the 1624 subsidies had already been spent, and huge costs continued to accrue. In addition to the accumulating subsidies promised to the King of Denmark and Count

Mansfeld, another £300,000 was still required for the fleet.[27] The total cost to proceed with the current war plan over the next twelve months was over £1 million.[28] One must wonder whether Charles and Buckingham ever stopped along the way to consider the total cost of the obligations they were incurring. In view of these huge expenses, when the Parliament of 1625 granted Charles a mere two subsidies (which would have yielded at most £140,000), he asked for more on the ground that this amount fell far short of the necessity. But some MPs questioned whether this was only a 'pretended necessity'. And others asked, if a necessity of this magnitude did in fact exist, then who had caused it?[29] The alleged necessity most debated in the Commons was the fleet, which would eat up all of the new subsidies and more. Charles felt it was absolutely necessary to finish preparing this fleet and send it to sea. He even went so far as to declare that it would be better for half the fleet to perish at sea than for none of the ships to sail.[30] In the Commons, however, it proved difficult to whip up enthusiasm. Cynics questioned why it had taken so long to prepare the fleet and what could be gained by setting it out so late in the year.[31] Phelips warned that it could actually do more harm than good because it might 'stir a powerful king to invade us'.[32] If no one cared to attack England, then why should it go out looking for enemies and provoke Spain into war, especially at a cost of £300,000?

It is important to remember that MPs in 1625 debated whether or not to launch the fleet, against whom, and at what cost. In other words, war could still have been averted. In his haste to generate sympathy for Charles, Kevin Sharpe confused the order of these events. The way Sharpe told the story, war was already under way, and the Parliament of 1625 engaged in 'post-mortem debates' about the Crown's 'first military ventures, the military expedition to the Palatinate of the mercenary Count Mansfeldt and the abortive assault on the Spanish treasure fleet at Cadiz'.[33] In reality, however, it is a simple fact that the Parliament of 1625 could not have engaged in a post-mortem debate about the failed assault on Cadiz because it had not yet happened. What MPs actually debated in 1625 was whether it was worth the cost to make an assault against an enemy who at that time was still unknown. Meanwhile there were real enemies who were too well known – pirates. MPs protested bitterly over the depredations of pirates. These protests could have been mainly a strategy for attacking Buckingham in his capacity as Lord Admiral, but they leave the impression that it might have been more popular to use the fleet against pirates than to embroil it in international warfare.[34]

War was not the only gulf opening up between Charles and his subjects. In 1625 MPs actually spent more time on matters of religion than they did on the king's request for supply. From the outset of his reign, Charles's religious convictions were suspect. One obvious cause of concern was his marriage. Jubilation over the collapse of the Spanish Match quickly turned to dismay when Charles, rather than proceeding to marry a Protestant, chose a French Catholic wife. Moreover, MPs could observe from the effects that Charles must have agreed to be more lenient towards Roman Catholics as part of the deal. 'What the Spanish articles were we know', observed Phelips. 'Whether those with France be any better is doubted.'[35] To force Charles back into line, Parliament presented him with a petition complaining about foreign ambassadors who interceded on behalf of Roman Catholics and 'the want of due execution of the laws against Jesuits, seminary priests, and popish recusants'.[36] Charles promised to do all that Parliament asked for, but in reality he could not fulfil this promise without breaking the promise he had already made to the French. Aware of that fact, MPs could only further doubt the king's sincerity.[37]

Charles was not honest on the subject of the religious concessions made to France, but his lack of candour is understandable. Charles, whose mother had been Roman Catholic, was truly exceptional in his willingness to deal with Catholics and even to marry one himself. There is no doubt that he would have been more popular as king if he had shared the virulent prejudice of most MPs against Roman Catholicism, but he would hardly have been more admirable as a human being.[38] Of course his leniency at this particular juncture arose from his need to placate the French rather than from any high-minded principle, but throughout his reign he was too friendly toward Roman Catholicism to suit the prejudices of his subjects. This was not the only cause for concern about Charles's religious orthodoxy, however. He also raised suspicions because of his apparent preference within the Church of England for the doctrine of Arminianism (that is, the belief in salvation through free will, which the English associated with Roman Catholicism, as opposed to the Calvinist doctrine of predestination). One early indication of that preference was his intervention on behalf of the controversial Arminian clergyman, Richard Montagu. To shield Montagu from a parliamentary inquisition, Charles announced that he was a royal chaplain and should therefore be immune from imprisonment and questioning. Charles thus managed to block the persecutorial zeal of the Commons, but in the process he also issued a challenge to parliamentary jurisdiction. Edward Alford warned, 'if we admit this, we shall take the way to destroy parliaments'.[39]

Everywhere MPs looked in 1625 they were horrified, and some began to fix the blame on Buckingham. Mansfeld's abortive expedition, the projected alliance with France, the Catholic queen, the fleet that required more money though it had no purpose – all seemed to be the Duke's doing. His singular influence over the king and the many offices gathered into his own hands were other causes of resentment.[40] Sir Edward Coke observed that 'a kingdom can never be well governed where unskillful and unfitting men are placed in great offices'. He also pointedly complained about the 'multiplicity of offices to be held in one man'.[41] Sir Francis Seymour was more explicit: 'Let us lay the fault where it is; the Duke of Buckingham is trusted, and it must needs be either in him or his agents.'[42] Sir Robert Phelips made perhaps the most radical speech of the entire Parliament, attacking Buckingham for his foreign policy and his monopoly of offices, and invoking historical precedent to challenge the royal prerogative if necessary to reform the government. A few days later he remarked: 'We are the last monarchy in Christendom that retain our original right and constitutions.'[43] These were ominous warnings that Buckingham's inordinate power and war policy were raising divisive constitutional issues.[44]

The Parliament of 1625 did not fail Charles; least of all did it fail to communicate its concerns. The attack on Montagu and the petition on religion should have alerted Charles that his religious policy was antagonising the very people he needed to support his foreign policy. The refusal to provide more than two subsidies should have alerted him to the fact that he did not have the political support or the material wherewithal to fight the kind of war he and Buckingham had designed. And the personal attack on the Duke should have been a warning to distribute offices and power more widely. Charles was given good advice during this period, but he refused to listen. If there was a communication problem, it sprang from the fact that Charles was not a good listener. When Charles encountered criticism, he did not absorb it. His reaction, instead, was to dig in his heels and attack his critics. Charles should have paid more heed to MPs like Coke and Phelips who had aided him in

1624, but he preferred to view them as turncoats. He should have paid more heed to the sage advice of Lord Keeper Williams, but he removed him from office.[45] Most of all, Charles should have reconsidered his war plans because, in Conrad Russell's own words, the actions of the House of Commons in 1625 had shown they were 'against the war'.[46] Granted that he had gone too far to call a halt to the war, he might at least have reassessed the situation in 1625, as indeed members of Parliament had done, and scaled back his plans; but he was not the sort of person to make mid-course corrections.

As Christopher Thompson has written, the Parliament of 1625 reaffirms the 'orthodox rather than revisionist interpretation'. Charles 'appears to have thought that the simple notification of his wishes ought to have commanded obedience'. Instead of blind obedience, Charles encountered stiff opposition in 1625, and that opposition was motivated by truly national interests not merely localist concerns.[47] This is not to say that critics of the king's policies were entirely in the right and Charles entirely in the wrong. On the subject of supply, for example, Charles knew he was a poor speaker, and it would hardly have been dignified for him to beg. Through his ministers in the Commons, he did repeatedly lay out the facts of his case. Buckingham, too, deserves credit for the amazing effort he made to answer questions in the Commons. The decision to pressure Parliament for more money after they had already granted two subsidies made sense in light of the Crown's enormous needs (though it made less sense to persist in these demands by forcing members of Parliament to reconvene at Oxford during an outbreak of the plague). There were even good reasons to insist that the fleet must sail. Such sympathy as did exist for war was based on dreams of a revived Elizabethan naval war against Spain. To capitalise on this sentiment, Charles had to despatch the fleet and attack Spain. Had it succeeded, it might yet have galvanised political support for war. Furthermore, Charles had to take action to convince his potential allies that he was serious about joining the war. Charles's determination went deeper than this, however. It was a matter of honour. And though he spoke in terms of the nation's honour and the Parliament's honour, he nevertheless left the impression that it was his own personal honour that was at stake. Charles still had a score to settle with the Spanish for the way they had treated him in 1623. More than that, however, he and Buckingham were now committed to a vast enterprise. The world was watching, and it would have been humiliating for Charles to back down. As the Lord Keeper expressed it, Charles desired 'not to live otherwise than in glory and reputation'. Or, as another diarist recorded it, Charles 'had rather go to his grave than not to go on in this design'.[48]

There was one troublesome legacy from the Parliament of 1625 which cannot be blamed on Charles. The biggest single component of the king's ordinary revenue came from the customs duties known as tonnage and poundage. Since the late fifteenth century, the initial Parliament of every reign had granted this income to the monarch for life. Charles's first Parliament was different, however. MPs who wanted to re-examine the whole subject of the king's revenue, including the controversial 'impositions' that had been added onto the customs duties back in King James's reign, produced a bill that would have permitted Charles to collect tonnage and poundage for just one year, thereby allowing time and room for negotiation over royal finances rather than throwing away this once-in-a-lifetime opportunity. But this bill did not pass the Lords before dissolution. That left Charles with no formal authorisation to collect tonnage and poundage, although out of stark necessity he continued to do so, naïvely believing that a later Parliament would understand he had no choice.

The Parliament of 1626

After the Parliament of 1625, Charles concluded an alliance with the Dutch and succeeded in setting out the fleet. These actions – if they had been crowned by success – might have radically shifted public opinion behind the war effort. When the fleet sailed, it still had no specific destination. Eventually it chased a small Spanish fleet out of Cadiz harbour; troops were put ashore, but they marched around, got drunk, and reboarded the ships without accomplishing anything. The fleet then sat off the coast of Spain for a while hoping to intercept the treasure fleet from Mexico which, however, had secretly sailed into Cadiz bay two days after the English left. As the English fleet straggled back home through the winter, it was obvious that it had been no less a debacle than Mansfeld's expedition.[49]

Meanwhile the effort to enlist France as an ally was unravelling. Charles was increasingly exasperated with Henrietta Maria's attendants, whom he blamed for 'making and fomenting discontentments

in my wife'.[50] The French were, in turn, upset by the way Charles
tried to minimise the influence of these attendants. They were also
upset by the seizure of several of their ships accused of carrying con-
traband or 'prize goods' destined for Spain. They retaliated by
placing an embargo on English wine shipments from French ports.
Another source of friction was the resumption of persecution against
English Catholics. The more Charles did in this respect to mollify
domestic opinion, the more he alienated the French by breaking the
terms of his marriage treaty.[51] Far worse than any of these other
strains on Anglo-French relations was the affair of the loan ships.
Charles and Buckingham loaned seven ships to the French as part of
the inducement to an alliance. There was a spreading Huguenot
(Protestant) rebellion in France, however, and the French government ended up using the English ships in their effort to conquer
the Huguenot stronghold of La Rochelle. Charles and Buckingham
were now in the untenable position of appearing to be aiding a
Catholic monarch in the suppression of his Protestant subjects. The
king and Lord Admiral were so horrified by this turn of events and
exasperated with the French that they contemplated sending a fleet
to France to retrieve the loan ships and free La Rochelle. In other
words, Charles and Buckingham were drifting perilously close to war
with France![52] Thomas Cogswell, who has most closely studied these
events, attributed them to 'an unprecdented run of bad luck' rather
than incompetence. But it seems fair to say, at the very least, that
Charles and Buckingham were no match for Louis XIII and Cardinal
Richelieu.

Charles summoned the Parliament of 1626 because he was desperate for money. In addition to the unpaid bills for the previous fleet
and the cost of the new fleet that was being planned, he was particularly concerned to satisfy the demands of the King of Denmark who
was threatening to withdraw from the war if he was not paid.
Charles's spokesman in the Commons announced that unpaid bills
from the Cadiz fleet and anticipated costs for the next eight months
totalled £1,067,221.[53] MPs were cognisant of the need to provide
something toward the nation's defence now that Spain had been
provoked, so they offered a grant amounting to £320,000. They conditioned this offer, however, on the king's satisfactory redress of
their grievances. They would not repeat the mistake of 1625 when
supply was voted before grievances were redressed. As Christopher
Wandesford explained, the 'cause of these great wants is that parliaments have of late met, saluted, given money, and so departed'. To

avoid repeating that mistake, it was necessary to 'give advice and counsel to the King as well as money'.[54] The Commons' paramount grievance was Buckingham, and their advice to Charles was to get rid of him.[55] What was the point, MPs reasoned, of giving Charles any more money if it would be placed in the same hands to be spent as badly as their previous grants? The Cadiz fleet, Sir John Strangways observed, 'gives us no great encouragement to give more monies'. And no man, said Sir John Savile, 'will be willing to give his money into a bottomless gulf'.[56]

The Parliament of 1626 intensified the bad qualities we have already seen in Charles and brought out worse. He was still intransigent, still insisting that Parliament was obliged to finance his £1 million-per-annum war without any concessions on his part. He was beginning to understand that Parliament had him in a compromising position, but he was still unwilling to compromise. 'Now ... that you have things according to your own wishes, and that I am so far engaged that you think there is no retreat', he told Parliament, 'now you begin to set the dice and make your own prize.'[57] As those words suggest, Charles adopted a resentful and vindictive attitude, not a conciliatory one. He was convinced that he could bend Parliament to his will by removing a handful of trouble-makers or intimidating the whole body. He tried again to prevent the Earl of Bristol from taking his seat in the House of Lords, but Bristol defiantly showed up, and Charles subsequently charged him with treason and imprisoned him. Likewise, he kept the Earl of Arundel out of the Lords for several months by imprisoning him and keeping him under house arrest.[58] To quiet the House of Commons, he selected six of the most vocal critics from 1625 and appointed them sheriffs, which technically barred them from sitting in the new Parliament.[59]

'The King and Kingdom must not be divided', Wandesford warned. But his very words suggested that this process was already under way.[60] The Commons were so disaffected that the removal of leaders like Coke, Phelips, and Seymour made no difference whatsoever in the tenor of their proceedings. They picked up precisely where they had left off the preceding year, attacking the Crown's war policy and Buckingham's leadership by interrogating the Council of War, hoping to show that subsidy money had been misappropriated and that the Lord Admiral was responsible for the catastrophes of Mansfeld and Cadiz. MPs were either disingenuous or deluding themselves to maintain that these attacks on Buckingham and the Crown's war policy did not reflect on the king himself.[61] Charles had no such illusions. When a member of the Council of War told Charles that he was willing to risk imprisonment at the hands of the Commons rather than jeopardise a further grant of supply, the king replied: 'It is not you that they aim at, but it is me upon whom they make inquisition.' Charles was determined to stand his ground, even if that meant losing the new subsidies he desperately needed. 'Gold', said Charles, 'may be bought too dear.'[62] He commanded members of the Council of War not to give any testimony in Parliament divulging the nature of their counsels; their lips were sealed. This action succeeded in cutting off one line of attack on the Crown's war policy, but it also drove the Commons into a more direct confrontation. Later that very same day, Doctor Turner read the list of accusations in the Commons that would become impeachment charges against Buckingham.[63]

Charles took the attack on Buckingham very personally. As Charles viewed it, Turner had made 'an inquiry upon articles against the Duke of Buckingham as he pretends, but indeed against the honor and government of himself and his blessed father'.[64] The impeachment charges were formally presented to the House of Lords by Sir John Eliot and Sir Dudley Digges. Both men used extravagant language. Earlier, when Clement Coke had said that 'it is better to suffer by a foreign hand than at home', Charles had branded this 'a seditious speech', but he left the punishment to the Commons, who did nothing.[65] This time Charles acted, arresting Eliot and Digges. 'I have been too remiss heretofore in punishing those insolent speeches that concerned myself', Charles explained.[66] One of the things that angered Charles was the comparison Eliot had drawn between the Duke of Buckingham and Sejanus, who was a notorious favourite of the Roman Emperor Tiberius. 'If the Duke is Sejanus', Charles concluded, 'I must be Tiberius.'[67] Another feature of these speeches that upset Charles was the insinuation that Buckingham had poisoned King James. Here, too, Charles felt that he was being implicated, especially in the words used by Digges. Despite the offensive content of these speeches, Charles eventually relented, releasing both Eliot and Digges. In the final event, however, the only way he could protect Buckingham from the judgement of the Lords was to dissolve Parliament, even though it cost him the badly needed subsidies.[68]

The reader should not be too quick to judge Charles by modern expectations. For example, it was standard practice for monarchs to

intimidate Parliament, even to arrest members (though usually *after*
Parliament was adjourned). This was Charles's principal means of
leverage over Parliament, and we cannot blame him for exercising it.
Of course such measures could backfire. As one member said in
1626, 'monies should not be gotten from us by threats as we have
had divers this parliament'.[69] These measures did not succeed in
getting Charles the money he wanted, but they had an effect none
the less by putting MPs on guard about what they said and did. It is
no accident that MPs in this Parliament threw one of their own
members into the Tower for speaking words that were no more offensive than those spoken by Coke, Eliot, or Digges.[70] This latter incident illustrates not only the efficacy of the king's interventions but
also the fact that MPs themselves displayed a frightening readiness to
interrogate, persecute, and imprison anyone they disliked (most
notably, Roman Catholics, Arminians, and 'evil counsellors'). Nor
should we be too quick to judge Charles's steadfast refusal to
sacrifice Buckingham. Today, no matter how unjust the accusations,
it is commonplace for a Prime Minister or President to dump a subordinate who has become a political liability. Charles was more resolute in the face of what amounted to a political vendetta. On this
point Roger Lockyer is absolutely right: Buckingham was no crimi-
nal. The impeachment charges against him were of dubious merit
and 'essentially political'.[71] In reality, as the Venetian ambassador expressed it, 'what weighs upon them [MPs] most of all is that everything depends upon a person, every one of whose operations has
turned out unlucky and unsuccessful'.[72]

What was wrong with Charles's conduct in 1626? While any one of
his actions taken by itself might be excused, the pattern of all those
actions taken together was deeply disturbing. It was becoming clear
that Charles was a stubborn, imperious, and dangerous man.
Moreover, what Charles did do was all the more alarming in view of
what he did *not* do. He threatened, intimidated, issued ultimata; but
he did not show a willingness to bargain. The challenge, as he saw it,
was not to reach a mutual understanding with Parliament but to
make them yield to his demands.[73] The message he sent to the
Commons on 20 April was typical: if MPs did not quickly vote further
supply, 'his Majesty will give you no longer time, he will endure no
longer delay, nor recede from what he now sends unto you'.[74]
Charles was convinced of his own rightness and blindly indiffer-
ent to the political process. During this Parliament, at the very
time Buckingham was being impeached for holding too many

offices, Charles secured another prestigious office for him, the Chancellorship of Cambridge University. What Charles considered a demonstration of support for the Duke, we can only judge an act of stupefying insensitivity. The king's defiant refusal to work within the political process drove him outside that process. There were disturbing intimations in 1626 that Charles was contemplating 'new counsels', and he himself declared: 'Remember that parliaments are altogether in my power for the calling, sitting, and continuance of them.'[75] Charles did not inspire respect or trust; he inspired fear. And the underlying fear he raised was that, since he showed no ability to rule with Parliaments, he would try ruling without them. In the summer of 1626, the Reverend Joseph Mead wrote, 'It is generally thought ... that the last parliament of King Charles his reign will end within this week.'[76]

The Forced Loan

In the aftermath of the 1626 Parliament, Charles did resort to different if not entirely 'new' counsels. He levied a forced loan and enforced its collection by imprisoning resisters. Richard Cust's study of *The Forced Loan and English Politics 1626–1628* provided an eye-opening portrait of Charles in this period. Cust emphasised that Charles was 'a difficult man to advise, particularly if the advice was unwelcome'.[77] Through tact and persistence, a faction of moderates on the Privy Council managed to dissuade Charles from taking harsher action against men who resisted paying the forced loan. In the main, however, it was the king who decided policy, refused to summon a new Parliament, and pursued the project of the loan relentlessly. He put pressure on the judges to endorse the legality of the loan; when they refused, he summarily dismissed the chief justice of the Court of King's Bench.[78] He threatened to deal with loan resisters by forcing them into military service and shipping them off to fight on the continent.[79] One courtier reported that no one dared intervene on behalf of any loan resister because the king's 'heart is so inflamed in this business as he vows a perpetual remembrance, as well as present punishment'.[80]

More than money was at stake here. Charles had become 'almost obsessively concerned with the loyalty of his subjects'.[81] As we saw above, Charles thought in 1626 that he could obtain a more cooperative Parliament by excluding a few key members, but he discovered that it was still disrupted by 'the irregular humors of some particular persons'.[82] Cust found the same sentiments amplified in the declaration Charles published afterward to justify his dissolution of Parliament. Charles continued to insist that he had been drawn into war by the Parliament of 1624 and that subsequent Parliaments had reneged on their promise of support. He also continued to believe that this failure resulted from 'the violent and ill-advised Passions of a few Members of the House', the malevolent spirit of 'such as are ill-affected to the State'.[83] Charles was deeply hurt by this turn of events and took it as an aspersion on his honour. When his uncle, the King of Denmark, suffered a crushing defeat, in part at least for lack of England's promised assistance, Charles felt further humiliated and betrayed by his own subjects. When his appeal to the nation for a voluntary benevolence failed to raise money, he became all the more convinced that the spirit of subversion was spreading. He came to abhor the very idea of a Parliament and to doubt the loyalty of his subjects. The forced loan became a test of his subjects' loyalty. When Charles behaved this way, of course, it fostered the very sort of attitude he feared. As people observed his high-handed methods, they did indeed begin to question his judgement and trustworthiness.

Cust's work on the forced loan demolished the revisionist picture of politics in the 1620s. Revisionism had emphasised shared assumptions, harmony instead of conflict, the absence of adversarial politics, and the non-existence of opposition. Where conflict occurred, it was reduced to petty motives, localist interests, or factionalism. And the root cause of trouble was alleged to be war, not the king. By contrast, Cust showed that the contemporary stress on consensus and harmony should not be taken at face value.[84] It was more a symptom of disorder, an expression of what people wished to be the case, than a description of what was in fact the case. More importantly, Cust showed that war was a superficial explanation for the disorders of the period; ideological division was a 'more profound cause'.[85] Cust believed in the existence not only of opposition but of a 'principled opposition'.[86] He found a great deal of news circulating in England, linking localities to the centre, creating a widespread political consciousness that emphasised conflict, criticised the king, and even tended to re-establish the impression that there were two 'sides' in early Stuart politics.[87] Cust came to agree with 'the Whig view, that news contributed to a process of political polarization', and he noted that 'in this, as in many other aspects of the period, the instincts and judgements of S. R. Gardiner remain a reliable guide'.[88] Cust went even further. Although he did not wish to rebuild the 'high road to Civil War' with its familiar milestones, he came very close to doing precisely that. He saw a continuous pattern of conflict from the forced loan to the Grand Remonstrance; and he concluded more generally that there was 'a measure of continuity and thematic unity in much of the ideological conflict of the early seventeenth century'.[89]

Cust's most significant achievement was to restore Charles to centre stage. He showed that although Charles was a difficult man to advise, he did receive good counsel. He showed that Charles was not an unfortunate victim of circumstances beyond his control but a vindictive and inflexible ruler who had a knack for making circumstances worse. He showed that Charles had come, in the words of contemporaries, to 'abominate' the very name of Parliament and had vowed not to summon another until he was 'reduced to extremity and pulled by the hairs of his head'.[90] He showed that Charles interpreted criticism as disloyalty. Indeed, he showed that Charles was 'in the grip of something approaching paranoia'.[91] And he showed that Charles's fierce determination to collect the forced loan led many of his subjects to question their 'trust and faith in the King himself'.[92]

Another historian who refocused attention on Charles was J. A. Guy, who unearthed one episode in the history of the forced loan that was particularly instrumental in undermining faith in the king.[93] The legality of the loan was never tested in a court of law. The famous case associated with the loan was the five knights' case, so named because it involved five imprisoned loan resisters who sought relief in King's Bench. The royal strategy in the five knights' case was clever. The Attorney-General, Sir Robert Heath, entirely avoided the issue of the loan and simply argued instead that the plaintiffs had been imprisoned 'by his majesty's special commandment' and were therefore not eligible for bail. The judges on King's Bench concurred. The prisoners were denied bail, and that would have been the end of the affair if not for the epilogue to the story uncovered by Guy. The court had made a mere procedural ruling denying bail. They had not made a substantive judgement on the issue of the king's discretionary power to imprison his subjects for unspecified reasons of state. Heath subsequently tried to change the way in which the case was recorded in the official records of King's Bench, however, to make it appear as if they had rendered a judgement establishing a binding precedent for the monarch's power to imprison without showing cause. Heath's attempt to pervert the legal record was a felony in English law, and to their credit, both the clerk and the judges refused to cooperate. Unfortunately for Heath, one of the lawyers who opposed him in the case, John Selden, sat in the Commons in 1628. When Selden stumbled upon evidence of Heath's effort to falsify the record, this shocking revelation helped strengthen resolve to curb the king's power of imprisonment. Heath's conduct contributed to the growing impression that Charles could not be trusted to rule within the established law of the land. Of course it was possible that Heath acted entirely on his own, a point that has been made in the king's defence by Kevin Sharpe. Unfortunately for that interpretation, Buckingham made the astounding admission that Charles had reprimanded Heath for failing![94]

Did the military exigencies of the time justify Charles's actions? Here it is well to remember Conrad Russell's argument: 'Charles had an attachment to the rule of law, yet he believed that the law must be compatible with his obligation to defend his kingdom.' Early modern monarchs preferred to rule within the law, but 'when a legal right came into conflict with an urgent necessity of defence, they gave priority to the urgent necessity'. Unlike his stingy and myopic subjects, the 'king could be presumed to know about military necessities'.[95] What were the military necessities that justified the extreme measures taken by Charles in this period? Charles managed to continue the war for nearly eighteen months without parliamentary assistance. In the fall of 1626 he launched a second fleet against Spain, a fleet that was even less effectual than the previous one against Cadiz. Badly damaged by a storm in the Bay of Biscay, it limped back to England without so much as encountering the enemy.[96] Since this fleet produced no tangible results, except to drive Charles more deeply into debt, it is hard to see how it could be considered a military necessity. Far more costly, of course, was the opening of war on a second front – France.[97]

Rational explanations can be found for Charles and Buckingham provoking another major enemy. Relations with France had continued to deteriorate. Despite the concessions Charles made to lure the French into a military alliance, it became increasingly clear that the alliance was a dream. When France actually allied with Spain instead of England, Charles felt duped by the French just as he had previously been duped by the Spanish. This was an especially bitter disappointment for Buckingham, who had been outmanoeuvred by Richelieu. Indeed, one historian has called the war with France 'Buckingham's private war with Richelieu'.[98] No less infuriating to Charles were Henrietta Maria's meddling French attendants. His patience exhausted, Charles forcibly removed these irritants and sent them back to France. Drive them away 'like so many wild beasts', Charles ordered, 'and so the devil go with them!'[99] Moreover, there was still the important matter of honour to be vindicated after the affair of the loan ships. If France refused to be an ally, then the most direct way to restore English honour was to make common cause with the French Protestants and relieve La Rochelle. As Charles himself later explained, Louis XIII's 'intentions were always false and feigned ... [and] I deemed it a lesser evil to have him for an open enemy than to have him for a false friend'.[100] Nevertheless, despite all these rational explanations, when one considers how miserably the king's military enterprises had fared up to this point and how completely his resources were already depleted, it is hard to avoid the consensus among historians that war with France was lunacy.[101]

In the war with France (as indeed in the war with Spain) there was only one battle of any consequence: in the summer of 1627 Buckingham personally led an attack against the French fort on the Isle of Rhé located just off the coast from La Rochelle. The English were bogged down for more than three months and lost at least 5000 men before retreating.[102] The assault on Rhé, like its predecessors, was not a military necessity; it was a gamble. If Charles had understood that even kings must work within the limitations of reality, if he had been less quick to stand upon his honour, if he had been less prone to make enemies, and if he had not felt the need to prove his mettle by vanquishing an enemy, he would never have taken that gamble.

As Gardiner rightly observed, 'Charles and Buckingham were ruining the sources of their influence by forcing the nation to support unwillingly an extravagant and ill-conducted war'.[103] The forced loan raised nearly £270,000, but it was the proverbial drop in the bucket.[104] A minor official at court described how desperate the Crown's predicament had become by the autumn of 1627: 'his Majesty's revenue of all kinds is now exhausted, we are upon the third year's anticipation beforehand, land much sold of the principal, credit lost, and at the utmost shift with the Commonwealth.'[105] Yet Buckingham was contemplating several new military efforts, including an attack on Calais; and Charles, undaunted by reality, blithely promised to provide the necessary resources.[106] In the end it was decided to take another stab at lifting the siege of La Rochelle, but the only way to pay for this undertaking was to summon a new Parliament.

The Parliament of 1628

Charles's inability to learn from experience, generate goodwill, or inspire confidence was all too evident in the short speech he made at the opening of the 1628 Parliament. If this new assembly failed to provide the necessary supply, Charles warned, 'I must, according to my conscience, take those other courses, which God hath put into mine hands'. Thus Charles, instead of laying the spectre of 'new counsels' to rest, actually breathed new life into it. Worse still, he told his listeners, 'take not this as a threatening, for I scorn to threaten any but mine equals, but as an admonition'.[107] A threat by any other name was still a threat, which set precisely the wrong tone and made the more conciliatory language in the king's speech ring hollow. By his 'studied rudeness', as Gardiner characterised it, Charles had managed to throw away a critical opportunity to improve his situation.[108] The Lord Keeper next spoke at greater length, describing the state of war on the continent in a way that was calculated to frighten members with the menace of Rome and the Habsburgs. Yet he, too, ended on a sour note with the hackneyed argument that Parliament had made an engagement to support the war, and he repeated the worst themes of Charles's speech. If kings find their subjects loving and eager to vote supply, he explained, then they 'may the better forbear the use of their prerogative, and moderate the rigor of their laws towards their subjects'. If not, then: 'Remember his Majesty's admonition, I say remember it.'[109]

Charles's politics of fear – his constant threats, his readiness to employ new courses, his elevation of the royal prerogative over the common law, and his harsh treatment of those who disagreed with him – bore their natural fruit in the Parliament of 1628. Charles had succeeded in frightening and alienating a sizeable number of his most influential subjects. For refusing to pay the forced loan 76 men had been committed to prison or held under house arrest; 23 of those now sat in the House of Commons (nearly one in twenty members).[110] One of these, Sir John Eliot, told the House that he and other prisoners had been threatened that if they did not pay the loan, they would be sent abroad against their will. Now he looked to his fellow MPs for help 'that it may be cleared here that the subject ought to be freed from that fear'.[111] Sir Robert Phelips admitted that there was cause to fear foreign dangers but, he added, 'let not these fears so work on us as to weaken our resolutions against our fears at home'.[112] The overriding concern of Parliament in 1628 was to banish fear by re-establishing the rule of law, to balance the subjects' liberties against the king's prerogative, 'to vindicate the fundamental liberties of the kingdom'.[113] In Eliot's words, it was 'our ancient laws, our liberties, our lives, that call to us for protection'. The normal bulwark of the law had been swept aside, leaving Eliot to ask: 'Where is law? Where is *meum et tuum* [mine and thine]? It is fallen into the chaos of a higher power.'[114] Without the law to protect them, the English were little more than slaves, a comparison that came naturally to several speakers in 1628. Sir Dudley Digges, for example, declared that any 'king that is not tied to the laws is a king of slaves'.[115] It was Digges who stated the dilemma most precisely: 'We are now upon this question whether the king may be above the law, or the law above the king. It is our unhappiness, but it is put upon us.'[116] He need only have added – if it had been safe to do so – that this question was put upon them by King Charles.[117]

Discontent in the Parliament of 1628 crystallised around four issues: unparliamentary taxation, imprisonment without showing cause, billeting in private homes, and martial law. Charles reacted predictably to this discontent. At first he promised that he would accept any solution that Parliament agreed upon 'by way of bill or otherwise', but then he began to wriggle out of this promise and force a confrontation.[118] He sent a message to the Commons assuring them that a bill was not necessary. In the words of the Lord Keeper, the king 'assures you that he will maintain all his subjects in the just freedom of their persons and safety of their estates, and that he will govern according to the laws and statutes of this realm, and that you shall find as much security in his Majesty's royal word and promise as in the strength of any law you can make'.[119] For some MPs this assurance was enough, but most (no matter what they said publicly to the contrary) put no stock in Charles's 'royal word and promise'. Charles should have let the issue die, but he insisted on sending another message to the Commons asking 'whether we will rest on his royal word or no'.[120] As J. A. Guy observed, this message 'poisoned the atmosphere completely'.[121] MPs actually sat for a while in stunned silence. It was obvious that Charles was trying to renege on the promise he had made at the outset to let the Commons proceed 'by way of bill or otherwise'. He could hardly expect MPs to rely on his royal word now when he was, in the very act of making that request, breaking his previous royal word. When the Commons persisted in drafting a bill to vindicate their liberties, Charles tried to evade his promise another way. He conceded that he would accept a bill, as he had originally promised, but now he specified that this bill must only confirm existing laws 'without straining them or enlarging them by new explanations, interpretations, expositions, or additions in any sort, which he clearly tells us he will not give way unto'.[122] Sir Nathaniel Rich summed up the emptiness of the king's promises: 'We have nothing thereby but shells and shadows.'[123]

When it became obvious that Charles would not accept a bill with any teeth in it, the Commons hit upon their own alternative in the Petition of Right. Charles's behaviour toward the Petition reveals much about his character. First he tried to limit the scope of the Petition by writing a personal letter to the House of Lords, appealing to them to preserve his right to imprison without showing cause. The Lords produced a 'saving clause' which would have been added to the Petition, declaring that there was no intention to limit 'that sovereign power wherewith your Majesty is trusted'. Of course the Commons refused to attach this clause. John Glanville, representing the position of the Commons to the Lords, described it as a 'clause specious in show and smooth in words, but in effect and consequence most dangerous'. Glanville warned the Lords not to put their blind trust in the king: 'The word "trust" is of a great latitude and large extent, and therefore need be well and warily applied and restrained, *especially in the case of a king*.'[124] The Lords knew what Glanville was talking about. They had made their own inquiry into Heath's effort to distort the record of the five knights' case. More importantly, several individual Lords had suffered directly at the hands of the king. Roughly 15 peers had refused to acknowledge the legality of the forced loan (chief among these were Warwick, Essex, Saye, Lincoln, and Clare). The most radically outspoken of these, Lincoln, was imprisoned in the Tower. Essex, who had performed valiantly in the expedition to Cadiz, was mortified to be deprived of his Lord Lieutenancy. Others experienced the shame of being removed from their positions as Justices of the Peace. 'No English

monarch', wrote L. J. Reeve, 'could afford to alienate such men so
seriously.' Nor was this the end of the list. Other lords offended by
Charles included: the Earl of Pembroke, who had long resented
Buckingham's ascendancy; Bishop Williams, who had been removed
from his office as Lord Keeper; Archbishop Abbot, who had been
confined to a home in the countryside and eclipsed in favour by
William Laud; and the Earls of Bristol and Arundel who had both
personally experienced arbitrary imprisonment.[125] To be sure, there
was much more sympathy for the king's position in the Lords than in
the Commons, and many of these men had more to gain from pleasing the king than pleasing the Commons. Even Bristol and Arundel
initially sought a compromise. When the Commons refused to compromise, however, the Lords opted to support the Petition as it
stood. Some did this to avoid confrontation, others to obtain the ur-
gently needed subsidies. Nevertheless, this united front of both
Houses was a portentous event.[126] It showed that Charles could no
longer count on the support of even his most natural allies.

Charles responded to the Petition in a characteristic manner when
it was presented to him. He gave only a vague reassurance that was
not substantially different from what he had said previously. This precipitated another entirely unnecessary crisis and drove the Commons
into a more radical course of action. They began to assemble a catalogue of their grievances to be presented to the king in the form of a
remonstrance. Charles tried to cut off these proceedings by making it
clear that he was determined to stick by his answer 'without further
change or alteration'.[127] Furthermore, he announced his intention to
adjourn Parliament in one week's time. He directed them to finish
the business at hand (that is, to produce the five subsidies he had
been led to expect he would receive in return for his acceptance of
the Petition) and to embark on no new business. The next day
he sent the same message through the Speaker, emphasising that he
would not alter his resolution to adjourn Parliament on the day he
had set and that no new business should be entertained 'which may
lay any scandal or aspersion upon the state, government, or ministers
thereof'. Charles was trying to prevent an attack on Buckingham, but
his heavy-handed intervention only succeeded in bringing the issue
out into the open. When MPs tried to continue debate, the Speaker
told them, 'There lies a command on me: I must command you not
to proceed.' This command had precisely the opposite of its desired
effect. It was Sir Edward Coke who now boldly opened the taboo
subject. 'Let us palliate no longer', he said. He named the Duke of

Buckingham as 'the cause of all our miseries' and the 'grievance of grievances'.[128] Faced with this outcry, Charles relented, indicating that he was willing to reconsider his answer to the Petition. Once again the Lords and Commons presented a united front and asked for 'a more clear and satisfactory answer'. Charles capitulated in a dramatic meeting of both Houses where he personally reaffirmed his intention to honour the Petition, and the clerk pronounced the words in French which gave it the effect of law.[129] Both Houses were ecstatic at this scene, though if they had listened carefully to what Charles said, they would have noticed that he thought he was conceding no more than he had previously. He ended, too, with a typically churlish remark that 'if this parliament have not a happy conclusion, the sin is yours, I am free from it'.

Charles told Parliament that he had given a more binding answer to the Petition 'to show you there is no doubleness in my meaning'.[130] Like so many of Charles's denials, this statement was an inadvertent admission that people did indeed worry about his duplicity. And they were right to do so. To ensure that the Petition would not be forgotten, Parliament obtained the king's permission to enrol it not only in their own records but also in the law courts at Westminster, and more importantly to print it for public distribution with his second answer. However Charles, true to form, later suppressed this version and distributed another version, substituting his first, unsatisfactory answer and adding other equivocating statements.[131] There was 'doubleness' in his meaning after all.

We have dwelt at length on the Petition of Right because few episodes could better illustrate Charles's defects as a ruler. He did not bargain in good faith and could not be trusted to keep his promises. When he encountered opposition, his first response was to stand upon his prerogative and refuse to make concessions. When this hard line failed and he was forced to back down, he lost more credit than he would have if he had been more accommodating from the outset. Furthermore, when forced to relent, he did not do it graciously. He was, in Charles Carlton's words, 'a bad loser' who treated people 'with little grace'.[132] Worse yet, when he was forced to make concessions, he typically did so merely to buy time until he was in a sufficiently strong position to retract those concessions. In his conduct toward the Petition of Right, Charles demonstrated those same 'weasel ways', as Derek Hirst called them, that he would later demonstrate when dealing with the Scottish Covenanters and with his other adversaries in the Civil War.[133] It is worth emphasising that such behaviour, devious

as it seems to us, did not seem so to Charles. He was so convinced of
the rectitude of his own position that he saw no contradiction between
appearing to concede while privately refusing to do so. He also took
pains to avoid outright lying. When he could, he couched his concessions in ambiguous language. When he could not, he interpreted the
language afterwards to suit his ends. He may have allowed himself
more latitude in this respect because, unlike mere mortals, he was ultimately responsible only to God. In any case, Charles's high view of
royalty prevented him from seeing himself as other people saw him.
He failed to comprehend how far his behaviour in the arena of every-
day politics eroded his majesty. In this respect as in others, he did not
grasp the connection between empirical reality and abstract ideals. He
continued to invoke 'the word of a king', oblivious to the fact that his
own actions had cheapened the phrase.

Anyone who has read the parliamentary records of 1628 must be
struck by the great earnestness with which speakers on all sides fer-
vently tried to restore a spirit of goodwill and shared government.
That sense of deep concern and genuine striving for harmony is
missing only from the curt speeches that Charles himself delivered.
The task of Privy Councillors in 1628 was to effect a reconciliation
between king and Parliament, and they could best do this by speaking for Charles rather than allowing him to speak for himself in his
predictably abrasive fashion. They had to 'work against the grain of
Charles's basic political instincts', as Richard Cust explained. They
succeeded best at the outset, but the longer Parliament withheld
supply and pressed their grievances, the more it confirmed the
king's belief in the existence of an anti-monarchical faction. The
main reason Charles was at all pliant was that he desperately needed
money, and as soon as supply appeared to be forthcoming, he re-
verted to his 'grating' style and began to 'backtrack' on his earlier
promises.[134] When Charles could not be held at bay or humoured
into cooperation by his wiser counsellors, he forced people into opposition and repeatedly made a bad situation worse. If he had simply
given a satisfactory answer to the Petition of Right immediately, his
evasiveness would not have prompted the Commons to start working
on a remonstrance. In the final days of this session, the House continued to compile this list of grievances against the Crown's religious
policy, the disastrous war effort, and above all Buckingham (the
Duke's assassin would later claim that this remonstrance had inspired him to commit the deed). When Charles formally accepted
the remonstrance, he made no effort to conceal his contempt for its

authors. He told the Commons that they did not know what they were doing, and in another tactless gesture of defiance he extended his hand for Buckingham to kiss![135] When the Commons prepared a second remonstrance, arguing that Charles was already violating the Petition of Right by collecting tonnage and poundage without parliamentary approval, they had at last gone too far. Charles (quite rightly, in this case) could never agree that the Petition had limited his power to collect these indispensable sources of revenue. Charles accepted the five subsidies for which he had submitted to the indignities of this Parliament, and then promptly prorogued it.

After the Parliament of 1628, the opening stage of Charles's reign rushed to a conclusion. The assassin's knife succeeded in doing what Parliament had failed to do by removing Buckingham from the king's side. Charles was better at making enemies than he was at making friends. S. R. Gardiner wrote that Buckingham was 'the only real personal friend' Charles ever had. This is an insightful observation, but we have to make an exception for Queen Henrietta Maria because, as Conrad Russell wrote with equal insight, 'the most disastrous consequence of Buckingham's assassination was that Charles fell in love with his wife'.[136] It is probably more than a coincidence that the queen, after nearly four years of marriage, became pregnant for the first time within months of the assassination. We can only speculate about the other consequences of Buckingham's murder, but it is reasonable to suppose that it contributed to the king's sense of estrangement from his people, his hostility toward Parliaments in general, and his later treatment of Sir John Eliot in particular.[137] As Clarendon observed, Charles 'admitted very few into any degree of trust who had ever discovered themselves to be enemies to the duke'.[138] Buckingham was buried in Westminster Abbey. There is a story that Charles wanted to build a monument for his lost friend, but he was dissuaded because he did not have the money and because, as Lord Treasurer Weston remarked, it would not look good for Charles to erect a monument to the Duke when he had erected none to his father.[139]

War, too, was coming to an end. Even before the Duke's death, peace overtures had been made to both Spain and France. A fleet commanded by the Earl of Denbigh had failed to relieve La Rochelle while the Parliament of 1628 met. Charles sent one more fleet (the one Buckingham had planned to command in person), but it made only a feeble effort to breach the impenetrable French blockade. The city surrendered within weeks of this English failure, and

Charles subsequently concluded peace with the French (April 1629) on worse terms than he could have had months earlier if he had only been willing to admit his inability to give the Huguenots any real assistance. Moreover, although the Huguenots were stripped of their power to defend themselves, Louis XIII and Richelieu did not take away their freedom of worship. This undermined Charles's justification for fighting the French in the first place and made the war seem pointless.[140] Peace with Spain took a little longer to conclude (November 1630), but the fact of the matter was, with the exception of the puny raid on Cadiz, hostilities had never quite broken out between the two nations.[141]

The Parliament of 1629

Parliament met one more time before the close of this era in early 1629. This session should have been smoother sailing. The subsidies voted in 1628 were still being collected, so Charles could not ask for more. Buckingham, the great 'grievance of grievances', was gone. The war effort was winding down. Charles, in a rare act of political acumen, had removed one of his most effective critics from the Commons, Sir Thomas Wentworth, by elevating him to the Lords and appointing him President of the Council of the North. And Sir Edward Coke, alleging old age, had removed himself. There were, however, two festering issues that came to a head in 1629: religion and customs duties.

Charles's marriage and the tolerance he had shown toward Catholics raised concern about his religious convictions from the outset of his reign. That concern escalated as Charles aligned himself with clergymen who espoused Arminianism.[142] Although, narrowly speaking, Arminianism was simply the doctrine of free will as opposed to the Calvinist doctrine of predestination, it was not this doctrinal difference that made Arminianism such a potent issue. The problem was that many English associated free will, and hence Arminianism, with Roman Catholicism. The problem was further compounded at this point because Arminian clergy glorified the royal prerogative, specifically in sermons supporting the forced loan.[143] The Commons' remonstrance of 1628 had described Arminianism as 'a cunning way to bring in popery', and it had named two leading clerics who were thought to favour Arminianism: Richard Neile, Bishop of Winchester, and William Laud, Bishop of Bath and Wells.[144] When members reassembled in 1629, they were appalled by the favour Charles had shown to these and other controversial clergy almost immediately after their prorogation the previous summer. Neile and Laud were admitted to the Privy Council. Laud was advanced to the prestigious bishopric of London. Richard Montagu, whom Charles had protected from the attack of Parliament in 1625, was appointed Bishop of Chichester. Roger Manwaring, who had been impeached in 1628 for his published sermons extolling the royal prerogative, was pardoned, named a royal chaplain, and given the rectory vacated by Montagu.[145] It was beginning to seem, as Conrad Russell wryly observed, 'for a clergyman to be complained of by the Parliament was probably the shortest road to preferment'.[146] Charles's brazen defiance of parliamentary opinion was typical. One historian has dubbed his pardon of Manwaring an act of 'political madness'.[147] On the other hand, Charles did take several steps to counterbalance the effect of these appointments before Parliament met in 1629. He appeared to get tough with recusants and restored Archbishop Abbot to favour. He also issued a proclamation suppressing Montagu's book (*Appello Caesarem*) and calling for an end to religious dispute.[148] Charles may not have been as avidly devoted to the doctrine of Arminianism as recent historians have made him seem, and he certainly wanted to avoid doctrinal wrangling.[149] Given his previous behaviour, however, people were bound to doubt his sincerity.

Customs duties were the other festering issue in 1629. As we saw above, the Parliament of 1625, in a sharp break with precedent, had failed to grant Charles authority to collect tonnage and poundage for life. Of course he had no choice but to collect this revenue whether Parliament authorised it or not. In 1628 the issue was made worse by some MPs who charged that this was a violation of the Petition of Right. It was high time to resolve the issue and allow Charles to collect tonnage and poundage without appearing to be operating outside the law. Indeed this is the only obvious reason Charles had for facing Parliament again in 1629.

The parliamentary session of 1629 was a shambles.[150] Charles was part of the problem, a fact he himself inadvertently acknowledged at the outset when he asked MPs to 'be deaf to ill reports concerning me'.[151] One ill report was confirmed early on when Selden described to the Commons how Charles had 'made waste paper' of the first

printing of the Petition of Right and substituted a second version
with his unsatisfactory answers attached.[152] Before much could be
made of this issue, attention in the House quickly passed to the
subject of religion. Francis Rous (John Pym's stepbrother) best expressed the elaborate conspiracy theory in the Commons that linked
Arminianism to Roman Catholicism, and Roman Catholicism to absolutist government in Spain and England. The way Rous viewed it,
Arminianism was a Trojan horse filled with men who were 'ready to
open the gates to Romish tyranny and Spanish monarchy'. An
Arminian was 'the spawn of a Papist'. Look closely, Rous warned,
and you will see 'an Arminian reaching out his hand to a Papist, a
Papist to a Jesuit, a Jesuit gives one hand to the Pope and the other
to the King of Spain'.[153] Another MP aimed more directly at Charles
when he declared that suppressing Montagu's book was little use 'for
if they can get bishoprics for writing such books, we shall have many
more that will write books in that kind'.[154] Yet another speaker
alleged that Arminians whispered into the king's ear, poisoning his
mind against anyone who opposed him, 'and so they put him upon
designs that stand not with public liberty, and tell him that he may
command what he listeth and do what he pleaseth with goods, lives,
and Religion'.[155] Certainly some MPs were more concerned over religion and others more concerned over issues of a legal or political
nature. Christopher Thompson has tried to distinguish between
these two factions in 1629.[156] But religion and politics were not entirely separable. As Sir Walter Earle said in the Commons, 'never was
there ... a more near conjunction between matter of Religion and
matter of State in any Kingdom in the world than there is in this
Kingdom at this day'.[157]

On the issue of Arminianism, although Charles was part of the
problem, he certainly was not the whole problem. We might say of
the Commons what Richard Cust said of the king earlier – that they
were 'in the grip of something approaching paranoia'. In any case,
their exaggerated fears arose not just from what the king did but
from their own crude religious hatreds. For the other major issue
that convulsed and eventually broke this Parliament, Charles was
even less to blame. He had no choice but to continue collecting
tonnage and poundage and impositions. When merchants, egged on
by Parliament, refused to pay, it was reasonable for the customs
officials to confiscate those merchants' goods. Linda Popofsky
has shown that Charles was 'faced with a full-fledged merchant
revolt' that went beyond narrow merchant interests to the larger

constitutional issues of illegal taxation and arbitrary rule.[158] Granted
that this was 'principled opposition', it is still hard to see what else
Charles could have done. When the Commons tried to prosecute the
customs officials, Charles too acted out of a combination of economic self-interest and higher principle. He had to protect the
revenue he was collecting, but he also thought it was wrong for his
servants to be punished for carrying out his own instructions. He insisted 'that the truth be not concealed, which is that what they did
was either by his own direct order and command, or by order of the
Council-board, himself being present and assisting, and therefore he
will not have it divided from his act'.[159] Charles consistently refused
to let his servants be used as scapegoats for his own actions. On
one level this was laudable. 'No king of England', Christopher
Thompson has written, 'could have contemplated the punishment of
his servants for obedience to his commands with equanimity whatever pretext was found.'[160] However, on another level, by refusing to
let his servants take the blame and placing himself in the line of fire,
Charles made matters worse politically. With this buffer removed,
criticism could only be aimed directly at the king himself, which
raised the stakes and made accommodation much more difficult.

Having reached this impasse, the session of 1629 came to a quick
and dramatic end.[161] When Charles ordered the Commons to
adjourn for a week, two members forcibly held the Speaker in his
chair. Some members tried to leave, but one locked the door and
put the key in his pocket. In the shouting and mayhem that followed, the Commons insisted on voting their own adjournment, but
only after giving apparent approval to three resolutions put forward
by Sir John Eliot and a small number of accomplices. These resolutions declared that anyone who promoted religious innovations
(specifically popery and Arminianism) and anyone who promoted
or paid tonnage and poundage was a 'capital enemy' to the
kingdom.[162] Exasperated by this course of events, Charles dissolved
Parliament and arrested nine members of the Commons.[163]

Conspiracy Theories and Opposition

L. J. Reeve's study of this period entitled *Charles I and the Road to
Personal Rule*, like Richard Cust's study of the forced loan, reaffirmed

the traditional view of King Charles. Reeve described Charles as: 'woefully inadequate', 'thoroughly ill-equipped to be king', 'authoritarian', 'paranoid about loyalty', 'defensive', 'unaccommodating', 'obsessive', 'inflexible', 'dogmatic, opinionated, and self-righteous'. Reeve emphasised that Charles had no aptitude for politics. He 'was not, by inclination or equipment, a political man'. Worst of all, he had a 'fatal inability to operate on a basis of trust'. Given all these faults, Charles deserved the lion's share of blame for the political turmoil of his reign. 'Somewhere in this book', wrote Reeve, 'I suspect lurks the deduction that if Charles had not succeeded to the English throne ... the troubles of his reign would have been avoided.'[164]

On the other hand, Reeve accepted another idea currently popular among historians that relations between Charles and his Parliaments broke down at least in part because of mutual fears or mutual conspiracy theories.[165] In the Commons people like Eliot generated fear of a court conspiracy. Indeed, it was Eliot's *modus operandi* to raise the alarm about evil counsellors.[166] In 1629 Buckingham was no longer available for attack, so Eliot found others to assail (Attorney-General Heath, Bishop Neile, Secretary Coke, Lord Treasurer Weston).[167] Eliot was always looking, as he himself said, for 'some *Malus genius* some ill angell that walks betweene us and the King'.[168] Of course the real problem lay with the king, but most historians believe Eliot failed to grasp that fact.[169] He lashed out at evil counsellors in a blindly destructive fashion, naïvely thinking that a change of ministers would remedy the situation. Conditioned by his prior experience in leading the assault against Buckingham, he doggedly continued the pattern in 1629 that had made him a celebrity. This time, however, his long, strident, eloquent speeches stirred many in the House to follow him to a dead end.

Meanwhile King Charles had his own conspiratorial view of the situation. The declaration he issued after the dissolution of 1629 shows that he believed more strongly than ever that his problem with Parliament stemmed from a small band of conspirators bent on destruction. Just as Eliot blamed a handful of evil counsellors at court, so did Charles blame a handful of evil men in the Commons. There may have been an element of envy in this. Charles had experienced the intoxicating effect of popularity in 1624. Now faced with the sudden and nearly total loss of that popularity, and assuming himself to be free of blame, Charles preferred to blame people like Eliot who were enjoying the popular acclaim he had briefly known. The declaration Charles issued in 1629 began, like his speech at the beginning of the session, with an effort to dispel negative rumours. Charles tried to justify his actions to the public, so his readers would not judge him 'in those colours in which we know some turbulent and ill-affected spirits (to mask and disguise their wicked intentions, dangerous to the state) would represent us to the public'. In the contest for public opinion, the king had one huge advantage: whereas critics of royal policies had to be very careful in criticising the king, he could vilify them with impunity, although this tended to drive the two parties even further apart. The way Charles told the story, during the first session of this Parliament in 1628 a handful of 'disaffected persons' had spent their time 'blasting our government'. These were extremists who went too far in their assault on the royal prerogative, 'not well distinguishing between well-ordered liberty and licentiousness'. Charles genuinely believed these men were dangerous. He was especially alarmed by the remonstrance produced at the end of the 1628 session, 'hatched out of the passionate brains of a few particular persons', and he saw the influence of these 'evil spirits' spreading outside the walls of Parliament among the merchants who refused to pay the customs duties. In the session of 1629, these 'few malevolent persons' exceeded all bounds of moderation. They ventured upon 'strange and exorbitant encroachments and usurpations, such as were never before attempted in that House'. Their ultimate objective, Charles believed, was to seize control of the government: 'their drift was to break ... through all respects and ligaments of government, and to erect an universal over-swaying power to themselves, which belongs only to us and not to them'. At last it was evident, said Charles, that the earlier attacks on Buckingham were motivated by 'more secret designs'. The true aim of his accusers was 'to cast our affairs into a desperate condition to abate the powers of our Crown, and to bring our government into obloquy, that in the end all things may be overwhelmed with anarchy and confusion'. Charles ended his declaration in 1629 by repeating his unalterable conviction that the men who had urged him into war subsequently reneged on their engagement. In a new twist to this old argument, however, Charles complained that these men used the urgent necessities created by the war 'to enforce us to yield to conditions incompatible with monarchy'.[170]

Contemporary historians are perhaps too inclined to discount these conspiracy theories. There was some basis in fact for them. As

Eliot suspected, Arminians were gaining a foothold at court, and
Lord Treasurer Weston was urging Charles to dissolve Parliament
and make peace with Spain. More generally, the extraordinary measures taken to prosecute the war were threatening cherished liberties. By the same token, Charles's view of the situation deserves to be
taken more seriously, too. His fears, like Eliot's, were not entirely
groundless. The House of Commons was sometimes swayed by a
handful of its most ardent and articulate members who planned
their strategy in advance, coordinated their speeches, and even
arranged for the order in which speakers would be recognised.[171] It
was not unreasonable for Charles to perceive this as a conspiracy.
Nor was it unreasonable for him to think that events in the House
betrayed an eroding respect for monarchy. Obviously there were
people out there who, despite their firm adherence to monarchy,
took a less august view of monarchy than he did. The problem was
that Charles, like his critics in the Commons, blew things out of proportion and made the worst assumptions about the other party's
motives. The truth is that many of the Crown's harshest critics, including Eliot, clung tenaciously to the fiction of evil counsellors precisely because they did not want to acknowledge any fault in the king
himself. Others who came closer to identifying Charles as the real
root of the problem still had no desire to remove him from the
throne. What they did desire was to force him to operate within
certain legal constraints. Charles was wrong to assume that these
constraints were 'incompatible with monarchy' or that they were motivated by a conscious desire to destroy the institution of monarchy.
But the effect of these restraints would certainly have been to dimin-
ish monarchy. For example, the Petition of Right was passed in
protest against particular practices in the later 1620s, but it had the
effect of limiting the Crown's freedom of action for all time. Thus
there was no wholesale or intentional assault on the institution of
monarchy itself, but there were incremental encroachments on the
royal prerogative; and it was not far-fetched for Charles to view these
as threatening.

Ironically, Charles made the situation worse by the way he reacted
to criticism. If he could have learned to accept, perhaps even to
profit from, criticism, his reign would have gone much more
smoothly. Instead, when he encountered criticism, he interpreted it
as disloyalty, hardened his position, and turned against the critics.
This was as much a function of his personality as his high conception
of monarchy. Sometimes historians claim that Charles reacted this

way because he had an unshakeable confidence in his own rectitude. Other times they claim that he reacted this way because actually deep down inside he lacked confidence; he overcompensated to mask his feelings of insecurity. In either case, the way he reacted tended to escalate the problem. Concrete questions about money, for example, were converted into larger questions about the trust-worthiness of the king and the rule of law. If Charles resorted to even more extreme expedients (like the forced loan), then he further heightened the level of concern. Thus Charles was at least as much responsible as any malcontents in the House of Commons for straining the loyalty of his subjects and testing the limits of the royal prerogative. Margaret Judson long ago interpreted the political turmoil of Charles's reign as a contest over the borderland between the king's prerogative and his subjects' liberties.[172] As David L. Smith more recently described it, the smooth running of the government depended on maintaining certain 'grey areas' and 'blurred distinc-tions' where the king's prerogative and his subjects' liberties were concerned.[173] These areas were more hotly disputed in Charles's reign – partly because of the extreme circumstances, partly because his subjects were growing more assertive, and partly because Charles himself forced the very issues he should have left dormant.

Charles's opponents were not set on destroying him, but he did have opponents. Initially revisionists, in their eagerness to refute S. R. Gardiner's interpretation, practically banned the word 'opposi-tion' from writings about the reign of Charles I. Eventually, however, this position proved untenable, and in 1985 Kevin Sharpe conceded, 'it may be that, as long as we are careful, banishment is too dracon-ian a sentence'. We have Sharpe's permission to use the term again, provided that we use it carefully.[174] Certainly Gardiner's account needed revising in some respects. It is true that he tended to view the opponents of Charles I as more cohesive and modern than they actually were; it is true that he created the impression of two clear-cut sides engaged in a continuous and escalating conflict that led almost unavoidably to Civil War. Revisionists were right to criticise these Whiggish aspects of Gardiner's narrative. Nevertheless, it turns out that in many other respects revisionists overreacted in their effort to refute Gardiner. In 1991 Richard Cust concluded, 'it seems likely that many of the hypotheses advanced by revisionist historians will themselves have to be revised, and much of Gardiner's account will be shown to have been closer to the mark than at first seemed possible'.[175]

The more historians like Cust, Reeve, Thompson, and Guy put
the real flesh-and-blood king back into the narrative of the 1620s,
the harder it was to exonerate him. He was not the hapless victim of
bad counsel, functional breakdown, or structural weaknesses. He was
not – no matter how often he repeated the claim – the unwitting
victim of a war that other men forced upon him then refused to
support. He was, instead, a stubborn, combative, and high-handed
king who generated conflict. Moreover, that conflict had a definite
constitutional dimension. Constitutional conflict was the keystone of
the old Whig history, and revisionists therefore tried to eradicate it.
Sometimes, following Nicholas Tyacke, they emphasised the religious issue of Arminianism to the exclusion of constitutional issues.
For example, Russell concluded that during the 1620s King Charles
'made few catastrophic errors' except for his espousal of
Arminianism.[176] Other times, in the manner of Lewis Namier, revisionists denied the role of principle in politics altogether. On this
subject, their most effective critic has been J. P. Sommerville. In
Politics and Ideology in England 1603–1640, Sommerville argued that
early Stuart politics could not be reduced to administrative defects,
factionalism, localism, or war. Sommerville swept aside these
'metaphorical locutions' and reasserted the central role of ideas.
'The reality of ideological conflict', wrote Sommerville, 'is a blindingly obvious feature of early Stuart history.'[177] Who controls the
power to tax? To whom are the great ministers of state accountable?
Who determines the doctrine of the church? Under what circumstances may the king imprison his subjects? What is the relationship
between the royal prerogative and the law of the land? In a time of
necessity, can the king override the law; and if so, then who determines whether a true necessity exists? In the final analysis, is the king
above the law? Granted, questions like these did not arise out of
purely theoretical disputes in the reign of Charles I any more than
they did in the reign of John I which produced Magna Carta. People
do not become embroiled in constitutional conflict as an academic
exercise. Constitutional questions arise out of concrete political
actions saturated with petty motives, but they are constitutional questions none the less.

The way Charles approached the political process, his very style of
politics, tended to push constitutional questions to the forefront. As
we have seen, he expected his commands to be acted upon without
question, he did not feel the need to explain his actions or justify his
demands, he was quick to brand critics as evil spirits and attribute

anti-monarchical motives to them, he was much more inclined to employ coercion and intimidation than persuasion and compromise, and he could not be trusted to keep his promises. More generally speaking, Charles was a bit of a mystery or puzzlement for the people who had to deal with him. As Glenn Burgess has explained, Charles's theoretical claims regarding the royal prerogative were no more extravagant than his father's. But he used those claims to justify more outrageous actions, and he failed to couple those actions with convincing reassurances about his subjects' liberties and property. Charles did not behave in predictable ways or speak in quite the same political idiom as his subjects. Thus, what he said and did tended to raise questions about the very meaning of concepts like 'law' and 'prerogative' that had previously been taken for granted. As a result, Burgess contended, Charles undermined the Jacobean political consensus and precipitated a 'crisis of the common law'.[178]

We should not exaggerate, however. If the first few years of Charles's reign brought matters to a crisis, the crisis soon passed. He had come to the throne relatively young and inexperienced, and he had been faced with problems that would have been daunting for the best of kings. Among the vast majority of his subjects, there was still a great reservoir of natural reverence for the Crown. Freed from the extremities of war, Charles now had an opportunity to draw upon that reservoir and make a new beginning.

3

THE PERSONAL RULE I

King Charles was not heading inexorably towards Civil War. Recent historians have been right to expose this underlying teleological assumption and dispel the air of inevitability surrounding many earlier accounts of Charles's reign. We know the ending of the story, so to speak, and we must be careful not to let that knowledge colour our view of earlier events. In 1629 it was still possible for the story to take many twists and turns and arrive at quite different endings. Indeed, in 1629 there was good reason to expect a happier ending. Charles had begun his reign with two huge liabilities: Buckingham and war. Now suddenly he was rid of the one and nearly rid of the other. Freed from the financial burden and political quagmire of war, freed from the influence and jealousies generated by Buckingham, Charles could now chart his own course under more normal circumstances. He had a fresh start, a second chance; how he chose to use this chance would determine the future course of events more than anything that had already happened.

Introduction to the Personal Rule

For 11 years, from the spring of 1629 to the spring of 1640, Charles ruled without Parliament. This was perfectly legal, but it was also rather unusual. Although it was normal for a few years to elapse between Parliaments, the longest previous gaps in the Tudor–Stuart period lasted only about seven years (under Henry VII, Henry VIII, and James I). Still, Parliament was not part of the routine machinery of government, and ruling without one for 11 years did not by itself make Charles a tyrant. A few historians in the past referred to this stage in Charles's reign as 'The Eleven Years' Tyranny', but today such words sound like Whiggish hyperbole.[1] For anyone still interested in constitutional issues, John Morrill has identified several grounds on which Charles could technically be charged with legal tyranny, but most of those reasons stem from what the king did before and after the 1630s rather than what he did during the 1630s.[2] As a substitution for 'Eleven Years' Tyranny', historians have sometimes called this the period of 'autocratic rule' or 'prerogative rule' or 'unparliamentary government', but these terms too carry negative connotations, so the preferred term today is the more neutral 'personal rule'.

It is impossible to know how long Charles expected to rule without a Parliament. Certainly he had developed a strong antipathy to the institution and was in no hurry to deal with it again. His father had told him back in 1624 that 'he would live to have his bellyful of Parliaments', and indeed he had.[3] In the proclamation he issued just after the dissolution of 1629, Charles made it clear that he would 'account it presumption' for anyone to recommend the meeting of another Parliament until the malefactors of the last Parliament had been punished and people in general had come to a better (that is, more favourable) understanding of his actions.[4] Charles Carlton has collected the king's pronouncements on Parliament early in the personal rule, as reported by the Venetian ambassador: 'in May 1629 he told the ambassador that "whosoever speaks to him about parliament shall be his enemy"; in 1631 that "on no account" would he ever again call parliament; in 1633 that he was "more opposed to it than ever"; and in 1635 that he would "do anything to avoid having another parliament"'.[5] To this should be added the ambassador's report at the beginning of 1637 stating that the king 'cannot suffer the mention of parliament, much less its assembling'.[6] Charles also expressed his views on Parliament in letters he wrote in the mid-1630s to Sir Thomas Wentworth, then Lord Deputy of Ireland. As Wentworth prepared to meet with an Irish Parliament, Charles warned him 'that here I have found it as well cunning as malicious'. In another letter to Wentworth, Charles said that he had learned from experience that Parliaments should not be kept in session too long because they 'are of the nature of cats, that ever grow cursed with age ... young ones are ever most tractable'. Furthermore, 'you will find that nothing can more conduce to the beginning of a new

than the well ending of a former Parliament'.[7] One must wonder
what precedents from his own experience Charles had in mind. It
could be said that all of his Parliaments grew more 'cursed with age',
although he may have thought this was especially true of the
Parliament that met in 1628–9. Which Parliaments did he think had
been tractable in their youth, and which one ended well enough to
be conducive to the good beginning of the next? Charles was hardly
in a position to dispense wisdom on this subject! All these expressions of hostility from Charles indicate that he was not inclined to
summon another Parliament in England unless forced to. There was
an added benefit in that the longer he was able to get by without a
Parliament, the more time he had to rehabilitate his image and
strengthen the bonds of loyalty to himself and his regime. On the
other hand, the longer he ruled without Parliament, the more likely
it was that this very fact would become a grievance in the next
Parliament whenever it did meet.

During the personal rule, Charles was able to exercise some of his
finer qualities and put his own stamp upon his regime. He approached his duties with real energy and conscientiousness. He
made a number of efforts to impose greater order and efficiency on
government at all levels. In marked contrast to his father's reign and
the earlier years of his own, Charles increased his revenues and lived
much more nearly within his means. In another marked contrast
with his father, Charles created a court society that was notable for
its decorum. His aim was 'to establish government and order in our
court which from thence may spread with more order through all
parts of our kingdoms'.[8] Charles also became a discerning connois-
seur of art who amassed one of the finest collections of his day and
used the fine arts to enhance his royal image. Through the many
paintings he commissioned (especially by Van Dyck) and the
masques performed at court, he attempted to project an image of
'ordered virtue'.[9] That image was further enhanced by his stable and
happy marriage. Judged by the standards of his day or our own,
Charles had a remarkably successful marriage. He and Henrietta
Maria were faithful, loving spouses, and they had nine children. In
conjunction with William Laud, who became Archbishop of
Canterbury in 1633, Charles also tried to restore the splendour and
dignity of the Church of England. Above all, during the personal
rule England enjoyed renewed prosperity and the blessings of peace.

Yet there was another side to the personal rule. For those who
did not share the king's own vision of order and virtue, it was a

repressive era. The king's fiscal and religious policies – combined with the darker qualities in his personality that we have already seen too much in evidence during the 1620s – generated considerable unease if not outright disaffection. And of course whatever Charles managed to achieve in these years was swept away when he became embroiled in war against his own kingdom of Scotland, which in turn forced him at last to face another Parliament. Thus the personal rule reveals to us a much more complex man with more redeeming qualities than we might have imagined from his unpropitious start, and yet there is something familiar and disquieting in the way events once more culminated in destruction. Kevin Sharpe was right to give Charles credit for being a 'monarch who was obsessed with order and decorum and of a strong moral stance, who attached great importance to the domestic realm and who was a vigorous reformer'.[10] But L. J. Reeve was also right in observing that 'these qualities were flawed when coupled with his capacity for political destruction'.[11]

Sharpe's massive book, *The Personal Rule of Charles I,* is the major work that has to be considered in any appraisal of this period, but its account of events is consistently biased in favour of Charles.[12] Nowhere is this more apparent than in the opening section where Sharpe described the events that drove Charles into peace. Sharpe acknowledged that Charles did not desire peace; he was driven into peace by Parliament's refusal to finance his wars. For Sharpe, however, this amounted to a story of shame and dishonour. Whereas Charles had been motivated by 'a powerful sense of duty to defend the commonweal', the members of Parliament had been 'oblivious to necessity' and were practically guilty of dereliction of duty. Thus Parliament's 'failure' to provide adequate resources was to 'blame' for Charles's ignominious retreat from war. The disappointed king felt the shame of Parliament's failure: 'For Charles I, England's neglect was his neglect.'[13] In truth, however, we should rather applaud Parliament's success and give the MPs of the 1620s credit for forcing Charles to abandon his entirely unnecessary military adventures. Sharpe himself inadvertently acknowledged that the grounds for war were flimsy. In his own words, 'Charles's sense of wounded honour had initiated the conflict' with Spain, and England had merely 'drifted' into war with France, 'not least as a consequence of the Duke of Buckingham's personal quarrels with Cardinal Richelieu'.[14] That being the case, why should Parliament be blamed for failing to perpetuate such wars arising from personal pique? The commonweal was actually better off when Charles stopped defending it. Just as war had been an incalculable burden for Charles, so was peace an inestimable advantage. But it was an advantage literally forced upon him. If peace is to be counted among the blessings of the 1630s, therefore, let us remember that the credit for initiating that peace belongs to the Parliaments of the 1620s.[15]

Reeve's *Charles I and the Road to Personal Rule* is biased in the opposite direction: it is mercilessly critical of Charles. However, it does a better job of capturing the moods and motives that prevailed at court when the personal rule began. Having been forced into peace, Charles was inclined to stay at peace because any resumption of war would require a resumption of Parliament to pay for it. More than this, however, Charles entered the personal rule surrounded by ministers who had their own reasons for avoiding war and Parliament. The two most powerful men in the first half of the personal rule were Archbishop Laud and Lord Treasurer Weston (whom Charles raised to the peerage as the Earl of Portland in 1633).[16] Laud and Portland had been prominent in advising the dissolution of Parliament in 1629, and both rightly feared they would be attacked in any new Parliament. Laud's reform of the church would surely have been endangered by another Parliament, just as Portland's effort to control royal finances would have been endangered by war. More generally speaking, Laud and Portland shared the king's view that Parliament had been taken over by an anti-monarchical minority. Thus the personal rule arose, in Reeve's apt phrase, amid 'a siege mentality'. By aligning himself with Laud and Portland, 'Charles identified with an insular circle of advisers who stood for Laudian, anti-war and anti-parliamentary policies in Church and state'.[17]

With Parliament out of the picture, Charles clamped down on dissent. He was especially determined to make an example of the MPs arrested for their behaviour in the Parliament of 1629. They were arrested for 'notable contempt committed by them against ourself and our government and for stirring up sedition against us'.[18] Charles was always quick to level accusations of sedition. Reeve has written a chilling account of the way Charles manipulated the legal system to crush these men. At one point Charles physically prevented them from appearing in court because he knew the judges were prepared to release them on bail, which Reeve deemed 'nothing less than a despicable and "dirty" trick'.[19] Furthermore, the Crown developed its case in such a way that the defendants were assumed to be guilty, and the only issue in dispute was whether or not they could be prosecuted for what they had said and done in Parliament. When one judge appeared to support the defendants on this point, Charles suspended him from office to encourage the others to toe the line (and he remained suspended until his death two years later). Using methods like these, Charles eventually prevailed. Two of the prisoners had been released early in the process. The seven other men were heavily fined and kept in prison at the king's pleasure until they showed sufficient contrition by submitting to his authority and acknowledging their guilt. Several capitulated in the early 1630s and were released, but others remained defiant. Sir John Eliot died in prison in 1632; Benjamin Valentine and William Strode were not released until 1640 when Charles needed to appease public opinion on the eve of the Short Parliament.[20]

The case of the MPs was not the only judicial effort to silence dissent at the outset of the personal rule. The famous antiquary Sir Robert Cotton and others were arrested in connection with the circulation of a tract that was thought to be seditious. Although this prosecution was abandoned, Cotton's library remained sealed.[21] Throughout the personal rule, personal libraries would continue to be searched and papers seized, most notably Sir Edward Coke's.[22] Another trial to break the will of resistance involved Richard Chambers, one of the merchants who refused to pay impositions.[23] Summoned before the Privy Council, Chambers boldly declared that 'merchants were in no part of the world so screwed and wrung as in England'.[24] Chambers was fined £2000 and sentenced to imprisonment until he would submit to the king and acknowledge his fault. When presented with the submission to sign, however, Chambers wrote upon it: 'I, Richard Chambers, do utterly abhor and detest as most unjust, and never till death will acknowledge any part thereof.'[25] For refusing to sign the submission or pay his fine, Chambers was kept in prison for six years. Yet another trial involved Alexander Leighton, a minister who had published an inflammatory tract attacking bishops and elevating the authority of Parliament over that of the king.[26] Leighton was fined £10,000 and sentenced to be placed in the pillory and whipped, to have one ear cut off, to have one side of his nose slit, and to have his face branded with 'SS' for sower of sedition. After being allowed a few days to recover from this ordeal, he was to be returned to the pillory where he would be whipped again and have his other ear cut off and the other side of his nose slit. Then he was to be imprisoned for life. The exorbitant fine never was expected to be paid, but the first half of the corporal punishment was inflicted on Leighton who remained in prison until he was released at the insistence of the Long Parliament in 1640.

These were 'show trials' intended to send a message to others. Such trials could not erase dissatisfaction with Charles's rule, but they could certainly discourage open protest and drive discontent underground. Charles was still practising the politics of fear. Kevin Sharpe emphasises the mildness of the personal rule, the rarity of such cases, and the relative lack of public protest.[27] But there is every reason to believe that resentment was simmering beneath the surface, biding its time. The Long Parliament voted reparations for Chambers and Leighton and included the treatment of the MPs from 1629 among the grievances listed in the Grand Remonstrance.[28] Two of those very same MPs (Denzil Holles and William Strode) sat in the Long Parliament and had the further distinction of being among the five members Charles attempted to arrest in 1642.

While the government was crushing dissent in the land, its own ranks were not entirely united or secure. Attorney-General Heath provides a striking example. Heath was a tenacious advocate of the royal prerogative who believed that the Court of Star Chamber should 'be strict in punishing notorious offendors, for example and terror to others'. Heath led the prosecution in all the major cases we have seen so far (the five knights, the MPs of 1629, Cotton, Chambers, Leighton). In 1631 he became chief justice of the Court of Common Pleas. Then, quite unexpectedly, Charles dismissed him from office in 1634. The exact reasons for Heath's dismissal remain obscure to this day, but it appears that he objected to the growing influence of Arminianism, and that brought him into conflict with Laud.[29] Laud himself, despite the special trust Charles placed in him, was notoriously insecure about the king's favour. No minister during the personal rule gained the type of exclusive ascendancy over Charles that Buckingham had enjoyed, but in the first half of the decade Lord Treasurer Portland came closer than is usually recognised. Portland was the leading figure among a group of courtiers who shared a sympathy for Spain and Roman Catholicism, though historians have grown reticent about labelling this group Hispanophile or crypto-Catholic.[30] Other figures in this group included Sir Francis Cottington, the Chancellor of the Exchequer, and Sir Francis Windebank who was appointed one of the king's two Secretaries of State in 1632.[31] For the sake of convenience, this group is usually referred to as the Spanish faction. The word 'faction' may suggest more unity and organisation than this group actually possessed, but there was at least a strong affinity among these men, and they had considerable influence over the king until Portland's death in 1635.

During the first half of the personal rule no other group at court came quite as close as Portland's circle to constituting a faction. For a while there was a group that coalesced around the queen and is often referred to as the French faction.[32] A leading member of this group was the Earl of Holland.[33] Of course Archbishop Laud was a very powerful man, but he was more of a loner. His main ally was Wentworth who spent most of the 1630s in the north of England and Ireland and did not become a factor in court politics until the end of the personal rule. In his account of court politics during the personal rule, Sharpe emphasised the cooperativeness of these men and played down the existence of factional rivalries.[34] It is hard to gauge the level of friction and competitiveness at court during the early 1630s simply because Portland and his friends enjoyed such a dominant position. Even during this period, however, rivalries could turn bitter. At one point in 1632 the queen's faction attacked Portland through his son; Holland actually challenged him to a duel.[35] Meanwhile Laud carried on a running feud with Cottington and made his own unsuccessful effort to topple Portland with charges of corruption.[36] In the later 1630s the situation deteriorated, and even Sharpe acknowledged the intensified rivalries that broke out, especially between the remnant of the old Spanish faction and the fluctuating 'party' that formed around the queen.[37]

Charles presided over the squabblings of this artificial family fairly effectively. He was a stern and forbidding monarch whose very demeanour tended to keep people in their place. On the other hand, he was also secretive and sometimes worked with a few intimates behind the backs of others, which had the opposite effect of breeding resentment. Another problem was the relative isolation of these officials. They were not very representative of the country at large or closely in touch with it, which was a special liability when there was no Parliament to give Charles a sense of wider opinion. As Ann Hughes has shown, for example, personal ties between the gentry of Warwickshire and the court 'were more tenuous than they had been for the previous seventy years'.[38] There was no Lord Burghley at the court of Charles I. Overall, however, the king appointed reasonably competent men to office (with the obvious exception of

Buckingham who was a hand-me-down). If they were not as talented
as the best of their predecessors, neither were they as corrupt as the
worst. It is fashionable these days to consider King James superior to
his son in political acumen, but Charles chose far better men to
serve in the highest offices of state.

Court Culture

In his handling of war and politics in the 1620s Charles revealed
much about himself, but there are other vantage points from which
to view and judge him. In the smaller world of the court, especially
the culture he chose to cultivate there, Charles revealed at least as
much about his mind and personality as he did in his relations with
Parliament. Studies of his court have shown that he attached special
importance to two qualities: order and virtue.

Although turbulent Parliaments and a frantic war effort made the
opening years of Charles's reign appear chaotic, within the confines
of the court his obsession with order was conspicuous from the
outset. Moving quickly to reverse the informality and disarray that
had developed under King James, Charles issued orders that re-
stricted access to the court in general and the royal presence in particular. In one of his very earliest proclamations barring 'disorderly
and unnecessary resort to the Court', Charles made it clear that he
did not like people 'pestering' him.[39] He valued his privacy, and
toward that end he installed new triple locks on the doors of his
private chambers.[40] Noblemen found they were barred from the in-
nermost rooms of the royal palace, and everyone associated with the
court discovered that they were expected to maintain a greater sense
of propriety. The Venetian ambassador noted that the new king 'observes a rule of great decorum'.[41] Charles set the tone for the new
court, and it was 'a tone of order, formality, and decorum'.[42] Not
content with the initial results, Charles renewed his efforts to regulate behaviour at court at the outset of the personal rule.[43] Much
later in his reign, Sir Philip Warwick remarked that Charles still 'was
carefull of majestie, and would be approacht with respect and reverence'.[44] Throughout his reign, Charles also contemplated plans to
reform the physical environs of the court by rebuilding the Palace of
Whitehall 'along more rational, classical ordered lines'.[45]

Charles's persistent effort to impose order on his court reveals much about his mentality. He wanted to get things under control, arrange them his way. Charles subjected himself to rigid self-control. The Venetian ambassador reported that he had 'drawn up rules for himself, dividing the day from his very early rising, for prayers, exercises, audiences, business, eating and sleeping'.[46] As Warwick expressed it, 'with this regularity he moved as steddily as a star follows its course'.[47] Thus in his daily habits, as Sharpe acknowledged, Charles 'adopted the rigid routine of the controlled personality'.[48] However, Charles was not just a controlled personality; he was a controlling personality. He endeavoured to impose his will on others as he had on himself, to control the external world as rigidly as he controlled his inner world. 'In all his pursuits', Sharpe wrote, 'we may discern that striving for, that obsession with ordering that was the dominant feature of Charles as man and monarch.'[49] Sharpe proceeded to deny that Charles was an authoritarian personality, but the description would seem to fit. Certainly Charles thought purely in terms of descending authority, never ascending authority. The orders came from the top down, and reality was expected to obligingly conform. Sometimes this worked, as in the regulation of access and etiquette at court. But other times, orders proved incapable of changing practice. Words alone could not eradicate the inveterate corruption of the royal Household; even the most elaborate plans, regarding the rebuilding of Whitehall for example, were impractical in the absence of money.[50]

Charles tried to make the court a microcosm of what he wanted the larger macrocosm of his kingdoms to be – an ordered and virtuous commonwealth under his paternal rule. There is much commendable in this, but it raises nagging questions too. While the court could serve as a model for the nation at large, it could also become an idyllic world of its own isolated from the harsher realities outside the walls of the palace. Sharpe wrote that 'Charles sought to establish a well-regulated court as a shrine of virtue and decorum'.[51] But not everyone cared to worship at this shrine; not everyone was willing to accept Charles's own personal vision of correct order and true virtue. The disparity between the orderly vision in Charles's mind and the obdurate reality of the external world is a theme that runs throughout his life. Toward the end when he was a prisoner in his own kingdom, Sharpe tells us, 'he sat scrutinizing plans for a palace at Whitehall twice the size of the Escorial'.[52] While no one would want to deny Charles the consolation or mental therapy of that moment, it does seem typical.

It is not news that Charles tried to foster order and virtue. Over a century ago, Gardiner wrote that Charles wanted his subjects 'to be happy and peaceful, above all to be orderly and virtuous'.[53] However, there has been a great deal of imaginative scholarship in recent years exploring how the king's love of order and virtue was related to court culture. Two seminal works in this area were Roy Strong's *Van Dyck: Charles I on Horseback* and Stephen Orgel's *The Illusion of Power: Political Theater in the English Renaissance*. Strong's book contained many fertile ideas. He spiritualised the meaning of Van Dyck's paintings of Charles on horseback. He argued, for example, that the horse represented the destructive force of passion ('unbridled' passion), and Charles, as rider, represented the conquest of reason over the passions. Strong viewed Charles as a chivalrous knight whose most important battle was not against foreign enemies but against evil on behalf of virtue. Here Queen Henrietta Maria played a vital role. She played Venus to his Mars, channelling his energies into a nobler battle for spiritual victory. Strong emphasised the Neo-Platonic love cult that grew up around the queen in the 1630s and the celebration of domestic bliss in the paintings of Charles and Henrietta Maria by Van Dyck and others. The royal couple were similarly idealised in the poetry and masques of the period. As Strong reminds us, Charles and Henrietta Maria were 'the first English royal couple to be glorified as husband and wife in the domestic sense'.[54] Strong illustrated this observation with a Daniel Mytens painting of the queen and king about to depart for the chase, and it is touching to notice that the royal couple are holding hands. At the same time it is jarring to pull back from this tender scene and remember that this is the same woman whom the public would later demonise for her Roman Catholicism, and the loving royal marriage that should have been an asset became a public liability. Finally, Strong noted the great importance Charles attached to the Order of the Garter. As head of this elite corps, Charles was 'an apotheosis of the chivalrous knight'. The symbolism of the Order was subtly changed, however, so that St George and the knights were conceived as battling against the devil rather than a dragon. Charles added more splendour to the installation ceremony and redesigned the badge or emblem of the Order by adding 'a huge aureole of silver rays'. He also issued instructions for all members of the Order to wear this resplendent emblem, as he himself did down to the day of his execution when he handed it over to Bishop Juxon on the scaffold.[55]

Perhaps Strong was right to emphasise the spiritual meaning in
Van Dyck's equestrian paintings of Charles, though one must
wonder whether that is what Charles himself saw in these paintings.
Charles very much wanted to be a real warrior, not just a spiritual
warrior. Despite his miserable military failures in the 1620s, perhaps
all the more because of them, he wanted to see himself as a heroic
commander. As Strong well knew, Van Dyck's equestrian paintings
of Charles blended the image of medieval knight with classical
emperor. In fact, one of these paintings was mounted at the end of a
gallery which was otherwise devoted to a display of Roman emperors.[56] Charles just as likely wanted to see himself in that class of men
as in the company of saints. On the other hand, it was only prudent
for artists working under Charles to avoid calling too much attention to the disparity between the martial image and the pacific
reality of the 1630s. By giving the viewer dual possibilities, by suggesting that real battles against armed enemies might be interpreted
as spiritual battles against evil, tactful artists met the requirements of
the time even as they made a virtue of necessity.[57]

Strong drew attention to the purposes behind the painting,
poetry, and masques of the Caroline court. One function of these
cultural expressions was to glorify Charles, but 'they did not only
glorify and acclaim, they were also seen as contributing in a specific
sense to the establishment of virtuous discipline and order in the
realm'.[58] This was not art for art's sake, but art with a social purpose,
to contribute to the reconstitution of society. Orgel analysed court
masques in the same manner, not as mere entertainment but as political statements and 'an extension of the royal mind'.[59] However,
Orgel emphasised the extreme idealism and unreality of it all.
Masques routinely ended in fantastical pastoral visions of a god-like
king who had the power to quell chaos and generally do the impossible. Orgel suggested that this was an expression of absolutist ideology or Neo-Platonism. It may have given Charles and other members
of the court an 'illusion of power', but it did not reflect a practical
mentality equipped to deal effectively with the real difficulties that
existed outside the artificial world of the court.[60]

Strong and Orgel were not the only authors to emphasise the
dreamy, idealistic, Neo-Platonic, and escapist quality of court culture
in the 1630s. Others included Peter Thomas and Graham Parry.[61]
For Thomas especially, it was all 'only a grand illusion, a piece of
theatre'. The principal actors in this court culture 'got its thoughts
entangled in metaphors and acted fatally on the strength of them'.[62]

However, more recent authors have strongly disputed this charge of self-absorbed escapism. In R. Malcolm Smuts's opinion, 'the stereotype of [a] totally isolated and unresponsive regime, living in an atmosphere of unreality, is at best greatly exaggerated'.[63] Masques were not 'a kind of Platonic dream world where Charles could retreat from the intractable problem of government'.[64] Art was political, to be sure, but 'the attempt to express political philosophy through art did not lead to an etherealized view of national affairs'.[65] Smuts took a far more complex approach to court culture and suggested a number of refinements in the way it reflected the king's state of mind. Smuts gave Charles positive credit for the enormous influence he had on the fine arts in England. Perhaps because of what he saw in Madrid in 1623, Charles was much more appreciative of continental art than most of his contemporaries. He assembled an incomparable collection of art works, brought Van Dyck to England, and patronised numerous artists and writers (and all this, by the way, at far less cost than his critics alleged). Charles enjoyed the company of artists and had a highly sophisticated understanding of their work.[66] On the other hand, left to himself, Charles would still have been a bore. He felt a natural affinity for the 'gravity and seriousness' of the Spanish court. Fortunately, he had Henrietta Maria who complemented his personality in this respect. The queen humanised Charles and added an air of love and pleasure to the court.[67] Of course court art did deal with serious subjects. Artists working under Charles were forced by circumstances to espouse the view that peace was more glorious than war and that a king was more laudable presiding over a highly civilised court than he would have been winning victories on the battlefield. At the same time, however, Smuts added the interesting insight that Charles personally felt the humiliation of his military failures in the 1620s and remained 'deeply ambivalent' on the subjects of war and peace.[68] Furthermore, Smuts did not view Charles as an idealistic Platonist. He was a realist motivated by the same concern we saw in his earlier public expressions: the stability of the state was vitally threatened by demagogues who stirred up people's passions. It was the king's duty to subdue these passions and preserve the state; the actions he took toward that end look 'far less irrational and unjustifiable' when we judge them in light of his own society's world view rather than our own.[69]

Court culture did not always glorify the king and his court. As other recent scholars have shown, it sometimes expressed criticism too. Albert H. Triconi showed how authors worked within the confines of Caroline censorship to express dissident views on topical subjects like illegal taxation and the disaffection of the populace under an oppressive king. For example, Philip Massinger wrote a play about a king who ruled arbitrarily, raising money by any method he pleased. 'We'le mulct you as wee shall thinke fitt', declared this king who admired the emperors of Rome because they acknowledged no law except 'what their swords did ratifye'. When Charles came across these lines, he wrote: 'This is too insolent, and to bee changed.' Once the change was made, Massinger did receive permission to perform the play. In Triconi's estimation, court playwrights were 'far from writing in splendid isolation'.[70] Martin Butler showed that the dramatic and poetic literature of the period contained not only criticism of specific actions but alternative political presuppositions. It had the capacity to 'shape and educate new kinds of political consciousness'. It did not withdraw 'into a world of escapism, fantasy and romance'. Caroline drama, wrote Butler, 'has been dismissed for its escapist tendencies' and 'derided for its servility' whereas in actuality it was neither escapist nor servile. On the other hand, Butler did concede that criticism was much more likely to appear in works produced outside the court than in. Moreover, the situation deteriorated over time. By 1640 the court had become narrow and insular. Charles was isolated, and 'the court forfeited the confidence of the nation'.[71] Court masques had the potential to express criticism and facilitate a political dialogue, but increasingly they degenerated into mere apology, vindication, and pontification. Masques which could have served as avenues of communication were used simply to 'generate credibility' for a shaky regime. In these later masques, 'dissent is demonised as rebellion, criticism is depicted as imposture and lies, and the authority of the king is not so much validated as whitewashed'. For Butler, this missed opportunity marked 'Charles's failure to use his culture to more constructive political ends'.[72] Thus recent scholarship has been ingenious in finding a dissident undertone in court culture, but the predominant tone in the end appears to have been escapist and servile after all.

Kevin Sharpe made significant contributions of his own to the exploration of court culture. He, too, believed that it expressed both *Criticism and Compliment*, as the title of one of his books declared.[73] In his mammoth book on the personal rule, however, Sharpe put most emphasis on the way Charles allegedly used court culture to advance his ends. Echoing the earlier words of Orgel, Sharpe wrote that the cultural artifacts of Charles's court can be interpreted as 'expressions of the royal mind'. But these expressions were projected outward to achieve an effect, to educate the viewer, to 'promulgate an image of ordered virtue'. Portraits of Charles were 'the most powerful visual statements' of a virtuous monarch's right to rule. Court masques were 'political liturgies' that expressed a 'political ideology'.[74] Charles keenly understood the power of images. He 'was preoccupied with visual representation, with the authority of images (and images of authority)'.[75] Sharpe emphatically denied that this constituted escapism: 'The culture of the Caroline court was characterized until recently as escapist, as withdrawal from harsh political reality into an ethereal world of ideals and illusions. We should study it rather as the most powerful and perhaps last manifestation of the Renaissance belief in the didactic power of images.'[76] According to Sharpe, therefore, Charles did not escape into a cultural dream world but, rather, used art to project his view of government outward and to instruct its beholders.

There is no way to prove that Charles had the conscious purpose in mind that Sharpe attributes to him. Painters and playwrights knew what appealed to Charles, and they produced works that pleased him. Charles liked these images. They suited his taste and appealed to his ego. They must have been reassuring. But whether Charles had the further intention of employing these images for didactic purposes it is impossible to say. One obvious reason for doubting Sharpe's interpretation is the simple fact that the court was an extremely self-contained world and the culture it produced was rarely viewed by outsiders. As Judith Richards wrote, most of the famous images of Charles I 'stayed in the royal possession or went directly into private hands, well away from the general view'. Van Dyck's majestic images of Charles on horseback, so familiar to historians of his reign, were 'not popularly available to his own subjects'. Technically speaking, Charles may have been projecting images, but the point is moot because there is little evidence of his subjects 'actually receiving the images'.[77] More important, images were no substitute for the real thing. From the beginning of his reign, Charles distanced himself from his subjects. He ordered people to stay away from the court, and he stayed away from them. Unlike his predecessors, he did not make leisurely 'progresses' through the countryside. Nor did he take advantage of the belief that the royal touch had magical healing powers. In fact, he issued at least 20 proclamations preventing or restricting people from seeking him out for this purpose. All in all, Richards concluded, Charles 'withdrew from the vast majority of his subjects to a degree unprecedented for generations'.[78] Whether or not Sharpe is right to claim that Charles took 'painstaking care with the dissemination of his image', it mattered far more that he 'literally retreated behind closed doors'.[79]

Even if Charles did try to project an image enhancing his authority, the effect was not entirely what he intended. As P. W. Thomas observed, 'art was dutifully doctrinal but for many in the country it offered the wrong doctrine'.[80] To the extent that the populace at large had any inkling of the high culture at court, they were as much disturbed as awed by it. Court culture was impressive, but it was also alien. It was continental and Baroque. By embracing the art and artists of this movement, Charles was in effect embracing the style of the Counter-Reformation. He even had his bust sculpted by Bernini, the sculptor and architect who is most famous for his magnificent additions to St Peter's Basilica in Rome. It was not just the Catholic artists but the values implicit in this art that troubled some people, especially those of a more puritanical bent. Charles's taste in art reflected his overall values – order, decorum, grandeur, and authority. These were the same values he and Archbishop Laud promoted in the Church of England, and it is not surprising that to some of his own subjects this looked like yet another movement in the direction of Roman Catholicism. Thus the Baroque tastes that flourished at court widened the gulf between elite and popular culture. In the words of Malcolm Smuts, they 'broadened the cultural gulf separating the court from most of the nation' and left Charles increasingly isolated.[81]

Foreign Affairs

In the early 1630s England remained at peace and developed friendly relations with Spain. To those of his subjects who preferred to fight on the Protestant side in the Thirty Years War, this policy looked like another sign of Roman Catholic influence at court. The foreign policy of these years was indeed dominated by Lord Treasurer Portland and the 'Spanish faction', but Charles was not operating under the spell of these men. Rather, he agreed with and employed these men because it suited his ends. Charles had grown to hate France more than Spain, and he had no affection for the

United Provinces because of their naval superiority and their repub-
lican form of government. By contrast, as his resentment over his
treatment in Madrid subsided, he retained other impressions of a
more positive nature. He was impressed by Spain's great power
status, its magnificent art, and the grandeur and formality of its
court ceremony. Furthermore, Spain offered the same attraction to
Charles that it had to his father: the lure of affecting the course of
events without having to engage in war.

A foreign policy of peace and friendship with Spain has not won
much favour with historians. S. R. Gardiner would clearly have liked
to see Charles fight on the Protestant side, especially in league with
the Dutch or the Swedes. This may reflect Gardiner's own personal
bias or the bias he absorbed from the despatches he read by
the English ambassador Sir Thomas Roe, an ardent supporter of the
Protestant cause.[82] In a similar fashion, much more recently, L. J.
Reeve was inclined to see the continental conflict through the eyes
of Viscount Dorchester, one of the Secretaries of State and another
passionate supporter of international Protestantism. Reeve complained that Charles and the Spanish faction reduced England to
the status of 'a non-combatant satellite of Spain'.[83]

The common bias in the works of Gardiner and Reeve is most conspicuous in their treatment of negotiations with Sweden early in the
personal rule. Both historians deeply regretted that Charles did not
ally with the brilliant King Gustavus Adolphus of Sweden when he
was triumphing over his Catholic adversaries and marching southward through Germany in late 1631 and most of 1632. If Charles
ever hoped to intervene effectively in the Thirty Years War and accomplish the restitution of the Palatinate to his sister and her family,
this was his best opportunity. 'The reality and the excellence of that
opportunity', wrote Reeve, 'throw Charles's rejection of it into very
sharp relief.' Gustavus Adolphus was driving a hard bargain,
however, insisting that Charles not only join the war on land but also
provide naval protection in the Baltic Sea, an action which was likely
to lead England back into war with Spain. Furthermore, to finance
these efforts it would have been necessary to summon another
Parliament. To Reeve these consequences seemed a small price to
pay for the chance to join forces with the valiant King of Sweden and
gain a share of the victory. Reeve thought 'the case for a Parliament,
in the light of the opportunity in Germany, was virtually irrefutable',
but Charles simply 'could not see matters in terms of reason of
state'. It was 'a lost opportunity to achieve success' and 'a damaging

failure' which further undermined confidence in Charles.[84] The truth, however, is that it would have been enormously risky for Charles to ally with Sweden.[85] It would have engaged him even more heavily than before in the deadly battle by land, which looks more like a gruesome prospect than a missed opportunity, and it would probably have propelled him right back into the domestic turmoil of the later 1620s he was trying to escape. Besides, Gustavus Adolphus died in battle near the end of 1632. While Protestants mourned the loss of their charismatic leader, Charles was entitled to a huge sigh of relief. If he had succumbed to pressure to ally with Sweden, committed England to renewed war on land and sea, and summoned a Parliament to plead for support, even if things had gone smoothly up to that point (which is highly unlikely), where would the death of Gustavus Adolphus have left him? Whether through prudence or simple fear of another Parliament, Charles did the right thing to steer clear of war in 1632. As an earlier historian observed, he 'did his country no disservice when he kept her out of the European holocaust'.[86]

The negotiations with Sweden were only one small part of Charles's diplomacy during the personal rule. There was a phenomenal amount of diplomatic activity in the 1630s, but it is difficult to know what to make of all this activity. Gardiner described Charles's myriad negotiations with all the major belligerents as 'so complicated and unreal, that they only served to make the brain dizzy'. Beneath it all, Gardiner could find 'no European policy at all'.[87] In the absence of parliamentary subsidies, J. R. Jones concluded, 'Charles could not afford an active foreign policy'. Spain and France 'engaged in desultory negotiations for an alliance, but they were satisfied if Britain was neutralized'. Consequently, 'Charles's remarkably inconsistent intrigues during the 1630s possessed no practical importance'.[88]

Recent authors have taken a more favourable view of Charles's foreign policy. They emphasise that he continued to be a player in international affairs and that, beneath the myriad negotiations, he did consistently pursue worthwhile objectives. His most consistent objective was to gain the restitution of the Palatinate for his sister Elizabeth and her husband Frederick. (After the death of Elizabeth's husband in 1632, Charles continued to support the cause on behalf of her son.) Although none of the proposed alliances toward this end ever materialised, the king's constant diplomatic pressure kept the issue alive and gave his sister's cause more weight. This also helps

to explain Charles's willingness to deal with Spain and the Holy
Roman Empire. Since the Habsburgs controlled the Palatinate, they
were the ones in the best position to restore it.[89] Charles's friendli-
ness toward the Spanish and hostility toward the Dutch offended the
pan-Protestants of his day who saw the battle on the continent in
simplistic terms as a religious crusade of good against evil. But
Charles was more realistic and actually ahead of his time in seeing
that the Dutch were becoming England's true rival.[90] Charles tried
to enforce his sovereignty over the Narrow Seas, pressuring the
Dutch to buy fishing licences and all foreign vessels to lower their
flags or dip their sails in deference to British ships. Another alleged
goal of Charles was to maintain the Spanish hold on Flanders. He
desired the continued existence of Flanders not because he irra-
tionally sympathised with Spain but because he understood that it
would be even worse for England if Flanders were swallowed up by
the Dutch and French. Meanwhile Charles reaped a tidy profit by assisting the Spanish in transporting men, matériel, and money to
Flanders.[91] On the other hand, while Charles favoured Spain, he
prudently continued to explore opportunities with France. While
dealing with any one nation, Charles achieved the ulterior advantage
of putting pressure on other nations to come to better terms with
him. Overall, then, Charles pursued specific goals, kept his options
open, and was sensitive to the balance of power.[92] What he did *not*
demonstrate was a burning desire to ally with the Protestant side and
win the Thirty Years War. This has seemed like apostasy to most historians, but it can be interpreted instead as a cautious calculation of
true national interest.[93]

While these recent authors make better sense of Charles's foreign
policy and draw attention to its positive features, they also make it
seem more coherent and dignified than it actually was. As long as
Charles dared not ask another Parliament for money, he did not
have much to offer a prospective ally. Although no one wanted
Charles for an enemy, neither was there much to be gained from his
friendship. His biggest bargaining chip was undoubtedly the navy,
especially after it was strengthened in the later 1630s. Usually,
however, Charles asked his prospective allies for absurdly more than
he was willing or able to offer them in return. What he wanted, in
essence, was someone else to do his fighting for him. In 1636 the
Spanish ambassador reported that the English 'assume the right to
ask for a lot, and to hand over the Palatinate politely to them is a
little thing'.[94] It is doubtful whether any of the major continental

powers ever took Charles's overtures seriously. Spain and France each toyed with him, perhaps to prevent him from allying with the enemy, perhaps to strengthen their own negotiating positions with other nations, and almost certainly to keep him neutralised. Sharpe put as favourable a face on these protracted and futile negotiations as possible, emphasising that England's neutrality was worth bargaining for and its navy could conceivably have tipped the balance. Yet Sharpe's own evidence shows that the Spanish were stringing Charles along just as they had his father. By 1635 Spanish duplicity was so evident that even Windebank realised 'their only end is to feed us with fancies and to amuse us to gain time'. Renewed effort to get a commitment from Spain merely confirmed that 'the Spaniard sought only to spin out the time, in the hope of keeping England neutral'.[95] The Earl of Dorset observed that Charles began 'to believe he hath been much abused and deceived in all his treaties about the Palatinate' with Spain and the Empire.[96]

Disillusionment with Spain, the death of Portland, and a realignment of forces on the continent encouraged Charles to enter into negotiations with France, where his experience was similar. On the surface, it appears as if Charles came closer to striking a deal with the French. Although he was still wary of committing himself to a war on land, he appeared to be inclining toward a war at sea. If the treaty had been concluded, the French would have pledged to restore the Palatinate in exchange for assistance from the English navy and the right to recruit soldiers in England. But there is serious reason to doubt that the treaty would ever have been concluded.[97] Charles himself had an odd view of what he hoped to achieve by talking with the French. When Wentworth advised him against 'the bleeding evil of an instant and active war', Charles told him he misunderstood the question.[98] 'For it is not whether I should declare war to the House of Austria or not', Charles explained, 'but whether I shall join with France and the rest of my friends to demand of the House of Austria my nephew's restitution, and so hazard (upon refusal) a declaration of war.'[99] It looks, therefore, as if Charles was still hoping to avoid outright war and get something for nothing. It probably did not matter what Charles thought, however, since the French kept putting obstacles of their own in the way of any agreement. To explain why nothing came of these negotiations, Sharpe wrote in one place, 'the French treaty was the first casualty of the Scots troubles'. There is a more likely explanation, however, which Sharpe himself conceded in another place: 'It may well be, as

Gardiner argued, that Richelieu placed little hope in Charles and sought, like Spain, only to lock England into a safe neutrality, by playing for time.'[100] The French, like the Spanish, manipulated Charles for their own purposes. In the end Charles simply ends up looking a little foolish and gullible.

What do we learn about Charles from the way he conducted foreign relations in the 1630s? In his dealings with foreign nations, he demonstrated more flexibility than he generally did when dealing with his own kingdoms and subjects. He was willing to deal with any foreign power that might deliver what he wanted. On the other hand, he still had an inflated view of his own importance, his assessment of the situation was typically unrealistic, and in the end, as usual, he failed to reach an accommodation with anyone. Furthermore, Charles was so aloof and inscrutable that sometimes even his own agents could not clearly discern what his intentions were, if indeed he had any clear intentions. In France the Earl of Leicester was advised by his wife that the word at court was he had 'not directly followed the King's mind, which it seems you must understand, though it be not expressed'. A few months later the Countess reiterated that it was imperative for the Earl to understand what was most acceptable to the king, 'but they say that is so [hardly] done as it brings me many apprehensions'.[101] Similarly, Sir Walter Aston admitted in his embassy to Spain that 'I never have clearly understood what his Majesty for the present would be contented to accept of for satisfaction from Spain, nor what content to return them.'[102] In 1636 when Charles sent Leicester to France, Aston to Spain, and another agent to the Empire, Sharpe maintained that he was only keeping his options open. The Venetian ambassador in London had a different view of the situation: 'Mutability and confusion reign in the foreign policy of the ministry here.'[103]

Historians have sometimes gone further to accuse Charles of unethical conduct because he negotiated with one nation behind the back of another or tried to get the best deal he could by playing one nation off against another. However, those other nations engaged in the same practices, as indeed most nations always have in the conduct of their foreign affairs. Perhaps the closest Charles came to genuinely reprehensible behaviour was at the outset of the personal rule when he made a separate peace with Spain, leaving his Dutch allies in the lurch. His attitude toward the Dutch on this occasion exhibited, in Reeve's words, 'that blend of unctuous rectitude, devious literalness, selfishness, pure ignorance, clear ideological preference and rationalization of betrayal which rendered so many of Charles's political endeavours positively destructive'.[104] The sheer necessity of extricating himself from the war may be sufficient to justify Charles's conduct on this occasion, but he apparently went further than that. There are indications that he led the Spanish to believe he might be willing to change sides entirely and join them in an attack against the Dutch. This possibility, which began as the highly secret 'Cottington Treaty', was discussed off and on with Spain throughout the 1630s, though we can never know how serious Charles was about it.

It is naïve and unfair to condemn Charles for his double-dealing with other powers on the continent who were doing the same toward him, but his double-dealing with his own court is another matter. Members of the Spanish faction were usually informed about all the initiatives that were under way, but the king's other ministers were often kept in the dark, deceived, and even lied to. For example, Sharpe made it appear as if a natural division of labour evolved between the two Secretaries of State: Windebank assumed responsibility for correspondence with the Catholic countries while the older Secretary, Sir John Coke, retained responsibility for just the Protestant countries. It appears to be a sensible division of labour and an astute 'balance of factions' effected by Charles.[105] But Charles did not operate that openly or honestly. He led Coke to believe that he was still in charge of all the foreign correspondence, while he used Windebank to establish a secret line of communication with several of England's ambassadors behind Coke's back. The resulting duplicity took several forms. In Spain it led to an elaborate and time-consuming system of dual despatches. In France it led to comical competition between dual agents, one tied to Coke, the other to Windebank. The shabbiest example, however, occurred in 1638 when Charles's secret dealings with the Habsburgs behind the backs of the French inconveniently came to light. Charles and Windebank, who were conducting these secret discussions, indignantly denied them and, in a manner that can only be described as contemptible, manipulated Coke into joining in their denial. Duped by Charles and Windebank, Coke avowed that the king was free 'from treating underhand', and he instructed the ambassador in France to demand an audience to swear on 'the word of a king' that there were no negotiations with the Habsburgs.[106] It mattered little because foreign powers were no more inclined to trust 'the word of a king' when it came from Charles than the Parliament of 1628 had been. Meanwhile Coke continued in his office all the way till 1640, but looking back over his long career he sadly concluded that 'kings cannot be served against their wills'.[107]

Domestic Affairs

Although historians debate whether Charles had a foreign policy, there is no doubt that he had a domestic policy. Two motives drove that domestic policy. The paramount motive was to raise money. It was becoming increasingly difficult for the king to support the growing cost of government from his traditional sources of income. In the 1630s Charles had the additional burden of paying off war debts from the 1620s and keeping his head far enough above water to avoid calling another Parliament. The other motive that drove domestic policy was the king's personal vision of good government. Charles was a conscientious monarch who tried to promote the public good, as he saw it. If he could promote the public good and make money at the same time, so much the better.

Charles's interest in good government is evident in the numerous commissions and sub-committees of the Privy Council he appointed to investigate departments of government and propose reforms. Charles was obviously concerned to put his house in order, and oftentimes the reports submitted by these bodies identified what needed to be done. The real question, however, is what was accomplished? In the opinion of G. E. Aylmer, who was best qualified to judge, in the early part of the reign 'very little was achieved'. During the 1630s promising starts were made, but few 'were carried through with sustained resolution'. Overall, the achievement of the personal rule 'must be reckoned meagre'.[108] Of course Charles was not entirely to blame for this failure. What we today would call corruption was a routine way of doing business in early Stuart England, not least because it compensated for the low salaries of public officials, and many office holders virtually owned their offices. To make headway against this system, Charles would have had to eradicate deeply entrenched practices and dislodge powerful people. On the other hand, King James, who was hardly famous for his frugality, had shown that this could be done when he backed the reforming efforts of Lionel Cranfield. Of course Charles and Buckingham had engineered the impeachment of Cranfield to clear the way for war in 1624, which overturned all of Cranfield's economies. The closest Charles had to a Cranfield of his own was Lord Treasurer Portland, who did manage to save money but never attempted to reform government on the scale Cranfield had. Besides, Portland was no model of probity.

One happy exception to the failures of the personal rule was reform of the postal system. Aylmer called it 'one of the few authentic improvements achieved under the early Stuarts'.[109] This reform was chiefly the work of an obscure man named Thomas Witherings, who only managed to withstand the opposition of Secretary Windebank and others because he had his own patron in the form of Secretary Coke. Credit for reforming the postal system should not go to the king. On the contrary, it was Charles who set up the rivalry between the two Secretaries that manifested itself in the fight over the posts, and a few months after Coke left office Charles actually allowed Witherings to be dismissed. The Long Parliament investigated the situation and gave Witherings some vindication, but he never succeeded in getting his office back.[110] One reason reform of the postal system was possible was because no nobleman was in charge of it. A minor figure like Secretary Coke was incapable of prevailing over the powerful figureheads in other departments (for example, the Earls of Pembroke and Denbigh in the Wardrobe and the Earl of Newport in the Ordnance).[111] The only person powerful enough to force such men to reform their ways or lose their offices was King Charles, but this would have been politically dangerous, especially for a king who had already offended his nobility in so many other ways.

The benefits and the risks of real reform are illustrated by the work of Laud and Wentworth. These men used the word 'Thorough' to refer to the thoroughgoing determination and housecleaning that would be necessary to create an efficient system of government. The concept of 'Thorough' had its drawbacks. It made Laud and Wentworth feel proud of themselves and contemptuous of their rivals. And in the case of Wentworth, it could be used to justify highhanded and self-serving actions. Nevertheless, it was the closest thing to an articulated reforming ideal at the Caroline court. Wentworth followed the practice of 'Thorough' in his administration of the Council of the North and Ireland. Laud tried to practise it in England, but (as he saw it) he was thwarted by men like Portland, Cottington, and Windebank. One example of this contest occurred in 1635, shortly after Portland's death. The Court of Star Chamber found James Bagg guilty of taking a £2500 bribe on behalf of the late Lord Treasurer, though he probably pocketed the money himself. This was an easy chance for Charles to prove that he too was on the side of 'Thorough', but instead he pardoned Bagg and gave instructions to set aside the verdict, an action which obviously pained Lord Keeper Coventry and Secretary Coke.[112] Laud, too, must have been appalled at this reversal, having fought fiercely for the conviction of 'bottomless bag'.

While the investigations of the 1630s failed to reform the departments of central government, Charles has been credited with promoting more responsible and effective local government through the Book of Orders issued in 1631. The Book of Orders has been subject to much misinterpretation. It has been erroneously attributed to Laud and Wentworth, and it has been blamed for deepening the sense of alienation between local governors and the central government. The recent researches of Paul Slack and Brian Quintrell have revealed that both the origins and effects of the Book were more prosaic.[113] It was written largely by the Earl of Manchester, utilising proposals he had originally formulated back in the reign of James I. The object of the Book of Orders was to establish oversight of the local Justices of the Peace in their enforcement of existing laws regarding the poor, vagabonds, idleness, and drunkenness. JPs were required to meet monthly and report quarterly to the Privy Council on the status of these matters in their localities. Although the plan looked good on paper, it broke down in practice. JPs were reporting on themselves, and the Privy Council had no independent source of information to judge their veracity. Nor did the Privy Council have the time or personnel to read the reports or discipline JPs who failed to comply. It has been estimated that only one-tenth of the reports which should have been submitted ever were. The central government simply was not equipped to carry out a project on this scale effectively. The Book of Orders did no harm, and perhaps it accomplished some good in so far as it made JPs feel more accountable for what they did. We might therefore call it a limited failure.[114]

Kevin Sharpe wrote that the Book of Orders 'very much expressed the royal mind', but which royal mind? The Book of Orders was issued in the name of King Charles with an elaborate preamble making it appear as if he had given the matter a great deal of personal consideration, but this was a mere formality and most of the language actually came from Manchester's draft which had been produced in 1620 as part of a commission appointed by King James who had spoken vigorously in favour of stricter supervision over local governors.[115] This example highlights several problems with Sharpe's effort to portray Charles as the architect of a programme with 'quite definite aims for the reformation of local society and government'.[116] Many of the elements in that so-called programme were not new but went back as far as James's reign and even Queen Elizabeth's reign. Viewed this way, the government of the 1630s, rather than spearheading a new royal programme, was simply resurrecting earlier policies and returning to the normal interests of peacetime after several years of wartime interruption.[117] The proclamations issued under Charles ordering the nobility and gentry to stay in the countryside where they could attend to their administrative duties, relieve the poor, and continue the ancient custom of hospitality is a prime example. Proclamations to this effect go back as far as Elizabeth's reign and were reissued several times under James. Sharpe contended that Charles attached special importance to this measure in his 'quest for reform of local society by a reinvigoration of traditional modes of government', but all he can really show that was new under Charles was the severity with which the policy was enforced.[118] In many areas, Charles's programme was a continuation of James's policies, though prosecuted with a much heavier hand. Furthermore, much of Sharpe's reconstruction of Charles's mentality is based on official documents like proclamations which naturally cast government actions in the best possible light. As Thomas Cogswell pointed out, such 'public relations' documents do not necessarily represent the exact words or true ideas of the king.[119] If we tried to reconstruct King James's mentality this way, he too would appear to be a monarch who worked energetically to reform government and promote the common good.[120]

The government undertook many projects in the 1630s with the justification that they promoted the common good, but in most of these the government turned a handsome profit too. 'Projects of all kinds, many ridiculous, many scandalous, all very grievous, were set on foot', wrote the Earl of Clarendon.[121] One of these was the company formed by Lord Treasurer Portland and his friends who obtained a near-monopoly over the manufacture of soap, thereby provoking an intense public outcry. Given the Catholic character of the company's backers, their product was dubbed 'popish soap'. After Portland's death, Laud fought a long and bitter battle with

Cottington over the company. Meanwhile the Crown's annual profit from this project rose to nearly £30,000 by the end of the 1630s.[122] Sharpe cited the soap company as one example of many where, despite the ill results, Charles was motivated by good intentions. Sharpe's frequent invocation of good intentions reminds us of the adage that the road to hell is paved with good intentions. Did the Crown's numerous efforts during the personal rule to regulate trade and shake down merchants fatally alienate the business community? Much as historians have pondered this question, they cannot agree on the answer.[123] The Privy Council evidently realised how irksome many of these measures were because they persuaded Charles to rescind 26 commissions and patents as a gesture of goodwill during the First Bishops' War.[124] These measures applied to such commodities as butter, tobacco, logwood, sheepskins, wine casks, hops, kelp, seaweed, and red herrings.[125] As Gardiner remarked, the government of Charles I 'was a government not of fierce tyranny, but of petty annoyance'.[126]

Charles's personal role in most of these projects is murky at best, though obviously he wanted the income. Fortunately, his role was more prominent in one project, the drainage of the fenland. This again was a project first broached in the reign of James I and resurrected under Charles. Patents were issued to the Earl of Bedford, a profiteer named Sir Anthony Thomas, and a clique of minor court officials to undertake the draining of various portions of the fenland. All these men did make a concerted effort to carry out their share of the project because they could then reap thousands of acres of recovered land for themselves. There is always a fortune to be made in land development. Thomas and his backers were the most unscrupulous, systematically appropriating 24,000 acres of the choicest land of the East and West Fens for themselves. In his study of the project, Mark Kennedy wrote that these men had 'used their influence with the king' to serve 'what was blatantly their own and not the country's interests'.[127] That was not the way Charles saw it. At one point when he intervened on behalf of these men, Charles warned the local commissioners to cooperate so that he would not be 'constrained to interpose our regal power and prerogative ... to force forward and adverse men to give way to that which is for the public good'.[128] Sharpe agreed that Charles was the best judge of the public good; he wrote that 'the king remained committed to a scheme that he believed to be for the welfare of his subjects, even if they did not recognize it'.[129] The Great Fen, where Bedford was in charge, proved more troublesome; in 1637 Charles announced that he was taking over this portion of the project himself. The king's motive in promoting these projects was not simply to promote the common good but to line his own pockets. By taking over the Great Fen, for example, he increased his share from 12,000 to 57,000 acres.[130] Nor did this endeavour look like the common good to the common people who were most affected by it. Perhaps the peasants who frequently rioted in protest against the loss of their common land were merely opposing progress, but Keith Lindley has shown that the actual results of the drainage projects were of doubtful value.[131] More importantly, there was gross injustice in the way a privileged few with court connections were able to seize the best land for themselves and leave the pickings for the poor.[132] Even local inhabitants of more stature who voiced objections to this exploitation found that they were defenceless in the face of royal authority. In sum, perhaps Charles supported a worthwhile public work, but he also ran roughshod over local authorities and gratified the rapaciousness of a handful of well-connected speculators. Like so many of the projects of the personal rule, the draining of the fens became a grievance in the Long Parliament, and popular pamphlets condemned it as a prime example of 'arbitrary government and tyranny'. As Kennedy concluded, because of the way the project had been carried out, Charles's government came to be viewed 'as a tyrannical oppressor wielding its powers arbitrarily for the benefit of those who could obtain or buy its support'.[133]

Perhaps the biggest success of the personal rule was in the area of royal finance. During the early 1630s annual ordinary revenues averaged a little over £600,000, and during the later 1630s this amount increased to nearly £900,000. Revenue actually came fairly close to meeting expenditures in these years. By the end of the 1630s it was even possible to redeem the Crown jewels that had been pawned in the 1620s.[134] There were still enormous debts and many sources of income had been 'anticipated' (that is, assigned to satisfy creditors) years in advance; but there was no doubt that the Crown's financial situation was steadily improving and Parliament could be avoided indefinitely – unless there was a war. It is a great pity that Charles had been forced to sell so much royal land to pay for the wars of the 1620s. By liquidating that capital, he sacrificed a huge source of royal income, but all of his predecessors since Henry VIII had done the same. What compensated for the loss of revenue from land and boosted ordinary revenues in the 1630s was the customs duties.

Income from customs increased automatically with the improvement
of trade. England's neutrality was a great boon in this respect. The
government also took advantage of the situation by increasing the
customs rates on certain goods and expanding their application to
other goods.

The increase in ordinary revenues during the 1630s tends to be
overshadowed by the highly controversial extraordinary measures
Charles employed to boost his income. For example, he fined men
who had not applied to be knighted at the time of his coronation
(distraint of knighthood). This was an ancient practice, one of the
surviving components of 'fiscal feudalism' that English monarchs
had relied upon for centuries. Charles raised at least £165,000 from
this source, but by its very nature it could not be repeated.[135] Much
less was gained by stricter enforcement of the forest laws (that is,
fining people who had encroached on the royal forests or made
illegal use of them), and it is doubtful whether the small sum raised
was worth the ill will it generated. While people complained about
distraint of knighthood and revival of the forest laws, both these
devices were perfectly legal. The most notorious fiscal measure of
the personal rule, ship money, which Charles began to collect in
1634, was another matter. While the Crown did have the undoubted
right to require coastal communities to provide ships during times of
emergency, it was only recently that money had been demanded in
lieu of actual ships, and it was a far more radical departure to impose
this levy on inland counties, indeed all of England and Wales, as
Charles began to do in 1635, and to collect it year after year.[136]
Before addressing the controversial questions raised by ship money,
three things must be said in its defence. First, Charles could not
support a formidable navy from his ordinary sources of income, and
Parliament had demonstrated no comprehension of the need to
provide a new source. This was a long-term problem and Charles was
attempting to solve it with an approach that was new but still rooted
in precedent. Secondly, ship money was used for its announced
purpose, to enlarge the navy and equip a series of special fleets; the
money was not diverted to other areas. Viewed this way, ship money
could be interpreted as a rate or fee-for-service rather than a tax,
which would mean that it did not violate the Petition of Right. And
thirdly, it was an impressively successful device. In the early years of
ship money the government collected over 90 per cent of its targeted
amount, and there was no sharp falling off until the disturbances of
1639–40. In the best years, ship money brought in approximately

£180,000; in all years combined it brought in a total of nearly £800,000.[137] It is therefore not without justification that Sharpe called ship money 'perhaps the most successful extraordinary tax in early modern (perhaps in modern) British history'.[138]

But why did Charles set out the ship money fleets, what did he accomplish, and at what price? Good objective reasons can be found for the ship money fleets. They were needed to ward off pirates, to strengthen the bargaining hand of England in its negotiations with continental powers, to counter the growing naval strength of France and the United Provinces, and more particularly to prevent sovereignty of the Narrow Seas from slipping into the hands of these other nations by default.[139] The traditional verdict was that the ship money fleets achieved little. Their bulky warships were virtually useless against the swifter ships of pirates.[140] They sold a few fishing licences to the Dutch and forced a few foreign ships to lower their flags or dip their sails in deference, but they fought no battles and brought home no glory. As Gardiner said of King Charles in general, 'large designs were followed by paltry performances'.[141] Recent historians have tried to reverse this verdict, emphasising that the mere presence of the ship money fleets was a benefit.[142] The words of one contemporary are cited in support of this view that if the ships 'do no more than sail up and down, yet the very setting of our best fleet out to sea is the greatest service that I believe hath been done the King these many years'.[143] The ship money fleets may have made England seem a more formidable force, but this impression was shattered by events in the autumn of 1639 when a large Spanish fleet being pursued by the Dutch took refuge in the Downs expecting that Charles would protect them. To be fair, Charles was not in a position to offer much assistance. Having poured all of his resources into the First Bishops' War earlier in the year, he could not afford to provoke another war; also the English fleet in the Downs was perilously small. To do nothing in the face of this challenge would have been humiliating, of course, but Charles found a way to stoop even lower. He told the Spanish he would protect their fleet if they paid him £150,000 while at the same time he told the Dutch and French they could have his permission to destroy the fleet if they put his nephew in command of an army to recover his patrimony in the Palatinate. Gardiner called this 'an auction, the strangest in the annals of diplomacy'.[144] Even Sharpe had to admit that Charles put 'the fate of the fleet out to auction' and 'was waiting on the best bid'.[145] The Dutch were too strong to need Charles's permission, and they simply proceeded to demolish the Spanish fleet. A few days later, the French, rather than put Charles's nephew in charge of an army to conquer the Palatinate, arrested him.

Charles's reasons for launching the ship money fleets were not as purely rational as recent defenders make them seem. His obsession with sovereignty over the Narrow Seas was part of his overall obsession with sovereignty. In the midst of his naval rearmament in the later 1630s, Charles ordered the building of a stupendously large, three-deck warship which he named significantly the *Sovereign of the Seas*. It was twice as large as a normal warship and probably the largest in the world at the time. Charles took a very great personal interest in the navy in general and this ship in particular.[146] He specified the ship's burden (1500 tons), visited it during construction, and increased its number of guns at the last minute (from 90 to 102), which may be why it proved top-heavy. Unhappy with the proposed launching date, the impatient king demanded an earlier time. 'I am not of your opinion,' wrote Charles, as if he had sufficient expertise to judge better than his master shipwright. The *Sovereign of the Seas* cost over £40,000, which would have paid for the construction of six normal warships, and that amount did not include the guns which cost nearly £25,000 additional. Her decoration alone cost over £6000. Charles personally designed the cluster of heroic symbols inscribed on each cannon of the *Sovereign* together with a motto declaring that Charles, like a much earlier Anglo-Saxon king renowned for sweeping the sea of pirates, 'has established dominion of the seas'. The *Sovereign* represented the way Charles wanted to be seen, and its very name signified what he wished most to achieve through the ship money fleets.

In a curious way, Charles's modern defenders share his assumption that it was important to assert English sovereignty, to join in the arms race, to be a player in the game of international warfare. Naval historians naturally like sea power. Kenneth Andrews, for example, wanted his readers to understand that the sorry affair in the Downs disgraced Charles but did not disgrace the navy; and as for the ship money fleets, they 'did win the nation a significant role in Europe'.[147] Dare we ask, who cares? Dare we ponder for a moment what would have been the dire consequences if Charles had been content to sit on the sidelines and not play costly (male?) power games? Two consequence are obvious: firstly, he would not have had to raise £800,000 through a tax of dubious legality; and secondly, when the Civil War broke out, an expanded and seasoned navy would not have been available to defect almost entirely to the parliamentary side.[148]

Charles did not have a total disregard for the law. Although he manipulated the legal process and intimidated judges when necessary, he nevertheless recognised the need to operate at least ostensibly within the framework of the law. Charles made three efforts to establish the legality of ship money. At the end of 1635 he obtained a brief reassurance from the judges that he had the authority to determine when the kingdom was in danger and to levy the cost of national defence on the nation at large.[149] At the beginning of 1637 he made a more elaborate inquiry of the judges in which he argued that the honour and safety of the nation were endangered in many ways, but most particularly 'by attempts to take from us the dominion of the seas, of which we are sole lord and rightful owner and proprietor'. When the kingdom was endangered, Charles then asked, did he not have the right to command his subjects to furnish ships (he made no mention of money), and was he not the sole judge of the danger? Yes, came the answer from all twelve judges.[150] When even this opinion was not sufficient to silence opposition, Charles allowed a trial to go forward at the end of 1637 in which John Hampden was the defendant. The amount of money Hampden owed was minor (20 shillings), but the issues raised by his case were major. If earlier generations of historians exaggerated constitutional issues, modern historians sometimes demonstrate an opposite inability to recognise a constitutional issue when it is staring them in the face. Kevin Sharpe alleged that 'Hampden's case is still grossly misrepresented in the textbooks of English history as a trial between the common law and the royal prerogative', yet two pages later he observed that the trial had raised 'lofty principles of prerogative, law and parliament'. Such inconsistency hardly succeeds, as Sharpe claimed, in lifting 'the obfuscating haze of Whig myth'.[151] It is not a myth that Hampden's case involved fundamental constitutional issues. Hampden's attorneys did not raise all the possible issues, but they did argue that the king could not compel his subjects to pay for the nation's defence except through Parliament unless the kingdom was in imminent danger, that the danger invoked by the king to justify ship money was obviously not urgent (and was not even specified in the writ of 1635), and that there would be no security of property in England if the king were allowed to be the sole judge of an imminent danger in peacetime.[152] The object of Hampden's attorneys seems to have been not simply to vindicate their client but to speak on behalf of all those people in England who wanted Charles to summon another Parliament. Although we know that ship money was in fact spent entirely on special fleets and did not in any way improve the overall financial position of the Crown, there was a strong suspicion among contemporaries that Charles had invented ship money as a permanent tax to replace subsidies, thereby allowing him to rule indefinitely without Parliament.[153]

A narrow majority of the judges (7–5) decided the ship money case in favour of the king. One of the judges who supported the king's position most strongly was Sir Robert Berkeley, and it is obvious that he and Charles saw eye to eye on the subject of Parliament. While he professed admiration for Parliament, Berkeley observed that the institution could breed delays and disturbances, and its individual members could have 'sinister' motives, as witnessed by 'the late woeful experience of this kingdom'. Parliaments, wrote Berkeley, gave subjects an opportunity to communicate their grievances 'if there be any' (!), but meanwhile the law was the king's instrument and not to be used for 'king-yoking'.[154] Given judicial opinions like this, even the royalist Earl of Clarendon acknowledged that the logic of the Hampden case 'left no man any thing which he might call his own'. When the Long Parliament met, six of the judges were removed from the bench and prosecuted to varying degrees. The House of Commons charged Berkeley with treason, but the Lords were content to find him guilty of high crimes and misdemeanours. 'The evils which we have suffered under', complained one MP, 'they were committed by the judges, or by them ought to have been and might have been prevented.' Denzil Holles, who had first-hand experience of the matter, charged that under these judges, 'he that had most might had most right', and the law itself was used to 'rob us and despoil us of our estates'.[155]

Ship money became a *cause célèbre*, but we should be careful not to exaggerate the level of discontent it generated. The Earl of Warwick is known to have spoken directly to Charles in an attempt to persuade him to abandon ship money. (Rebuffed on this occasion, Warwick later had the satisfaction of seizing control of the royal fleet for Parliament.) Viscount Saye and Sele was a moving force behind Hampden's case. But these two noblemen were hardly representative. Collection rates of roughly 90 per cent certainly do not amount to a taxpayers' strike. Local studies reveal widespread foot-dragging alongside equally impressive efforts to comply. It has been alleged that most people simply did not understand the constitutional issues raised by Hampden's case, and those few who did resist ship money had minor procedural qualms about the way it was assessed and collected. What we have to bear in mind, however, is that it was dangerous to express open hostility to the Crown, and there were more prudent ways of dealing with objectionable policies than strident protest. Historians have recently begun to appreciate the extent to which people who objected to ship money on principle might nevertheless have found it safer to pay up and shut up or, at most, slow down the process with technical and procedural objections on the local level. In the absence of a Parliament, would-be opponents of royal policies stood naked before the power of the king. As Ann Hughes explained, 'there was no forum for concerted opposition and people were very cautious in expressing their views'. The result may be a 'surface calm' in the sources available to historians that does not truly represent the level of discontent.[156] S. P. Salt concluded that the case of Sir Simonds D'Ewes 'tends to confirm the suspicion of historians that the gentry concealed, behind the loyal rhetoric with which they carried on their correspondence with the Council, both their own hostility toward the levy and the extent to which there was wilful (or, at least, calculated) obstruction in the shires'.[157]

While we need to be wary of reading events backwards, it is not reasonable to believe that the explosion of protest in the Short and Long Parliaments against ship money and the judges came out of the blue and bore no relation whatsoever to sentiments in the 1630s when, as Clarendon observed, there was an outward impression of prosperity but an 'inward reserved disposition of the people to murmur and unquietness'.[158] Of course it is not clear here which people Clarendon had in mind. The collection of ship money penetrated further down the social scale than subsidies normally did, but still the people most affected by Charles's fiscal policies were the propertied classes who were loath to pay for the costs of royal government even while they happily exploited the people beneath them. We need not waste too much sympathy on these privileged few. Nor would Charles have suffered such dire consequences for offending these people alone if he had not also offended a much broader spectrum of the population through his religious policy, especially when he forced thousands of his English subjects to leave their homes, march northward, and risk their lives to impose that religious policy on his Scottish subjects.

4

THE PERSONAL RULE II

The year 1637 marked the high-water mark of Charles's personal rule. In the Hampden case, he established his right to continue collecting ship money. Earlier in the year in an equally celebrated case the Court of Star Chamber crushed three opponents of his religious policies (John Bastwick, Henry Burton, and William Prynne). Observing these events, the Venetian ambassador in London concluded that Charles had 'changed the principles by which his predecessors reigned'. It was still too early to know 'if the road he has taken will lead him to absolute royalty, which is definitely the goal he has set himself'. Considering how upset the English were over their loss of liberty and changes in religion, the ambassador thought that Charles would be 'very fortunate if he does not fall into some great upheaval'. None the less, success was possible 'if his Majesty adopts gentle methods in his government and in religion'.[1] The treatment of Bastwick, Burton, and Prynne was far from gentle. All three had their ears cut off. Prynne (whose ears had already been cropped as a result of a previous prosecution) also had the initials 'SL' for Seditious Libeller branded on both cheeks. All three men were next transported to remote prisons where the intention was to keep them isolated from the outside world for the rest of their lives.[2] In the higher circles of English society there was concern that gentlemen from three respected professions (a physician, clergyman, and lawyer) could be treated so harshly; but the case aroused more widespread sympathies too. Although many of Charles's subjects were dissatisfied with his foreign and domestic policies, it was his religious policy that generated the most zealous opposition and produced the most dramatic examples of repression. When Charles tried to extend that policy to his kingdom of Scotland, where his rule had already aroused discontent on other grounds, he virtually invited rebellion. Faced with the Scottish challenge to his authority, Charles overreacted as usual, marching northward with an army intending to crush the Scots. He was *Rex Bellicosus* again, and again the results would prove disastrous.

Religious Policy

On the surface, the religious policy of the personal rule was eminently reasonable. Charles and Archbishop Laud were appalled by the deteriorating physical condition of the churches. They launched a campaign to repair and adorn them. They were worried, too, by the extent to which the laity had gained the power to appoint and support many of the clergy (through the purchase of impropriations and advowsons). They tried to remedy this by making the clergy more financially independent of lay control. They thought that respect for the clergy had declined. They sought therefore to enhance the status of the ministry and the power of the church hierarchy, particularly the authority of bishops. They thought the actual form of worship in the church had become too lax and disorderly. They tried therefore to impose higher standards, reduce lectureships and sermons, enforce the official liturgy, and generally restore the splendour and ceremony of the church service, what Laud called the 'beauty of holiness'. Ministers were enjoined to wear the surplice and worshippers to bow at the name of Jesus. Nothing came to symbolise this shift toward ceremony and formality more than the issue of the communion table. In many churches the table where people received communion was located in the middle of the church, although it was supposed to be stored in the east end of the church when not in use. Standing out in the open, the table was subject to such indignities as people laying hats on it and dogs urinating on it. Charles and Laud preferred to see the table protected by a railing, and preferably located permanently in the east end of the church, in a north–south orientation (what was called 'altarwise'). This arrangement of the table carried the further expectation that members of the congregation could be won over to the habit of receiving communion at the rail, perhaps even in a kneeling position.

These policies are often referred to collectively as Laudianism, but Charles and Laud were so much of one mind on church matters that it is extremely difficult to say who was the determining force. Kenneth Fincham and Peter Lake found it impossible to distinguish between the responsibility of the king and archbishop; it was a 'symbiotic relationship between archbishop and monarch', a working relationship 'best understood as a partnership'.[3] Kevin Sharpe and Julian Davies assigned the major share of responsibility to Charles, especially where the altar was concerned.[4] Although they both gave Charles chief responsibility for determining policy, Sharpe and Davies disagreed on whether the policy itself was good or bad. As we might expect, Sharpe took a more benign view of the religious policy of the personal rule.[5] Davies saw it as more provocative, both in conception and execution, but he blamed this on Charles (sometimes abetted by over-zealous clergymen such as Harsnett, Neile, and Wren). According to Davies, all the qualities traditionally associated with Laud – 'intransigence, intolerance, authoritarianism, paranoia, duplicity' – really belonged to Charles. Laud, by contrast, was flexible, lenient, cautious, and tactful. Davies went even further, claiming that Laud was 'seriously out of step with the pace and some of the objectives of Caroline policy'.[6] For example, it was the king, not Laud, who insisted on reissuing the *Book of Sports* in 1633, permitting certain forms of recreation on Sunday and thereby upsetting strict sabbatarians. And it was the king, not Laud, who turned it into a test of loyalty or obedience when some ministers declined to read the accompanying declaration of sports.[7] On the other hand, Davies happily gave principal credit to Laud for the drive to repair St Paul's cathedral in London, although this has usually been considered one of the king's pet projects.[8] In general, then, as Andrew Foster said of other recent writers who tried to rehabilitate Laud's reputation, we are asked to believe that he was actually 'a kindly old man whom we have all misunderstood'.[9] Meanwhile Charles gets the worst of it.

Whatever one thinks of this effort to rehabilitate Laud, it has forced further thinking about the role played by Charles. Davies emphasised that the king's approach to religion dovetailed with his approach to politics. Just as Charles feared there was a popular movement abroad in the land that threatened the monarchy, so too did he fear that this movement threatened the church. As Charles viewed it, the laity were getting too much of their religion outside the church by their own means and without sufficient subordination to the ritual and hierarchy of the church. He wanted them to conform – to the church, to the bishops, to the whole structure over which he was the supreme governor. At heart Charles had no sympathy for the individualist and populist impulses of the Reformation. He took these very qualities which gave vitality and a sense of fellowship to the church and interpreted them as signs of rebellion against authority. Charles 'loathed evangelical Puritanism'. He equated it with 'a popularist threat to hierarchy and authority'.[10] Thus the king's religious policy was reactionary, an attempt to clamp down in the church as he had in the state, to impose his will and his way on his unruly subjects.

This line of analysis may exaggerate the extent to which Charles was motivated by a conscious fear of rebellion or a conspiracy theory. On the other hand, it is true that Charles bristled at the thought of nonconformity, be it political or religious. Here, as elsewhere, he thought in terms of descending authority, not ascending authority. His whole mental framework and his aesthetic sensibilities naturally inclined him toward a conception of the church that emphasised order, control, obedience, formality, spectacle, decorum, dignity, hierarchy, and authority. In these respects, the religious policy of the personal rule was so quintessentially Charles that it might be more accurate, as Davies suggested, if Laudianism were renamed Carolinism. (Whether this amounted to 'sacramental kingship', as Davies also claimed, is another matter.)[11]

Although Charles was keenly aware of the political implications of religious behaviour, he certainly did not reduce religion to purely practical considerations. Quite the contrary, he was an intensely religious man.[12] In the words of Peter White, he was 'more cleric than king'. Unlike his father, however, he did not have the temperament of a theologian. He was not a deep thinker.[13] He and Laud both took pleasure in the rituals or rites of the church, but not in disputing fine points of doctrine. The king's aversion to doctrinal wrangling was evident early in his reign in a proclamation expressing his 'utter dislike to all those, who to show the subtilty of their wits, or to please their owne humours' advanced new religious ideas. He forbid the writing, preaching, or printing of unorthodox ideas, and he accused anyone who violated this injunction with wilfully breaking 'that circle of Order, which without apparent danger to Church and State, may not bee broken'.[14] In the proclamation of 1629 suppressing Montagu's *Appello Caesarem*, Charles likewise said that he was taking this step so that people would no longer trouble themselves with unnecessary disputes or questions; he again forbade the reading, preaching, or printing of views that were 'either *pro* or *contra*'.[15] Some historians believe that Charles was not as neutral as these public pronouncements made him seem, but the point remains that he preferred to avoid theological disputes. Charles wanted his subjects not to be less religious but to share his particular form of religious expression. He wanted them to approach the altar with an attitude of awe and reverence, to find comfort in the repetition of dignified ceremonies, and not to engage in unseemly theorising or debate.

Although Charles did not believe in hounding people over obscure points of doctrine, the penalty could be severe for anyone who broke 'the circle of order' by refusing to accept or openly criticising his vision of the church, and his regime consequently acquired a reputation for religious oppression. One way historians have tried to soften this criticism is to point fingers at other culprits – Laud, Neile, or Wren, for example. Another way has been to minimise the oppression altogether. Kevin Sharpe adopted this latter strategy to vindicate the Court of High Commission and the Court of Star Chamber. Historians have known for some time that these courts were not just cruel instruments of oppression. As Sharpe noted, the vast majority of their cases were pedestrian; many even served the interests of the downtrodden and poor. Unfortunately, a few notorious cases 'besmirched' the reputation of these courts, which was all the more unfortunate because the defendants in these cases were so uncooperative and insolent that they were practically asking to be punished.[16] Sharpe gave most attention to the trial of Bastwick, Burton, and Prynne; he did little more than mention the case of John Lilburne which occurred in the winter of 1637–38. Convicted of printing unlicensed books critical of the church, Lilburne was whipped through the streets, placed in the pillory, gagged, put in irons, kept in solitary confinement, and nearly starved to death.[17] One does not have to make heroes of these men or succumb to anachronistic sentimentality about liberty to wonder whether a regime that resorted to such measures was going badly awry.

Granted that such sensational cases were a tiny minority, they were adequate cause for public concern. From his study of petitions to the Long Parliament, a great many of which concerned religious grievances, James S. Hart concluded that the actual policies of the personal rule were 'less troubling to the average Englishman than the severe and seemingly arbitrary penalties imposed for resisting them'.[18] The rule of law appeared to be in jeopardy. Furthermore, whatever the reality of the situation, it took only a few ghastly cases to affect contemporary perceptions, and the perception that ultimately hurt these courts most was that they were dominated by inordinately powerful bishops.[19] In this area, as in others, the true impact of the personal rule may be best measured by what happened afterward when people were freer to express themselves. Bastwick, Burton, Prynne, and Lilburne were released from prison in 1640 on the orders of the Long Parliament. The Courts of High Commission and Star Chamber were abolished. And Prynne exhibited his own brand of ruthlessness in the destruction of Laud.

What went wrong? In Sharpe's roseate view of the personal rule, nothing much went wrong at all until 1637. Then suddenly the trial of Bastwick, Burton, and Prynne backfired, and soon thereafter Scots propaganda further enflamed public opinion until there was a 'crescendo of national paranoia'. As time wore on, fear of a Roman Catholic conspiracy centred at the court and animosity against the bishops further fuelled this paranoia.[20] Charles was not the cause but the victim of religious hysteria. For Davies, the trouble began much earlier and was inherent in the way Charles used the church to promote his political agenda. Under Charles, 'the Church had become enmeshed in the promotion of arbitrary government'. Power had been taken away from the laity and concentrated in the hands of the king and the church hierarchy, particularly the bishops. Charles had turned his back on the Reformation spirit of the church, pitting himself against many of its most ardent members, stigmatising them as trouble-makers, defiling their sabbath, silencing their preachers, and generally promoting what appeared to be 'the recatholicization of Anglicanism'. Charles would have been better off to leave things alone. Instead of uniting the people behind a restored and resplendent church, he created 'the impression that the king and the bishops were conspiring either to return the country to Rome or to set up an English popery'. The fault was clearly the king's, and the reaction it provoked amounted to 'an almost unanimous vote of no confidence' in his governance of the church.[21]

Sharpe and Davies disagreed on the king's culpability, but the common theme in their explanation is correct: it was fear of popery that ruined Charles's religious programme. For more than two decades the religious history of the early Stuart period has been dominated by the work of Nicholas Tyacke, who argued that the key to the religious history of the period is Arminianism. Tyacke's work had many salutary effects. It demolished the old tendency to think in terms of Puritans versus Anglicans. It forced historians to think of Charles and Laud, not the Puritans, as the true innovators who upset the status quo. And it exposed the simplicity of attributing the conflicts of this period to an amorphous 'rise of Puritanism'. Yet Tyacke's thesis had its own faults. It gave as much explanatory power to the rise of Arminianism as an earlier generation had given to the rise of Puritanism.[22] It grossly exaggerated the importance of doctrine, and it spawned an outpouring of books and articles distinguished by their mastery of obscure theological controversies which would have been intelligible to very few of Charles's own subjects.[23] Tyacke's thesis was that the church under Charles was taken over by Arminians. Under their regime, Calvinists, who had previously been in the mainstream of the church, were marginalised and branded as Puritan extremists. Tyacke tried to identify the exact point at which Charles was converted to Arminianism (1623) and to uncover the identity of the other Arminians who carried out this take-over of the church that eventually precipitated a counter-revolution. For this thesis to make sense, the definition of Arminianism had to be broadened to include more than the rejection of the Calvinist doctrine of predestination.[24] Arminianism had to be equated with anti-Calvinism more broadly speaking, and all the various changes that Laud and Charles introduced into the church had to be interpreted as somehow springing from this Arminian viewpoint. It does logically follow that a person who believes in the Arminian doctrine of salvation will be averse to Calvinism or Puritanism in many other respects. An Arminian will attach greater importance to the ceremonies and sacraments of the church because they are a means to salvation; and an Arminian will take a more august view of the clergy who preside over these ceremonies. Surely there is considerable truth in all of this, but it is not the whole truth. King Charles was not interested in the erudite argument over free will versus predestination, and the changes he introduced into the church did not arise exclusively or even predominantly from Arminian convictions. There were other temperamental, aesthetic, intellectual, and historical reasons for both Charles and Laud to pursue the changes they did.[25] But most important, when the public outcry came, it was not so much because these changes smacked of Arminianism as because they smacked of Roman Catholicism.

What gave Arminianism its potency as an issue was its perceived connection to the much larger and more menacing issue of Roman

Catholicism or what the English called popery. Davies probably went too far in saying that the kind of Arminianism we saw complained of in the 1620s was 'a dead letter by 1640', but it certainly was not as incendiary an issue as Roman Catholicism.[26] To understand how Charles got himself into trouble on this score, Tyacke's work is not as helpful as Caroline Hibbard's *Charles I and the Popish Plot.*[27] The fear of a popish plot centred at the court would become one of the most effective propaganda tools against Charles in the 1640s, and much that he did in the 1630s provided a plausible basis for that propaganda. As we have already seen, Charles patronised Catholic artists and enthusiastically embraced the art of the Counter-Reformation. The same aesthetic values that attracted Charles to Baroque art attracted him to a Baroque style of church service. The changes he and Laud introduced in the government and liturgy of the church had an aura of Roman Catholicism about them. The emphasis shifted away from Protestant preaching toward the spectacle, adornments, and sacraments of Catholicism. The Protestant minister took on the appearance of a Catholic priest, and the Protestant communion table took on the appearance of a Catholic altar. These changes looked so much like a move in the direction of Roman Catholicism that the papacy itself was encouraged to think that Charles, Laud, indeed all of England, might be converted back to Rome.[28] Laud was constantly on the defensive to prove that this was not the case.

Suspicions raised by changes in the character of the church were heightened by a simultaneous growth of real Catholicism at court. To Protestant bystanders, as Hibbard remarked, it must have looked as if the court 'was swarming with Catholics'. While the changes within the church may or may not have arisen from Arminianism, court Catholicism was 'a separate phenomenon, a willed disaster' for which Charles was personally responsible.[29] In 1634 Charles allowed agents to be exchanged between the papacy and the court of Queen Henrietta Maria. The priest Gregorio Panzani became the first official representative of the papacy to enter England since the reign of Mary I. In 1636 Panzani was succeeded by George Con, a native of Scotland who had been brought up in the Roman Catholic church on the continent where he spent over a decade in important church posts. When he arrived in England, Con allied with Spanish and Jesuit forces and became an intimate of the king. Charles treated Con as an ambassador to his own court and formed a closer relationship with him than had been seen in England since James I

befriended Gondomar. The effects of Con's diplomacy were everywhere visible in 1637–38. The queen became a more active protector
of English Catholics and the centre of a Catholic party at court. By
the terms of her marriage contract, she maintained a chapel at each
of her residences, and she had 12 Capuchin priests who served as
her chaplains. Large numbers of people began to attend mass at the
queen's lavish new chapel at Somerset House and other chapels
maintained by certain noble families in London. Famous English
Catholics who had been living in exile on the continent were
allowed to re-enter England (Wat Montagu and Toby Mathew in particular), and the court was abuzz with a number of sensational con-
versions. Meanwhile several notable enemies of Cardinal Richelieu
also took up residence in England, and Charles's foreign policy
began to swing back toward friendship with Spain.[30]

It was Charles's misfortune to be more tolerant than his subjects.
His broad-minded reception of Catholic emissaries at court and inclusion of Catholic figures in his government deepened the suspicion that his own predilections were alien to those of the nation at
large. But Charles was not entirely blameless. Had he been more politically adept, he would not have allowed these Catholic figures and
their activities to be so blatantly associated with his regime. Even less
would he have appointed Bishop Juxon as the new Lord Treasurer
in 1636, the first cleric to hold that post since the reign of Henry VII.
Juxon joined Laud and Neile on the Privy Council (and hence the
Court of Star Chamber), thereby strengthening the impression that
bishops were gaining excessive power.[31] As we have seen, it can be
argued that the art and drama of the court sent out a message to the
nation at large, though it is not certain how that message was perceived and by how many. The religious policies of the 1630s sent out
a message, too, and with much more certain results. By mandating
changes in the local churches that his subjects attended and allowing
the proliferation of Catholics at court, Charles broadcast a message
that was highly visible and unsettling. At another time in another
nation, the king's close affinity with Roman Catholicism would not
have been a liability, but given the circumstances of his time and
place, as Hibbard observed, Charles's behaviour was 'politically
suicidal'.[32]

Of course the blame goes all the way back to Henry VIII who
created an odd church that was neither Roman nor reformed; the
competing forces of conservatism and reformation had been battling
for control ever since. Elizabeth and James had managed to contain

and balance those forces. One way or another Charles destabilised this precarious balance – by squelching Puritanism, promoting Arminianism, or fostering Catholicism. Historians do not agree on the amount of damage Charles did. Naturally Kevin Sharpe tried to minimise the damage. As Sharpe explained, people who were disturbed about the direction the church was taking on a national level might still have been comfortable with whatever accommodation was worked out on their local level. A few extremists like Prynne were crushed; a few others emigrated to the New World. In any case, the godly or Puritans 'were never more than a well organized, minority sect'.[33] Furthermore, lest we focus too exclusively on these few malcontents, we should remember that a great many other people continued to be perfectly happy with the official church and its liturgy.[34] By contrast, John Morrill thought that the religious policies of the personal rule were very damaging. He detected widespread anger, bitterness, and tension in England, making the nation comparable to a coiled spring.[35] Whoever is closer to the truth (and it is probably Morrill), Charles had not done anything so far which was sufficiently outrageous to jeopardise his crown. It is true that he appeared to be too sympathetic toward Roman Catholics, but he was not actively waging war against Protestants. At least not yet.

Scotland to 1637

The personal rule was like an experiment that was not allowed to run its full course. We will never know how long it might have continued or what its natural outcome might have been because it was cut short by Charles's decision to fight another war. Had he avoided war, which in turn would have enabled him to avoid calling another Parliament, the personal rule might have continued indefinitely. No matter how great the level of dissatisfaction was, the plain fact remained that his subjects had no safe and effective way of doing anything about their predicament. As long as Charles could make ends meet financially, they had no leverage over him to make any demands. And as long as there was no Parliament, they had no forum where they could pool their dissatisfactions, find strength in numbers, and mount a campaign to rectify the situation. For a man who prized control, Charles was in an enviable position during the

1630s. Yet Charles was like a moth fatally attracted to light: all he had to do was avoid war, and he flew headlong into it.

Recent authors have had little good to say about the way Charles ruled Scotland. Indeed, there has been a veritable rush to condemn him. Even Kevin Sharpe abandoned his plucky defence of the king when he reached this subject.[36] Maurice Lee, Jr believed that *The Road to Revolution* began in 1625 with the accession of Charles I.[37] Peter Donald's *An Uncounselled King* made Charles seem more exclusively to blame because he resisted and ignored good advice from the people around him.[38] Allan Macinnes's *Charles I and the Making of the Covenanting Movement* accused Charles of attempting to reduce Scotland to provincial status.[39] In a refreshingly different article, Keith Brown tried to shift attention away from the king to long-term economic developments that predisposed the Scottish nobility to revolution. Nevertheless Brown still had no doubt that Charles was guilty of 'crass stupidity', 'ineptitude and bungling', and in his subsequent book *Kingdom or Province?* he portrayed Charles as an imperialist aggressor against the Scots who 'brazened out the threat from the imperial monarchy'.[40] The current tendency is certainly to sympathise with the Scots. Charles gets no credit for his attempts to compromise, and the Scots get no blame for their intransigence.[41] Perhaps no one will ever be so foolhardy as to defend the personal rule in Scotland, but David Stevenson's book, *The Scottish Revolution 1637–1644*, written before the current hostile climate, did at least strive for balance.[42]

One of Charles's principal problems (as with any powerful person) was that he tended to be isolated from criticism. This problem was greatly magnified in his relations with Scotland. As an absentee monarch, Charles did not have the regular face-to-face meetings with his Scottish Privy Council that he had with his English Council. The lines of communication with Scotland were more distant and tenuous. Furthermore, Charles scrupulously refrained from discussing Scottish business with his English Council – not because he jealously guarded this area or wanted to keep anyone in the dark, as is sometimes claimed, but rather because it was an established practice that prevented the English Council from unfairly directing the affairs of Scotland.[43] Surely the Scots would not have wanted the English Privy Council directing their business. The drawback of this system was that it left Charles too isolated from the information and advice he needed to make good decisions. These structural impediments to good communication were, of course, made worse by Charles's personal predilections. The Earl of Mar told Charles that the Council in Scotland had refrained from implementing his father's orders a hundred times, and when they explained their reasons, James thanked them for helping him to avert a problem.[44] But not so Charles, who expected to be obeyed and did not want to hear about difficulties. Charles failed to establish a good working relationship with the Scottish nobility, though he actually added more of them to the Council. On the other hand, the internecine quarrels among these men and their history of confrontation with the Crown prior to the seventeenth century did not exactly recommend them for power. Matters were made worse, however, by Charles's tendency to trust in the Scottish bishops and promote them to civil office. His appointment of Archbishop Spottiswoode as Lord Chancellor of Scotland, the country's highest civil office, had an effect similar to his appointment of Juxon as Lord Treasurer in England – it strengthened the impression of an overly powerful clerical regime and helped to precipitate a backlash against episcopacy.

Charles definitely got off on the wrong foot in his rule of Scotland. In the first two years of his reign he announced a number of changes in the administrative structure of the country, and he issued an act of revocation that was unprecedented in its scope. Since so many monarchs in Scotland succeeded to the throne as minors, they had gained the customary right when they finally came of age to revoke all grants that had been made in their names during their minority. This custom protected the monarchs' interests, allowed them to reverse grants made to their prejudice, and helped secure allegiance by requiring other recipients to plead or pay for the continuation of their grants. What made Charles's revocation outrageous (in addition to the fact that his own father had ruled through his minority) was that it applied to kirk land as well as Crown land and extended back not only through his own minority but to the middle of the sixteenth century. It looked like a wholesale assault on property rights. The idea for this vast act of revocation may not have originated with Charles, but by adopting it as his own he left an indelibly bad first impression.

Most authors agree that what Charles did in Scotland was not as bad as how he did it. Sharpe, for example, observed that the changes introduced at the outset of his reign had some merit but they 'were, *as often with Charles*, enacted with excess haste, inadequate explanation and insufficient sensitivity to the suspicions of others'. Macinnes described the king's manner as 'authoritarian sophistry'.[45] Rational

explanations are not lacking for what Charles did, however. The revocation of church land, for example, was intended to provide better
financial support for the clergy. Charles had no intention of reclaim-
ing all the land involved and planned to pay compensation for what
was reclaimed. Moreover, the king's haste in announcing these measures was dictated by the circumstances. He was desperately short of
money for the war effort, and he was required by law to make the revocation before his twenty-fifth birthday. Perhaps most important, it
is usually not sufficiently appreciated that Charles made these decisions as a very young and inexperienced man. We could chalk them
up to the rashness of youth if, unfortunately, they did not fit the
pattern he exhibited throughout his life.

After this inauspicious beginning, Charles's rule of Scotland proceeded more smoothly into the early 1630s. The revocation and
other changes Charles had announced were not carried through as
ruthlessly as was feared, though the king did not receive and probably does not deserve much credit for this fact. In 1633, when Charles
travelled to Scotland for his coronation, he had an excellent opportunity to further reverse the damage of his earlier actions, but he
succeeded only in raising new alarms. With the exception of the trip
to Madrid in 1623, Charles did not generally travel far from London.
Perhaps it was part of his obsession with control that he did not like
to leave his accustomed environs. In any case, he spent only a few
weeks in Scotland, and during that time he seemed more concerned
to use and manipulate people than to befriend them. His personality
was a handicap in this respect; he simply did not have the easygoing
interpersonal skills necessary to capitalise on this festive occasion
and cultivate popularity. Moreover, this was a business trip for
Charles, and he methodically conducted that business through the
two great staged events of the trip: the coronation ceremony and the
meeting of the Scottish Parliament. Charles orchestrated the coronation ceremony in a way that looked alarmingly like Roman
Catholicism to the Scots. There was an altar with candles on it, and
the clergy, who wore elaborate vestments, bowed toward it. In his
planning for the Parliament, Charles displayed what Morrill called
'naked authoritarianism' and Macinnes called 'managerial
overkill'.[46] The king prohibited discussion of legislation in advance,
tried to prevent any real debate from occurring, and personally kept
a running tab of people who cast negative votes. This gives us a dramatic illustration of the way Charles thought a Parliament should
proceed – swiftly, compliantly, and with no grievances. The corona-

tion Parliament was forced to vote on one huge legislative package that contained 168 individual measures. Some of these related to controversial business like the revocation and taxation which was reaching unprecedented levels; others related to the even more inflammatory topic of religion. Charles was given authority to determine clerical dress, and the five articles of Perth which James had passed but refrained from enforcing were confirmed. The most objectionable of these articles required kneeling at communion. Thus the alarms of Roman Catholicism that were raised by the coronation ceremony were further reinforced by the legislation rammed through Parliament. Charles was less menacing as an unknown quantity ruling from London than he appeared to be in person on the coronation visit. 'His presence', wrote Macinnes, 'provided tangible proof of not just his intransigence and ineptitude as a monarch, but also his crass insensitivity to Scottish sensibilities.'[47]

Charles did not want to hear that his visit to Scotland had been anything but a success. He refused to accept a supplication through which several Scottish leaders had hoped to communicate their unhappiness, and when he learned later that a copy of this supplication was in the possession of Lord Balmerino, he put him on trial. Although Balmerino was convicted by the narrowest possible vote and was guilty only of possessing the slanderous document, the penalty was death. Charles then relented and pardoned Balmerino, perhaps thinking that he had proved his point. Some Scots interpreted the Balmerino case as further evidence of the inordinate power of bishops. For others it reflected more directly on the king. As Stevenson explained, the whole object of the trial had been 'to terrify opposition into silence', but the effect of the trial was to horrify people at the injustice and severity of the king's rule.[48] In Lee's opinion, 'Charles's decision to prosecute Balmerino alienated the Scottish ruling class and turned it against him and his government' more than any other act, even the revocation.[49] For Macinnes, who had no qualms about anticipating the outcome of the story, the indictment of Balmerino 'was to prove the single most important event transforming the disaffected element from a political faction into a national movement'. Indeed, the Balmerino trial 'marked a decisive shift from reform towards revolution'.[50]

Whig teleology aside, it is difficult to judge, in Scotland as in England, just how volatile the situation was before 1637. It seems unlikely, however, that an explosion would have occurred if Charles had not tried to impose a new prayer book on the Scots. Recent scholarship has emphasised the importance of a multiple-kingdoms approach to the study of British history. This approach highlights the fact that Charles wanted his three quite disparate kingdoms to be more uniform (or as Morrill has said, congruent) in matters of religion.[51] Given Charles's obsession with order, it is understandable that he would have desired greater uniformity between England and Scotland where the worship service was too irregular and informal for his tastes. But to try changing this state of affairs by royal *fiat* was reckless almost beyond words. Charles, wrote Conrad Russell, 'decided to drop a match into this powder-keg by setting out to achieve one uniform order of religion within the three kingdoms'. Combined with what Charles had already done to destroy the consensus in matters of religion, the 'effect seems to have been very like that of taking the pin out of a grenade'.[52]

Prayer Book and War

Charles did not try to impose the English prayer book *verbatim* on Scotland. But neither did he follow a very consultative process in modifying it for the Scots. He and Laud worked with a handful of bishops. This must have seemed quite natural to Charles, given his hierarchical top-down approach to politics and the church, but it did not pave the way politically for the acceptance of the new prayer book. It would have offended all of Charles's sensibilities for something as sacred and authoritative as a prayer book to be composed with participation or approval from the Scottish Parliament or a General Assembly of the kirk. King James had been more politic in such matters, but Charles introduced his changes solely on the authority of his own prerogative. The collusion of Scottish bishops in the project made it even more unpalatable. Again it was not just what Charles did, but the manner in which he did it that generated opposition. Charles preceded the new prayer book with new canons for the Scottish church at the beginning of 1636 which gave the Scots a foretaste of what was to come. More than a year would elapse before the actual arrival of the prayer book, and opponents effectively used that interval to organise against it. Exaggerated rumours, especially regarding the Roman Catholic character of the new prayer book, ensured that when it did appear in the summer of 1637 opinion was already so inflamed that it would receive no fair reading. Of course *any* prayer book may have been anathema to the style of worship in the Scottish church. Charles had a classical and authoritarian frame of mind; for him it seemed proper for the congregation to follow a liturgy prescribed from on high. The Presbyterian form of worship was not so rigid and relied more on extemporaneous preaching. We are back, then, to the point made by Julian Davies that Charles never accepted the Reformation. Now, unfortunately, Charles appeared to be trying to reverse the Reformation in the one kingdom of his three where it was most firmly entrenched.

When the explosion came, how did Charles handle it?[53] His first response, as we might expect, was to stand firm and try to break the opposition. The issue for Charles was a simple one of obedience, and he was determined not to have his authority challenged. It took Charles an awfully long time to realise that this approach would not work and that he would have to negotiate. The people advising the king, most especially the Earl of Traquair and the Marquis of Hamilton, ran the risk of losing his favour if they were too honest with him about the nature of the situation. As they became increasingly blunt and the situation became increasingly desperate, Charles gradually agreed to make concessions. By then, however, it was too late. The opposition had spread and organised in the National Covenant. From that point forward, even when Charles agreed to retract the canons and the prayer book and allow a meeting of the General Assembly, the Covenant itself became a sticking point for him. And meanwhile, his adversaries were no longer content with concessions that probably would have appeased them if Charles had only made them sooner. Among other things, the Covenanters were now determined to abolish episcopacy. This is an all-too-familiar pattern. Charles had a habit of making concessions belatedly that could have gained him immeasurably more if he had only been willing to make them earlier. Furthermore, as usual, Charles insisted on making his concessions in ambiguous language that afforded him loopholes to escape through but aroused suspicion about his sincerity.

War might have been averted if Charles had made conciliatory gestures earlier, but the problem went deeper than that. Peter Donald observed that Charles 'tried to dictate', which was true at the beginning of the Scottish troubles, but after the Covenant it was the Scots who dictated.[54] The Covenanters were animated by a potent combination of religious zeal and nationalism that would have been difficult for any ruler to mollify. Charles, however, was especially unsuited to the task. He never could brook opposition, but he found it particularly repugnant when it came from religious nonconformists. He failed altogether to comprehend the viewpoint and the fervour of the people he was up against in Scotland. As Russell explained, Charles was least likely to deal well with the Scottish crisis because it concerned the area of his 'deepest inflexibility', the area where his religious convictions and his sense of authority intersected.[55] To Charles, the Covenant was simply 'damnable' and those who subscribed to it were 'rebels' and 'traitors'. He did not understand how he himself could be perceived as the innovator who was upsetting the status quo when it was the Covenanters who were challenging authority. As he explained, 'my taking of arms is to suppress rebellion, and not to impose novelties'. From Charles's point of view, as long as the Covenant was in force, 'I have no more power in Scotland than as a Duke of Venice, which I will rather die than suffer'. Charles's view of this challenge to his authority was identical to the view he would adopt on the eve of the Civil War: there are concessions a king cannot make without ceasing to be a king. 'I will rather die than yield to these impertinent and damnable demands', wrote Charles, 'for it is all one, as to yield to be no King in a very short time.' Moreover, personal honour was involved again: 'not only now my crown, but my reputation for ever, lies at stake'. Given these views, one must doubt whether Charles was as sincere as his emissary, Hamilton, in attempting to reach a negotiated resolution. Certainly, such an extreme opinion of the Covenanters was not conducive to a reconciliation. Both Charles and the Covenanters prepared for the possibility of war while continuing to talk. Charles told Hamilton 'that I expect not anything can reduce that people to obedience, but only force'. He instructed Hamilton to 'flatter them with what hopes you please' and 'gain time by all the honest means you can'. Or, in other words, 'win time ... until I be ready to suppress them'.[56]

Charles's view of the situation was not irrational: his authority was at stake. The crisis in Scotland, like so many he precipitated in England, began as an argument over a limited number of specific religious measures but escalated into a larger constitutional issue that was far more difficult to resolve without violence. Who was in charge in Scotland? This question was clearly foremost in the king's mind when he issued a proclamation at the beginning of 1639 attempting to stem the flow of Scottish propaganda that he feared was poisoning the hearts of his English subjects and encouraging them into similarly rebellious courses. As Charles explained, the Covenanters were striving, behind the pretext of religion, 'to shake off all Monarchicall government'. The question now, he declared, was not whether the new prayer book would be accepted, or even whether episcopacy would be preserved, 'but whether We are their King or not'.[57]

Just as there was a basis in fact for the king to take an extreme view of the Covenanters, so was there increasing justification for the Covenanters to take an extreme view of him. Fulfilling the worst fears of the Covenanters, Roman Catholics were now playing a major role in plans to subdue the Scots. As Caroline Hibbard has shown, the king's viewpoint was strongly influenced by court Catholics, some of whom saw the troubles in Scotland as an opportunity to advance their cause.[58] At one time or another Charles explored the use of Irish Catholics, Spanish troops, and papal money to subdue the rebellion in Scotland. He allowed a monetary contribution to be collected from English Catholics. He hoped for support from a handful of Catholic Scots, among whom the Earl of Nithsdale gave perfectly terrible advice.[59] While the king was still not consulting with his full Privy Council about Scotland, he was taking advice from George Con, the papal agent who just happened to be a Scot, and increasingly from Henrietta Maria. In Hibbard's words, the queen 'was pushing the king toward just those policies that he should most scrupulously have avoided'. When he did turn to his Council, he employed a sub-committee that was dominated by Catholic hardliners (Arundel, Cottington, and Windebank). It is true that Charles resisted good advice; but he was also given a lot of bad advice from people close to him who reinforced his imperious view of the situation, manipulated him for their own ends, or both. Con reported to Cardinal Barberini that the king had told him 'I mean to be obeyed'.[60] At the very time when Charles needed to hear a broader spectrum of opinion, especially from the more ardent Protestants he had spurned, he was turning for support and guidance to the small coterie of court Catholics who shared his most self-defeating impulses. In the insulated world that Charles had created for himself at Whitehall, he was drawn into a course that Hibbard described as 'politically lethal'.

The two armies met at the border in early summer of 1639. Peter Donald referred to the 'gritty resolution' on the part of the Covenanters in assembling their army, and in fairness we should acknowledge the 'gritty resolution' on the part of the king in assembling his.[61] Equally noteworthy, however, is how quickly both sides lost their grit. The First Bishops' War and the Pacification of Berwick that followed almost immediately are both misnomers. The two forces did not wage war, and no one was pacified. The strange charade that took place between the king and Covenanters in June of 1639 defies a fully rational explanation.[62] Charles had failed to mobilise public opinion behind his effort. He did not have the full support of his own nobility (Lords Saye and Brooke made their objections quite visibly known), and his ragtag army had no heart for the fight. The Scottish army probably did not have as great an edge as the English feared, but Charles appears to have been 'outbluffed'.[63] In the event, both sides opted to negotiate rather than fight. It was remarkable that Charles entered into these negotiations in person, and he gave evidence of those debating skills he would display almost ten years later at his trial. The two sides reached a temporary accommodation that enabled them to disband their armies and go home, but afterwards it became apparent that they had not reached a permanent understanding.

   At first Charles thought he might be able to influence the course of events if he attended the planned meeting of the Scottish General Assembly and Parliament in person, although he admitted that he was 'far from thinking that at this time I shall get half of my will'.[64] It was soon obvious that he would get nowhere near half, and he returned directly to London. The Scots proceeded to reject all the major religious measures of the personal rule, abolish episcopacy, and make constitutional changes that limited the king's voice in the business of the General Assembly and Parliament. It would not be fair to accuse Charles of intransigence at this point. He was prepared to make major sacrifices (including the articles of Perth, the canons, and the prayer book). He even seemed prepared to abandon episcopacy in Scotland, although this was probably just a temporary tactical retreat. What he could not accept were the drastic reductions in his power and the specific language the Scots insisted on attaching to their abolition of episcopacy. That language declared that episcopacy was not just inappropriate under the present circumstances in Scotland but unlawful in general, which was tantamount to attacking episcopacy in his other two kingdoms.[65] It was the Scots, not Charles, who were now thinking in terms of religious uniformity in multiple kingdoms.

Charles was paying heavily now for not being more brutal when he had the chance. By his failure of nerve in the summer of 1639, he had thrown away his best opportunity to impose his will on Scotland. Had he made a fight of it at that point, his army might have hardened and public sentiment might have swung behind him. But having raised an army, marched it to the border, and failed to use it, Charles could not reasonably expect to repeat the exercise another time with anywhere near the same prospect of success. At the very least, if he wanted to try again, he would have to summon a Parliament to finance the enterprise, and that decision effectively brought the personal rule to an end.

5

A MATTER OF TRUST, 1640–1649

In 1640 Charles once again summoned a Parliament to pay for a war he had already decided to undertake. It was immediately apparent that the Short Parliament was even less interested than its predecessors in financing a war. Instead it attacked the policies of the personal rule with such vehemence that Charles dissolved it and attempted to fight the Second Bishops' War on his own resources. For anyone acquainted with the 1620s it was, as they say, *déjà vu* all over again. This time, however, the war struck closer to home and had more earth-shattering consequences. The victorious Scottish army occupied northern England, and Charles was forced to summon another Parliament to extricate himself from this predicament. Members of the Long Parliament, fired by discontent and aware that Charles was in an unusually weakened position, exploited their advantage to the full. They removed the king's chief ministers and abolished all the hated institutions and measures of the personal rule. Having seized the day and redressed their own grievances, members of the Long Parliament might have rested on their laurels, but instead events conspired to drive them into new territory. Eventually MPs were locked in a battle with Charles over the boundaries of the royal prerogative and bitterly divided among themselves. The situation deteriorated until the failure to reach a political accommodation led to civil war. The war's outcome was by no means predetermined. Charles adapted to his radically changed circumstances and commanded the royalist forces through four years of tenacious fighting, but in the end he had to surrender. Even at this late point, he might still have retained the throne if he had been willing to make fundamental concessions regarding the royal prerogative and the church and, perhaps more importantly, if he

126

had stopped being duplicitous. But Charles would not compromise away the powers of the Crown or the sanctity of the church, and he repeatedly demonstrated that it was folly to trust him. Because he was uncompromising and untrustworthy, he forced his enemies to choose: if they wished to bring an end to the bloodshed and secure the objectives for which they had fought, they had to eliminate him. While most still shrank from so extreme a solution, a handful of battle-hardened radicals engineered the king's trial and execution. They destroyed the king, and yet Charles for once snatched victory from the jaws of defeat by conducting himself through these final days with such dignity, eloquence, and courage that he ennobled the cause of monarchy for his posterity to reap the rewards.

Before examining this momentous series of events in greater detail, it is important to note that we have entered quite different historiographical terrain. Here, in contrast to the 1620s and 1630s, there has been little effort at exoneration. Here, more than at any other stage in his reign, it is relatively easy to put Charles back into perspective because he never slipped very far out of perspective. Almost everyone agrees that he brought ruin upon himself.

The Demon King

Historians argue interminably about the causes of the Civil War. Fortunately, the present book does not have to summarise all those arguments.[1] Our subject is only the king, and on this subject there is very little argument. Whatever else they disagree about, nearly all historians of the 1640s take the same unfavourable view of King Charles. Most further agree that the king's flawed character and impolitic actions figured prominently in the outbreak of the Civil War. Revisionist historians of this period have been credited with emphasising short-term causes, and the chief short-term cause of the Civil War they emphasise is King Charles I. For example, in *The Outbreak of the English Civil War*, Anthony Fletcher traced the way John Pym and a handful of likeminded MPs used the fear of a popish plot to turn their fellow members against Charles, but no one helped them more than Charles himself. As Fletcher described him, Charles was incapable of comprehending the people who criticised him or the nature of their criticisms. His vision of politics was clouded by his conviction that Puritan extremists were intent on destroying monarchy. He was haughty, aloof, and rigid. He was inclined to deviousness and intrigue. He cultivated an alien culture at his court and loved an alien queen. And his repeated blunders 'did much to make the political crisis insoluble'.[2] Whereas Fletcher stressed the role of anti-Catholicism in parliamentary politics, John Morrill stressed the widespread disaffection that the king's religious policies generated throughout his three kingdoms. In Morrill's formidable body of work on the background of the Civil War, it was the fervour of the godly that provided the driving force, but it was still Charles who provoked that force. In Morrill's view, Charles was 'wholly incompetent' and 'overbearing'. The rebellions that broke out in quick succession in Scotland, Ireland, and England were 'variant responses to a shared problem – the incompetence and authoritarianism of Charles I'.[3] In fact Charles might have remained secure in his kingdom of England if he had not done such a bad job of governing his other two kingdoms. 'There was a civil war in England in the 1640s', Morrill explained, 'because Charles I misgoverned Scotland and Ireland.'[4]

The big question was what view would Conrad Russell take of Charles in these later years. In his earlier work on the 1620s Russell had emphasised mitigating circumstances and impersonal forces, structural defects and functional breakdown, instead of the king's own personal culpability. The only major error Russell attributed to Charles in the 1620s was his promotion of Arminianism.[5] It would have been fascinating to see Russell try to continue this marginalisation of Charles in the later period, but that is not what he did. As Richard Cust and Ann Hughes pointed out, Russell always took a more charitable view of Charles in the 1620s than in the years surrounding the outbreak of the Civil War. In the earlier period Charles was depicted as 'moderate and reasonable'; in the later period he bore 'a much greater resemblance to the popular historical image of an untrustworthy king who was both aggressive and ineffectual'.[6] Russell never did subscribe to the view of the Civil War as a social revolution.[7] It was a rebellion against Charles, and – to put it simply – if Charles was what people were rebelling against, there had to be something wrong with him. Russell was also influenced by the work of L. J. Reeve and Richard Cust. Russell considered Reeve's *Road to Personal Rule* and Cust's *Forced Loan* 'among the most important books on early Stuart political history in the past ten years'. As Russell explained the process, 'Dr Cust, Dr Reeve, and I have all been writing about Charles at much the same time, and our pictures enjoy a good deal of similarity'.[8] The similarity had increased over time because, as Russell acknowledged in another place, his relationship with Cust, one of his own former students, had been 'a fourteen-year dialogue'.[9]

In his later articles and two major books, *The Fall of the British Monarchies* and *The Causes of the English Civil War*, Russell did not perform a complete *volte-face*. He still appreciated structural weaknesses, especially the poverty of the Crown. The Stuarts, wrote Russell, 'inherited a financial system which was already close to the point of breakdown'. Charles was described as a penniless king whose poverty limited his freedom of action and diminished his majesty.[10] Nor did Russell entirely abandon the argument about tension between the centre and the localities, but he gave this argument new life by elevating it to a higher level. Now the tension existed between the centre, England, and the other two kingdoms, Scotland and Ireland. It was not easy to rule three kingdoms, imposing central authority on all three while at the same time allowing sufficient regional differences to satisfy everyone, particularly when one kingdom was as Protestant as Scotland and the other as Catholic as Ireland. This problem of multiple kingdoms, influenced by the work of H. G. Koenigsberger, carried enormous explanatory weight in Russell's later work.[11] Taken together, these impersonal problems of money, multiple kingdoms, and religious division were, in Russell's words, 'three long-term causes of instability, all of them well established before Charles came to the throne'.[12] Russell still defended Charles on other grounds, too. Like Fletcher, he blamed John Pym for much that went wrong.[13] And he resorted again to the argument from national defence: 'If heads of state, in any age, are forced to choose between ruling illegally and not defending their countries, they will rule illegally.'[14] Furthermore, as Russell viewed him, Charles was not 'nearly as duplicitous as he is sometimes taken to be'.[15] Russell described 'the charge of bad faith' as 'no more justified against Charles than it is against most politicians with long careers'. If Charles deceived people, 'it was because they allowed themselves to be deceived'. Or, to put it another way, 'those who were deceived were deceived voluntarily'.[16]

Nevertheless, for anyone acquainted with Russell's work on the 1620s what was most surprising in his later work was the emphasis on the king's personal responsibility. Charles was no longer the helpless victim of circumstances or a man caught in the wrong place at the wrong time. There were mitigating circumstances, to be sure, but they were not beyond the king's control. To a considerable extent, his fate was in his own hands. Russell expressed surprise at this discovery. In his own words, he had found, 'as the work progressed, that the King was a more active participant in the story than I had supposed'.[17] Russell discovered not only that Charles had more control over his own destiny than previously imagined but also that he was a far worse king than he had seemed in the 1620s. In fact, he 'was unfit to be a king'.[18] He did not understand that he 'was bound by the limits of the possible' and therefore frequently 'attempted to do the impossible'.[19] He 'did not believe in the political process' and suffered from a 'lack of political perception' or 'inability to read the political map'.[20] He never accepted that 'the political process demanded bargaining and concession'.[21] He was plagued by 'nagging doubt about his status and capacity' and suffered from a 'sense of personal inadequacy'. Consequently authority 'seems to have been something of which he felt very much in need', and he was 'possibly mildly paranoid'. Like Cust, Russell believed that Charles had an 'obsessive anxiety about his subjects' loyalty'.[22] Finally, Russell came to the realisation that Charles was 'an untrustworthy king' who was trusted all the less because of 'his known willingness to use armed force'.[23] The 'desire to secure compliance by the threat of force' was typical of Charles, and he was usually the one 'who raised the stakes by introducing threats of force'.[24] It is no wonder that G. E. Aylmer thought Russell came close to reducing Charles to 'the demon king'.[25]

Russell added his own refinements to earlier portraits of Charles. For instance, he developed an interesting answer to the question of whether or not Charles was capable of accepting good counsel. The problem, according to Russell, was that Charles took half-counsel. He would allow himself to be persuaded to take a particular action (for example, calling the Short Parliament) without making the fundamental change in policy (abandoning war with the Scots) which would have allowed that action to succeed. This 'half persuasion was worse than none'.[26] Russell also added to our understanding of the king's religious views. As Russell described him, Charles felt 'a very profound incomprehension and distaste for the religious convictions of large numbers of his subjects'.[27] Russell fully subscribed to Tyacke's view that Charles was an Arminian, both in the narrow sense of rejecting Calvinist theology and in the broader sense of preferring more ceremony and 'decency' in the church service. Charles was also firmly committed to episcopacy and a 'Caesaro-papist version of the Royal Supremacy'. All of this made him feel 'a deep disgust at Scottish methods of worship' and ensured that he would utterly fail to understand the Covenanters when he came into conflict with them.[28] Indeed, Charles 'suffered from an allergy to the kind of religion the Covenanters represented'.[29]

If Charles was an active participant in the course of events and 'unfit to be a king', then it naturally followed that he bore a larger share of the blame for what went wrong. The political difficulties of the 1620s, Russell had claimed, were 'first and foremost, not the difficulties of a bad King, but the difficulties of a nation reluctantly at war'.[30] In the years immediately preceding the Civil War, Russell gave more attention to the bad king. This time he also recognised that Charles was the chief reason the nation was reluctantly at war. Charles might have been dissuaded from war if he had had an open mind on the subject, but he was not in the habit of calling a Parliament to consult it about what policy to pursue. Rather, Charles typically called a Parliament for the purpose of enlisting its support for the policy he had already independently decided upon. He summoned Parliaments *à sa mode*, to serve as rubber-stamps for his preconceived plans.[31] In the realm of religion, Russell had already criticised Charles for the rise of Arminianism in the 1620s. At first glance it might seem that he shifted blame to Laud when it came to the 1630s. A picture of the Archbishop, not Charles, appeared on the dustjacket of *Fall of the British Monarchies*. Or perhaps the king and Archbishop were equally to blame. 'There seems no sense in trying to apportion responsibility between them', wrote Russell. The two men 'shared a common outlook, and it seems fair to hold them both responsible for the resulting policy'.[32] But Laud gradually receded into the background of Russell's account, and Charles came to the foreground as the man who most ruined the careful work of King James. In Russell's words, 'the Jacobean compromise was killed by Charles I'.[33] The king and his Archbishop worked 'in close collaboration', but when it came to the decision to impose the prayer book on Scotland, this 'was so entirely Charles's decision ... that to deny his responsibility would amount to a wholesale rejection of the evidence'. Furthermore the policy that led from this fateful decision to the outbreak of war 'was almost exclusively the King's personal responsibility'.[34]

Despite all these criticisms of Charles, Russell still resisted the conclusion that he was the paramount cause of the Civil War. He 'must take a large share of the responsibility', wrote Russell, but 'not quite as big a share as S. R. Gardiner would have given him'.[35] Yet everywhere we look in Russell's later writings, we see Charles's inimitable work of destruction. Why did three kingdoms rebel against Charles? 'If we look for common factors', Russell observed, 'we can find them in the two problems all three kingdoms shared: that of being part of a multiple kingdom, and that of being ruled by Charles I.'[36] As Russell had said earlier in his seminal article on multiple kingdoms: 'We are dealing with a king who invited resistance in all of his three kingdoms, and got what he was asking for.'[37] Russell organised his *Causes of the English Civil War* around seven critical events and phenomena which, taken together, caused the outbreak of war. Of course Charles was not equally responsible for all seven, and yet 'nothing except perhaps Charles I can be likely to have been a cause of all seven of these'.[38] In his 'Conclusion' to *Causes*, Russell made one last effort to maintain that 'Charles's failings as a ruler' were an important part of the story but not 'the whole of the story'.[39] The whole of the story must take into account the conjunction of those three longstanding problems mentioned above for which Charles was not personally to blame (the problems of multiple kingdoms, religious discord, and royal finances). But what caused the explosive conjunction of these three underlying problems at this particular time? The answer, said Russell, was Charles's attempt to impose the prayer book on Scotland. It is, in fact, 'difficult to see what action a king could have taken which would have been better designed to precipitate an English civil war'.[40]

Anthony Fletcher, John Morrill, and Conrad Russell do not share S. R. Gardiner's view of escalating constitutional conflict culminating in the Civil War. They reject his Whig teleology. But they do share his view of Charles I. In the 1640s there is no equivalent to Kevin Sharpe's valiant defence of the king in the 1630s. As we turn, therefore, to the years surrounding the outbreak of the Civil War, putting Charles into historical perspective requires, as much as anything, resisting the temptation to reduce him to a mere caricature of incompetence or (in Aylmer's phrase) a one-dimensional 'demon king'.

The Short Parliament

Charles ruled three kingdoms, and one of the most salutary trends in recent historiography is the increased appreciation of the interaction among these three, what Russell aptly called the 'billiard-ball effect'.[41] The rebellion in Scotland was an education and an inspiration for disaffected people in England. It demonstrated that the king could be successfully resisted and his policies reversed. A constant flood of printed propaganda coming out of Scotland continued this process of politicising the English. Moreover, the Scots were personally in contact with leading members of the Short Parliament such as John Pym, in effect conspiring with them. Having said all this, however, we should not lose sight of the extent to which MPs in the Short Parliament were expressing their own native protest against the personal rule in England. For both Sharpe and Russell, the Scots play the role of outside agitators who foment rebellion in England. We have already seen the weight Sharpe gave to Scottish propaganda, whipping up a 'crescendo of national paranoia' in what was otherwise a tranquil England.[42] For Russell too, as John Morrill described it, the Scots are a '*diabolus ex machina*'.[43] No doubt the Scots played a critical role, but that fact should not overshadow the extent to which the English were spontaneously expressing their own accumulated outrage.

The Short Parliament is so called because it lasted only three weeks.[44] It was immediately apparent that the king and the House of Commons had different agendas. The king's agenda was simply to get the money he needed to fight another war against the Scots. The paramount agenda item on the minds of most members of the Commons was to obtain redress of their grievances. There were so many grievances complained of so forcefully in the Short Parliament that it dispels any false impression that Charles's English subjects were content with his rule. Viscount Saye in the Lords and Harbottle Grimston in the Commons both made the point, as Clement Coke had in a previous decade, that the problems requiring most immediate attention were the problems at home.[45] Some of those specific grievances themselves went back to the 1620s. Sir Francis Seymour raised the issue of the MPs who had been imprisoned after the last Parliament. It is not mere Whiggery to observe that it was brave of Seymour to raise this issue in recognition of his old comrades early in this session before it was apparent how far MPs could safely go in expressing their displeasure. Seymour said, 'I know not how soone it may bee our case, yett had I rather suffer herein for speakeing the truth, then that truth should suffer for want of my Speaking'.[46] Another issue that went back to the 1620s was Roger Manwaring, who had been impeached in 1628 but was now entitled to sit in the

House of Lords as a bishop.[47] Seymour may have had Manwaring in mind when he complained about people who preached 'that the King hath an unlimitted power and that the subjects have no property in their goods'. Equally bad, Seymour thought, were the judges who violated the Petition of Right by telling the king that 'his prerogative is above all Lawes and that his Subjects are but slaves'.[48] This comment referred to the ship money case (what Sir John Glanville called the 'damned and impious opinion of the Judges'), and of course it was only one of a plethora of grievances that had accumulated during the personal rule.[49] It took Pym nearly two hours to list all the grievances on his mind, and other speakers added to the list. Of course the sheer fact that Parliament had not been summoned for 11 years was a grievance in itself. Many other grievances related to religion: the presence of papal agents at court, the celebration of the mass at Somerset House, all the Catholic practices and gestures that had crept into the English worship service, the *Book of Sports*, the Court of High Commission, the inordinate power of bishops, and the vilification of ardent Protestants as puritan zealots. Francis Rous thought all these religious grievances sprang from an underlying intention to reunite England with Rome.[50] Ship money was the greatest of the civil grievances, but there were many more: distraint of knighthood, enforcement of the forest laws, monopolies, impositions, projectors, and the Court of Star Chamber. The backlash against the personal rule was intense and broadly based. On several occasions MPs voiced the concern that they did not dare face their constituents again until they had removed some of these grievances, and they presented petitions from the counties to substantiate this claim. Even Kevin Sharpe was reduced to admitting that these complaints 'leave us in no doubt that, for all the surface calm, resentments had built up'.[51]

Charles had done so many things that alienated so many people, and he had insulated himself so completely from criticism, that a gulf of incomprehension had opened up between him and the political nation. Charles, who could only see the urgency of his predicament, said that it was 'preposterous' and putting 'the carte before the horse' to insist on prior redress of grievances. He swore that he would happily attend to their grievances later, but MPs simply did not believe him. What it boiled down to was a matter of trust. 'If they will not trust me first', Charles lamented quite correctly, 'all my business is lost.'[52] The issue of trust surfaced again and again in both Houses throughout the Short Parliament, but Charles never had inspired much trust, and the events of the personal rule had hardly made him seem receptive to criticism.[53] Charles offered 'his royall word', but the Commons of 1640 was no more impressed by this offer than the Commons of 1628 had been.[54] As for the urgency of supply, Grimston retorted, it was 'none of our faults, for the Kinge if he had beene pleased might have called us sooner and therefore we were not guiltye of the Kings streight'.[55]

The king's tactics did not help his cause. In another act reminiscent of the 1620s, he tried at first to prevent Lords Saye, Brooke, and Mandeville from taking their seats in the House of Lords, although he relented.[56] Saye became an exceptionally effective speaker in the Lords where he repeatedly argued against Thomas Wentworth, whom Charles had brought back from Ireland and created Earl of Strafford to shore up his government. What Charles needed most to do was make a stirring speech to the Commons, but here too he stubbornly repeated the pattern of the 1620s. At the opening of Parliament, he spoke even more briefly than usual, then turned the real speech-making over to the Lord Keeper, Sir John Finch. During the formalities surrounding the presentation of the Speaker, Charles again said almost nothing. And a week later when he summoned both Houses to the Banqueting Hall to press the issue of supply, he again let Finch do all the talking. Finch made long speeches that failed to impress his listeners, who were not likely to be sympathetic in the first place.[57] As Mark Fissel remarked, 'Charles might well have chosen the devil himself'.[58] Finch was the former Speaker who had been held in his chair to prevent adjournment in 1629, an episode that MPs in 1640 continued to complain about. Furthermore, during the 1630s, as chief justice of Common Pleas, Finch had been associated with unpopular policies like the exploitation of the forest laws and controversial cases like the one over ship money. Less well known is the fact that Finch had been the queen's Attorney-General, and during the actual meeting of the Short Parliament upon his creation as Baron of Fordwich he made what a contemporary described as 'a very fine Elegant speach touching all his preferment by the Queene'.[59] When Finch spoke to the Commons, he was inclined to warn them not to be led astray by malignant, malicious, ambitious, or peevish spirits, which only revealed how sinister a view he and the king took of criticism.[60] Charles could hardly have done worse by speaking for himself. In politics as religion, however, Charles preferred a decorous silence. His appearances before Parliament were ceremonial occasions. He presided over the ritual like a priest, but he did not stoop to the level of a popular preacher. That would have detracted from his majesty. As he often said, it was not his fashion to use many words. In this respect, speakers like Pym in the Commons had a rhetorical advantage over Charles. The style as well as the content of their speeches was better suited to appeal to the very people Charles needed most to convince, the ardently Protestant or puritan members.

Charles's best performance in the Short Parliament occurred when he went down to the House of Lords and made a personal plea for their help.[61] Commentators noted that he came to the Lords unexpectedly; neither he nor the Lords were wearing their formal robes. Here he made the kind of impression he needed to make on the Commons. It was said that Charles spoke to them not as a king but as a gentleman.[62] After this appearance, the Lords voted to put supply ahead of grievances and urge the Commons to do the same (although a significant minority of Lords voted in the negative). Charles knew that his greater strength and natural allies were in the Upper House, and appealing to the Lords must also have squared with his sense of hierarchy and authority. The Commons, however, put the worst possible interpretation on the advice they received from the Lords and voted it a breach of privilege.

As the saying goes, actions speak louder than words. It was not enough for Charles to make empty promises; he had to make concrete concessions. Given the circumstances, he made astoundingly few. Prior to the meeting of Parliament, he released the remaining two MPs imprisoned from 1629 (Benjamin Valentine and William Strode).[63] At the outset of Parliament, he instructed Manwaring not to take his seat in the House of Lords.[64] As Russell observed, Charles does not appear to have absorbed the fact 'that, after an eleven-year interval, he could not expect Parliamentary supply for *any* reason without doing something in return for it'.[65] Eventually Charles did offer a *quid pro quo*: if MPs would give him 12 subsidies, he would give up ship money for ever. Charles for once appeared to be adopting a real bargaining position, but after a day-long debate the Commons could not agree on how to react, and the next day Charles dissolved Parliament.

The abrupt dissolution of the Short Parliament was not all Charles's fault. There were people in the Commons who did not want a compromise, specifically Pym and his cohorts who wanted to prevent another war with the Scots, not facilitate it. There is reason to think that if Charles had allowed Parliament to sit one more day,

Pym and his allies would have disrupted the whole bargaining process by raising the issue of peace with the Scots. The last thing Charles wanted in 1640 was a parliamentary debate over foreign policy like the one he had happily asked for in 1624. He could not afford to have MPs openly discussing the merits of the Scots' cause. Pym had already hinted several times that he would speak against war. He had argued that kings can declare wars, but Parliaments are not obliged to support those wars unless they are asked for their counsel and give their assent. In this instance, as Pym complained, Charles 'hath not pleased soe farre to impart his affayres to the Howse or to demand any Councell from them'.[66] Some MPs also thought this was an opportune time to eliminate irksome military charges like coat-and-conduct money that paid the costs of raising an army on the local level.[67] Charles could not afford to throw these charges into the bargain, however, if he wanted to fight another war. Nevertheless, Charles might still have outflanked these hardline opponents of his war policy and reached a compromise with more moderate members if it were not for the recurring issue of trust. Arguments at the end of the Short Parliament show that many MPs rejected the deal offered by Charles simply because they did not trust him to abide by it.[68] For these men, it was not enough for Charles to say he would give up ship money. Unless it was declared illegal, they feared he would resume collecting it at a later date.

In his closing speech to the Short Parliament, Charles thanked the Lords for their efforts and blamed the dissolution on 'some fewe cunning and ill affectioned men' in the Commons.[69] This familiar refrain has earned Charles a reputation for paranoia, but by 1640 the king's fears were not entirely unfounded. Pym in particular had worked to prevent an accommodation between Charles and the Commons. By now the atmosphere was so poisoned against Charles that he could not seem to do anything right. When he dissolved Parliament, he kept the Convocation of the Church of England in session to write new canons for the church. He thought that these new canons would prove that he was a stout defender of the church, no promoter of Roman Catholicism, and no innovator. Instead, the canons raised one more furore, as people found all sorts of causes for alarm in them. The strongest reaction was against an oath to uphold the doctrine and hierarchy of the established church (what came to be known as the *etcetera* oath). Charles himself had insisted on this oath, as he had earlier prescribed a military oath that Lords Saye and Brooke refused to take at Berwick. Charles thought that oaths demonstrated loyalty, but many of his subjects were profoundly suspicious that he harboured an ulterior motive. Thus the canons, which were intended to allay fears, provided one more reason for distrust.[70] On the other hand, Charles should have known better. The Short Parliament had voiced serious concern about the plan for Convocation to write new canons.[71] By proceeding against their wishes to impose new canons on England as he had in Scotland, he was characteristically flaunting his authority and inviting criticism.

The very same day he dissolved Parliament, Charles held a meeting of the special committee on Scottish affairs. Russell made two very perceptive observations about that meeting. Firstly, it occurred so soon after the dissolution that emotions were running too high for reflective judgement. Secondly, Charles does not appear to have asked for advice about whether or not he should fight another war with the Scots but simply how.[72] Charles obviously preferred people who agreed with him, and that usually meant people who took a strong stand on behalf of the royal prerogative. There was some timid effort at this meeting to suggest that a defensive war was the most Charles should think of conducting, but the Earl of Strafford swept aside all such arguments. It was terribly unfortunate for Charles that Strafford dominated this meeting, but Charles had arranged it that way. He had brought Strafford back to England, thinking that the man who had tamed the north of England and all of Ireland could tame Scotland. Charles was looking for another Buckingham, and unfortunately that is what he got. Of course Strafford had far more solid ability than Buckingham, but at this point on this subject Strafford was as wildly optimistic as Buckingham had ever been. Rather than discourage the king, Strafford confidently asserted that the Scots could be subdued in one summer. If necessary, the army in Ireland could be employed. The king should do whatever was in his power to do; he was 'absolved from all rules of government'.[73] Strong talk like this appealed to Charles, but it only got him into worse trouble. Charles lost the Second Bishops' War practically before he began to fight it. When the Scots poured over the border, the English did not have enough men with enough weapons in place to stop them. Lack of money had been a crippling handicap, but there was also a lack of will to fight the Scots. The resentful troops forced into service against the Scots rioted along the way, destroying altar rails in many churches; while at the top of the social hierarchy members of the English nobility were actually colluding with the Scots to force Charles to surrender and call a Parliament.[74] Charles accepted the fact that he would have to face another Parliament, but the more urgent question was how to deal with the conquering Scots. With his army in a shambles and no one else to turn to, Charles summoned a Great Council of Peers who extricated him from his immediate difficulties by patching up a truce with the Scots (the Treaty of Ripon). The only thing truly agreed upon at this point, however, was that £25,000 per month would be paid to the Scottish army while they continued to occupy the north of England. All the other substantive issues were left to be negotiated in London in conjunction with the Parliament. Charles was effectively consigned to the sidelines, and it remained to be seen whether he could ever regain the initiative.

The Long Parliament to 1642

Judging from what Charles said at the opening of the Long Parliament, he was no more realistic than usual. He apparently expected Parliament to finance renewed war against the Scots, an expectation which Russell characterised as 'a flight from reality', 'a grievous misjudgement of the public mood', and part of the 'royal inability to perceive the true situation'.[75] Perhaps the problem was rather that Charles perceived the 'true' situation differently. The truth was that Charles was the lawful king and his Scottish subjects were rebelling against him. Of course it is equally true that the king's English subjects had already amply demonstrated that they had no intention of helping him, but that refusal made no sense to Charles. Given his world view, it was incomprehensible, and he doggedly persisted in trying to impose his ideal preconceptions on reality rather than accept the discordant realities of a new world where, no matter how much the king acted like a king, his subjects could no longer be relied upon to act like subjects. Furthermore, even if Charles did understand the hopelessness of his situation, he would not have declared that fact to the world. Charles never conceded anything until he was forced to. He followed the maxim that one should 'never make a defence or apology before you be accused'.[76] So Charles began the Long Parliament with no apologies or concessions. It was not his way to start with a declaration of surrender. He left it to others to show him how futile his position was.

Charles quickly found out how marginal he had become. When he unexpectedly appeared at the first day of negotiations with the Scots in London, he was rebuffed and did not return. In the affairs of Parliament he was almost equally irrelevant. In the opening months of the Long Parliament, there were loud complaints about all the grievances that had accumulated during the personal rule but little immediate concrete action. One obvious reason for this delay was the overriding need to conclude a treaty with the Scots and raise the necessary money to pay off both the Scottish and English armies. Another reason may have been some hesitation about how to proceed in making what amounted to substantive changes in the institutions of government. It was much easier and less radical to deal for a while in mere personalities. Thus long before the Court of Star Chamber was abolished, the victims of the court were ordered to be liberated. Bastwick, Burton, Prynne, Leighton, and Lilburne were not only freed; their cases were re-examined by the House of Commons, and they were voted reparations. At the same time, proceedings were initiated against the alleged perpetrators of injustice, including the judges themselves. Judge Berkeley was presiding over the Court of King's Bench when he was arrested. It was a dramatic demonstration of how far the tables were turned. When Secretary Windebank was summoned to explain his role in protecting priests and Jesuits, he fled to France. Lord Keeper Finch likewise fled to the continent to escape impeachment.[77] The two most prominent evil counsellors, Strafford and Laud, were arrested and charged with treason. Laud was allowed to languish in prison (he was tried in 1644 and executed in early 1645), but the destruction of Strafford was a matter of much greater urgency.

It took Charles a while to get his bearings in these very different political circumstances. He was adrift, and he could expect no clear lead from his Privy Council which was shattered and demoralised. Through the autumn of 1640, therefore, he played a largely passive role, allowing Parliament to vent its pent-up anger and avoiding any new provocations. When Charles re-entered the picture, he did so cautiously at first. During the first two months of 1641 he took a number of steps which indicated that he was prepared to make concessions and work toward a settlement. He drew a distinction 'between reformation and alteration of government', and declared that he supported reformation. He accepted the Commons' unanimous condemnation of ship money as illegal. He even announced his conversion to the view that 'frequent parliaments is the best means to preserve that right understanding betwixt me and my subjects which I so heartily desire'.[78] Charles accepted the Triennial Bill that provided for the meeting of a Parliament at least every three years. On another front he tried to win over opponents by appointing seven lords (including Bedford, Essex, and Saye) to the Privy Council. However, he did not make much use of the Council after these men joined it, and he did not bestow any offices of consequence on his critics in the Commons.[79] Given the king's sense of hierarchy, it was easier for him to reach out to wayward peers than to accept hostile commoners.

While Charles made these conciliatory gestures, a number of factors mitigated against his achieving a true accommodation. Religion was a huge impediment. Charles was prepared to limit the secular power of bishops, but he would not countenance their removal from the House of Lords, let alone their total 'root-and-branch' elimination. Of course the more incendiary religious issue was Roman Catholicism. The Commons were already agitated with fears of a popish plot, and it did not help matters that Charles, at the urging of the queen, intervened at this point to prevent the execution of another priest. This humane gesture was naturally given the worst possible interpretation in the House of Commons. It also drew attention to the influence of the queen, who came increasingly under open attack. Charles had good reason to fear for his wife's safety. Another factor working against accommodation was the role of the Scots who had a vested interest in preventing a reconciliation between the king and Parliament. In fact the Scots published a paper near the end of February 1641 intended to keep the two most inflammatory issues alive – the abolition of episcopacy and the destruction of Strafford. For the time being, this blatant interference in English affairs sabotaged the king's efforts at reconciliation, but it also generated a backlash against the Scots which in the long run he could hope to capitalise upon.

Charles had not done his cause any harm and may have been making some headway garnering a party of his own in the House of Commons until it came to the trial of Strafford. It was a matter of honour for Charles to stand by Strafford as he had stood by Buckingham and the customs officials in the 1620s. Charles promised Strafford 'that upon the word of a king you shall not suffer in life, honour, or fortune', and surely this is one promise that Charles had every intention of keeping; but in the end it proved to be, like so many other things now, beyond the king's power.[80] When

Strafford ably defended himself against the false charge of treason, his enemies in the Commons abandoned impeachment proceedings and turned to a bill of attainder. They were ready to employ any means, so long as it resulted in death for the one man they and the Scots most feared. In the face of this implacable hatred, Charles did what he could to save his ablest counsellor. He met with Pym, probably offering him the Chancellorship of the Exchequer in return for Strafford's life, without success. He assembled both Houses of Parliament to assure them that there was no basis for the most sensational charge against Strafford (that he had advised Charles to use the Irish army to suppress his English subjects), and he vowed that he would never again employ Strafford in any capacity, not even in the lowly office of a constable. He begged his listeners 'to find some such way as to bring me out of this great strait'.[81] The king's listeners had no interest, however, in helping him to escape the greatest moral dilemma of his life. Parliament passed the bill of attainder (with many men absenting themselves in both Houses), and Charles was asked to approve it amid an atmosphere of hysteria. Mobs of people gathered outside Whitehall crying for blood, and their anger was directed as much against the royal family, especially the Catholic queen, as against Strafford. Charles buckled under this pressure and gave his reluctant assent. Recounting these events, S. R. Gardiner, certainly no admirer of Charles, made a concession to the king's basic humanity: 'Let him who has seen wife and child, and all that he holds dear, exposed to imminent peril, and has refused to save them by an act of baseness, cast the first stone at Charles.'[82] Having assented to Strafford's execution, Charles made one last pathetic plea for mercy. He sent the prince, a small boy just a few days short of his eleventh birthday, to the House of Lords with a letter asking them to consider commuting Strafford's sentence to life imprisonment. 'This', wrote Charles, 'if it may be done without a discontentment to my people, would be an unspeakable contentment to me.' Yet Charles himself had little hope of this final appeal falling on sympathetic ears; he was resigned to Strafford's execution 'if no less than his life can satisfy my people'.[83] The next day Strafford was executed, an event that haunted Charles for the rest of his life.[84]

   The preceding account of Strafford's trial and execution omits one major event: the First Army Plot. Charles had participated in plans to use military force to free Strafford from the Tower and clear the way for his escape by ship. At first glance, this plan to circumvent and perhaps overawe Parliament by military force looks like an outrageous and contemptible ploy. Certainly, as it played itself out, it backfired and made Strafford's execution seem even more imperative. Historians tend to take a censorious and fastidious view of resorts to force, but the First Army Plot was not especially shocking or heinous. If carried out, it would have entailed force but not necessarily violence. The Scottish army was already being used by the Scots and their English friends to intimidate Parliament. Would it have been much more reprehensible for Charles to play the same game with the English army? Russell, who has written most extensively about the First Army Plot, criticised Charles but stopped far short of a total condemnation. As Russell explained, Pym and Charles were both engaging in 'the use of threat to force compliance'.[85] Charles may even have wanted the plot to become known in advance in the hope that its mere prospect would be sufficient to cow his adversaries into cooperation. Most important, although Charles toyed with the possibility of resorting to violence, he did not actually employ it. In part this was simply due to a lack of necessary support in the army and the quick preventive action of the House of Lords, but it also owed something to the fact that Charles, whatever his other faults, was neither ruthless nor brutal. Prior to the Civil War, Charles arrested people, seized their papers, sealed up their studies, and bent the law to silence his critics and collect taxes. He often characterised the behaviour of those critics as sedition. In the exceptional case of Sir John Eliot, he allowed one man to die in prison. But he was not a killer. Although historians are loath to notice it, the real violence in May of 1641 occurred within the hallowed walls of Parliament where an innocent man was condemned to die. In the contest of wills that began with the opening of the Long Parliament, the first blood shed was not on Charles's hands. Indeed, as Russell has well observed, when the panic over the Army Plot subsided, 'the feeling that there was something discreditable about the condemnation of Strafford remained'.[86]

After these significant changes were made in the personnel of government, Parliament proceeded to change many of its institutions and practices. The courts of Star Chamber and High Commission (and several lesser prerogative courts) were abolished. Ship money, distraint of knighthood, and the extortionate use of the forest laws were outlawed. Meanwhile the meeting of future Parliaments had been guaranteed by the Triennial Act. By the summer of 1641 Charles had made a great many sacrifices. How much was enough? Of course there were still unresolved issues, especially the Crown's finances and the highly volatile issue of church reform. However, it was becoming increasingly apparent that even if compromise could be reached on these remaining issues, it would not be enough to satisfy the king's leading opponents. Their problem was simply that they had gone so far in alienating Charles that they could never again feel safe as long as he had the power to retaliate. For that reason they passed a bill forbidding the dissolution of the Long Parliament without their own consent, which was presented to Charles along with the bill of attainder for Strafford under circumstances that made it difficult for Charles to refuse his assent. This act gave the king's most vocal critics an extended lease on life, but they were still left with the basic problem: what could they possibly do while they still enjoyed their power base in Parliament that would ensure them adequate protection later when presumably the members of Parliament would someday agree to a dissolution? The Ten Propositions in June of 1641 provided an early answer to this question.[87] The arrangement envisioned by the Ten Propositions was a shared government in which more evil counsellors would be removed, future appointments would be approved by Parliament, and the Crown's military resources would be put in the hands of people agreeable to Parliament. The Ten Propositions also expressed a virulent anti-Catholicism directed against the court and the royal family. Catholics would be replaced by stout Protestants around the queen; the papal agent, Count Rossetti (who had taken Con's place) would be expelled from England. Protestants would be put in charge of the care and education of the royal children. The Ten Propositions were an early, less detailed and less strident, version of the later Nineteen Propositions that would constitute Parliament's ultimatum to Charles. At heart their aim was to take control away from Charles, to make him less of a king, because a few men knew they would never again be safe if Charles retained the full powers of the monarchy.[88]

As in the Short Parliament, so in the Long Parliament: what it boiled down to was a matter of trust. Had Charles been a different sort of man, his opponents might have settled for the gains they had made through the summer of 1641. Both the Scots and the king's adversaries in the English Parliament knew, however, that those gains could vanish in an instant. What they therefore had to do was 'make Charles's concessions irreversible'.[89] This is an insistent theme in Russell's account of the descent into civil war. As he explained, the Scots knew from their bitter experience with Charles that they could never 'trust their security to his goodwill'.[90] In England the spectre of Sir John Eliot must have hung over the heads of men like Pym. They 'knew enough about the fate of their predecessors in co-ercing the King to know that a settlement with the King was no guar-antee against subsequent royal revenge'.[91] Consequently, 'Pym and his allies had firmly committed themselves to the view that it was unsafe to trust the King with any significant amount of power'.[92] They had 'to bind an untrustworthy king in chains' and reduce Charles to a mere 'figurehead'.[93]

An effort to circumscribe the powers of the Crown and reduce the king to a figurehead surely amounted to constitutional conflict, as earlier so-called Whig historians understood, even if it did spring from a basic desire for personal survival. Moreover, personal survival could not have been the sole motive. Recent accounts like Russell's come close to reducing the story to a two-man battle of wills between Charles and Pym. In this version, people groped their way toward a new arrangement of the constitution, not because they were rethink-ing the nature of government, but merely because they were think-ing about preserving their own skins. New ideas were forced upon them 'to serve the immediate purpose of clipping the wings of a king with whom they simply could not cope'.[94] Granted that personal sur-vival was a powerful motivator, one must wonder if this version of events trivialises or oversimplifies the nature of the conflict. Could new ideas have been taking root in the minds of these men before they confronted one another in the Long Parliament? Could a more general underlying shift in mentality have paved the way for the events that were now occurring, a shift in the way people thought about power and authority, a shift that made Pym and his allies more inclined to challenge the king and made other members of the Commons more receptive to their arguments? By concentrating ex-clusively on surface events, it is possible to underestimate the extent to which those events were conditioned, even in some ways made possible, by larger cultural transformations that are invisible beneath the surface.[95]

Perhaps the wider cultural transformation that fuelled events was merely religious. That is the way John Morrill saw it. He criticised Russell for focusing too narrowly on Pym's faction and giving too little attention to the wider 'political sociology' of the situation. Political sociology for Morrill, however, turned out to be the sociol-ogy of religion. Morrill believed that 'Charles had alienated the great majority of his subjects'. And religion was the chief stumbling block.

The constitutional grievances that had caused this alienation were satisfied with relative ease, but the religious grievances proved far more irresolvable and divisive. There was a great public outcry against the religious policies of the personal rule, and religion was the issue that moved most members of the Commons.[96] Naturally the more conservative House of Lords, where the bishops sat, showed less enthusiasm for legislation regarding the church, but this did not stop the Commons from expressing their pent-up anger. In addition to arresting Laud and liberating the victims of Laudianism, they removed offensive ministers from their livings and unilaterally ordered an end to Laudian practices in the church. Meanwhile the more radical members kept pushing for the total abolition of episcopacy. Charles tried to appease this sentiment, repeatedly declaring that he favoured the church as it was established in the reign of Elizabeth. In sharp contrast to his concern over the fate of Strafford, he utterly deserted Laud and rehabilitated Laud's foe, Bishop Williams, appointing him Archbishop of York. Yet these reassurances fell short. Here too the crux of the matter was lack of trust in the king's intentions. While a few MPs worried about their own personal futures, many more worried about the future of the church. Thus religion broadened the base of discontent and gave Pym's faction a potent issue to capitalise upon.

Whatever combination of personal, political, and religious motives drove some men toward more radical constitutional experimentation, their success was far from assured in the summer of 1641. To achieve their ends, these men needed a majority in both Houses of Parliament and the powerful assistance of the Scots. Both these sources of support were now slipping through their hands. The execution of Strafford and the dismantling of the machinery of the personal rule took many members as far as they wanted to go. If the more radical members of Parliament insisted on further change, they would be crossing that line that Charles had delineated between reform and alteration of government. Except perhaps in the realm of religion, it was doubtful whether a majority of both houses would be willing to cross that line. Of more immediate concern was the changing status of the Scots. Parliament at last scraped together enough money to pay and disband the Scottish army, but in doing so they were dissolving their major source of leverage over Charles. Nor was the king standing still. He was working hard to neutralise the Scots, and toward that end he hit upon the truly inspired stratagem of going to Scotland in person (Russell called it 'brilliant').[97] Charles arrived in Scotland in August and spent three months there, with mixed results. He tried to drive a hard bargain, but in the end he was forced to relinquish nearly all his authority in Scotland. For this huge sacrifice he received no gratitude in return because he had also conspired with anti-Covenanter Scots in an abortive plot known as the 'Incident'. It was a typical example of the king's habit of making concessions when it was too late to gain any goodwill by them, worsened in this instance by his apparent treachery. On the other hand, Charles had little real prospect of regaining control over Scotland anyhow. Having tried both by negotiation and by force without success, he surrendered. In the end he had no choice but to sacrifice Scotland in order to maintain his control over England – which would not have been a bad bargain if it had not been for Ireland.

Charles had hoped that he would return to England in a much stronger position. The rebellion that broke out in Ireland at the end of October 1641 dashed those hopes. It can hardly be disputed that Charles was to blame for provoking the earlier rebellion in Scotland. Was he now equally to blame for rebellion in Ireland? In a word, no. Charles (and Strafford) had managed to alienate a great many of the Irish, but that is not what caused the Irish to rebel. M. Perceval-Maxwell concluded that Charles 'must bear ultimate responsibility for the conflict', but that conclusion comes as a surprise at the end of a book which actually exonerates Charles in many respects.[98] What Perceval-Maxwell and other recent authors have amply demonstrated is the intimate relationship between the outbreak of rebellion in Ireland and what was happening in England and Scotland in the immediately preceding months. At first the English Parliament and the Scots had been happy for the cooperation of the Irish in supplying information against Strafford, but there were strong reasons why this cooperation quickly turned to animosity. Above all there was the rabid anti-Catholicism of the English and the Scots. Understandably, the Irish (more precisely, the native Irish and 'Old English' in Ireland) looked on with alarm as Pym and his cohorts fanned the flames of religious hatred against Roman Catholics in England, flames that could easily be expected to spread to Ireland. Another factor prejudicing the English and Scots against the Irish was the persistent rumour that Charles was plotting to use the Irish army against them. In the case of the Scots this had been true, but in the case of the English it is more doubtful, though historians continue to argue over the factual basis for these rumours.[99] Ironically,

at the same time as sentiment was building against their religion and
fears were mounting over their army, the Irish were encouraged by
the successful example of the Scots to believe that they might
improve their own situation, especially regarding their property
rights; but they found the English Parliament more disposed to view
them as a conquered colony than kindred spirits. Their expectations
having been raised, the Irish discovered to their disappointment that
the new powers in England were likely to be even more oppressive
than the old powers. As Russell has observed, where Ireland was concerned, Pym was an ideologue whose policy made Charles look 'intelligent' by comparison.[100] Charles is usually portrayed as having got
himself into trouble for wanting religious uniformity in all three of
his kingdoms, but he was actually much more comfortable with Irish
Catholicism than the Scots and English were. Nevertheless, when the
rebellion broke out, Charles happily volunteered to lead an army
against it. Of course the men who had spent the past year assailing
his rule could hardly afford now to place him at the head of an army.

   If the king's adversaries were to keep the army out of his hands,
they had to stem his growing popularity and tighten their control
over Parliament. The Irish rebellion helped them by appearing to
confirm the monstrous threat of a popish plot. In the days before
Charles returned from Scotland, Pym's faction capitalised on this opportunity by producing the Grand Remonstrance which portrayed
Charles's entire reign as one long conspiracy to advance the forces
of Roman Catholicism in England. The Grand Remonstrance was a
gigantic piece of propaganda listing 'those evils under which we
have now many years suffered'. All these individual evils were depicted as parts of a larger, overarching popish plot. The fomenters of
this plot were identified as Jesuits, bishops, and evil counsellors. The
authors of the Remonstrance professed that they had not 'the least
intention to lay any blemish upon your royal person'; their intention
was rather to show how the king had been 'abused'.[101] However, the
remedies proposed in the Remonstrance assumed that Charles could
not be rehabilitated until he allowed Parliament and men chosen by
Parliament to take over the management of his affairs. The Grand
Remonstrance was a test of strength for Pym's faction. Debate lasted
all through the day and into the night. When the vote finally came
after midnight, the measure passed by a vote of 159 to 148 in a badly
depleted House. Charles later said it resembled 'the Verdict of the
Starved Jury'.[102] The narrow margin of 11 votes showed that even at
this late date (November 1641) the king's adversaries enjoyed only a

very slim majority. Nor was the House of Lords a party to the Remonstrance. It was a unilateral act of the Commons, and indeed one of its purposes was to protest against the obstructive force of the Lords. Furthermore, an embryonic royalist faction was beginning to develop in the Commons to counterbalance Pym's faction, and Charles cultivated these potential allies (particularly Edward Hyde, Sir John Culpepper, and Lord Falkland). Charles appointed Culpepper Chancellor of the Exchequer and Falkland Secretary of State. There were rumours that Charles had also made another effort to win over Pym by offering him the Exchequer, but Charles did not generally subscribe to the theory that enemies should be won over by rewarding them with office (Strafford being a notable exception). To Charles it made much more sense to shun or isolate his opponents and reward the people who supported him.

The situation was not hopeless for Charles until he himself made it so. Charles snapped at the beginning of 1642. He had plenty of provocations. The Commons' leaders had decided to escalate their propaganda war by printing the Grand Remonstrance. There were rumours that they might make a more direct attack on the queen, and they were certainly determined to assume command of the army. The City of London was increasingly falling under their control, and mob violence was frightening everyone. Twelve of the bishops protested that it was too dangerous for them to attend the House of Lords, and therefore bills approved during their enforced absence should not be considered valid. The House of Commons responded by arresting the protesting bishops and levelling impeachment charges against them, thereby depriving Charles of 12 crucial votes in the Upper House.[103] Meanwhile Henrietta Maria kept pressuring her husband to take a stronger stand. At the end of December, there was a momentary lull in the public demonstrations. The impeachment of the 12 bishops had appeased some of the mob, and the conservative forces around the court and City were gaining strength.[104] In this frenetic atmosphere, at a juncture where he might have thought he was gaining the upper hand, Charles decided upon a bold course that is known as the attempted arrest of the five members. It was a terrible miscalculation.

What Charles actually did was not as outrageous as it is usually made to seem, but it was bad enough. On 3 January he sent his Attorney-General to the House of Lords asking them to arrest one of their own members (Lord Mandeville) and five other members in the House of Commons on charges of treason. (The five members of the Commons were Pym and Hampden, whose inclusion hardly requires explanation, Holles and Strode, who had previously been arrested after the Parliament of 1629, and a newcomer named Sir Arthur Haselrig who had produced the bill of attainder against Strafford.) The king was thus attempting to remove his enemies by the same legal course, impeachment, that the Commons had used a few days earlier against the 12 bishops and, according to rumour, were planning to use against the queen. It is easy to assume that this is a typical case of Charles attributing all his problems to a handful of malcontents, but it is interesting to consider what might have followed if Charles had succeeded in making an example of this handful. The courage of the Commons might have quickly deflated in the face of a forceful reminder that King Charles, not King Pym, was the ruler of England. We shall never know, however, because the Lords refused to cooperate; they were accustomed to accepting impeachment charges from the Commons but questioned the legality of accepting any from the king. The inclusion of one of their own members on the list hardly encouraged them to cooperate. The day after the Lords balked, Charles took matters into his own hands by going with a large armed guard to the Commons to arrest the five members there in person, though they had fled before he arrived. If Charles had succeeded in this attempted arrest, his next step would have been to proceed to a trial of the defendants in the Lords, so his intervention was not as highhanded as it might appear. Indeed, both S. R. Gardiner and Conrad Russell agreed that he had solid legal grounds for charging these six men with treason. As Russell expressed it, Charles 'could have made a better case against them than they had made against Strafford'.[105] While this may look like a typical instance of Charles's readiness to resort to force, he actually refrained from using force. He was contemplating a trial, not a summary execution of his enemies, and he did not allow his troops to disperse the defiant Commons, which they appeared eager to do.[106] Perhaps the real problem was that Charles once again lost credit by acting as if he would resort to force, then shrank from actually employing it because he was not sufficiently ruthless or brutal. Even Gardiner observed that if Charles was determined to arrest the five members, it would have been more prudent 'to seize them in their beds'.[107]

It is probably true that the best strategy for Charles was to pose as the conservative champion of tradition against the excesses and innovations of Parliament, and surely it did cost him dearly when he exchanged this role for the role of the aggressor. The abortive attempt to arrest the five members played into the hands of the king's adversaries so completely that it is tempting to believe they provoked it on purpose. Anthony Fletcher speculated that 'Pym teased Charles into the action which lost him more face than any other in his entire life'.[108] In the blunter words of Charles Carlton, 'Pym baited the trap' and 'Charles took the bait'.[109] Russell observed that Pym's attempt to raise an armed guard under the command of the Earl of Essex at the end of December constituted a first appeal to armed force that 'invited a pre-emptive strike'.[110] A pre-emptive strike has got to succeed. If it fails, as this one did, it can only discredit the perpetrator and put the other side on notice.

In the days following the attempted arrest of the five members the king's stock plummeted. He had alienated the Lords, driven the Commons to an even higher level of paranoia, and – perhaps most important – lost control of his capital. The five members had taken refuge in the City, and when Charles ventured there to urge their surrender, he encountered angry defiance. Brian Manning best described the significance of the event: 'It was a decisive moment in history and the decision lay, not with the king, not with the parliament, not with the nobility and gentry, not with armed soldiers, not with the lord mayor, aldermen, or Common Council, but with the mass of the ordinary people of London.'[111] Less than a week after the attempted arrest of the five members, Charles and the rest of the royal family fled Whitehall in fear for their lives. Although Charles is sometimes criticised for abandoning London, no one can say for certain how things would have turned out if he had remained there.[112] According to Clarendon, those people 'who wished the King best were not sorry that he then withdrew from Whitehall; for the insolence with which all that people were transported, and the animosity which was infused into the hearts of the people in general against the Court, and even against the person of the King, cannot be expressed'.[113]

Several months elapsed between the king's retreat from London and the actual outbreak of the Civil War. During that time there were negotiations between the two sides, but it is doubtful whether reconciliation was still possible. At first Charles seemed conciliatory, even agreeing to the exclusion of bishops from the House of Lords, but he was probably buying time, especially until Henrietta Maria safely escaped to the continent with the Crown jewels to look for assistance. For a proud man who had little patience with the political

process and a high conception of his own kingship, Charles had submitted to a great many indignities over the past year and a half, and
he was finally fed up. When a parliamentary delegation in March
asked him, among other things, to relinquish his authority over the
militia at least temporarily, Charles retorted: 'By God, not for an
hour! You have asked that of me in this was never asked of a king.'[114]
The king's opponents could hardly ask for less, however. After the
attempted arrest of the five members, they realised even more starkly
than before that as long as Charles was king, they would never be
safe, no matter what promises they might extract from him on
paper. Many also doubted the king's promises regarding religion.
The ultimatum presented to Charles in June known as the Nineteen
Propositions was based on the premise that the government had to
be taken out of his hands because he had become a deluded participant in the popish plot. In Morrill's words, Charles was assumed to
be 'a deranged king, one who needed to be rescued from the conta-
gion of popery, to be shielded and deprogrammed, to be decontami-
nated'.[115] The Nineteen Propositions would have reduced Charles to
a mere figurehead or bystander. He was asked to cede control of all
the great offices of state, the church, the judiciary, the military, even
the education of his own children. If he accepted the Propositions,
Charles complained, 'we shall have nothing left for us but to look
on'. If government were placed in the hands of men selected by and
accountable to Parliament, then 'our councillors (or rather, our
guardians) will return us to the worst kind of minority, and make us
despicable both at home and abroad'. Charles could not accept this
loss of honour and authority. Nor could he accept the levelling im-
plication of the Propositions which would have made him 'an equal'
to the members of Parliament.[116] In short, if Charles wanted to continue as king, he would have to fight.

Oddly enough, for Russell, who disparaged old-fashioned constitutional history, the Civil War erupted over a constitutional issue. In
his own words, an 'unbridgeable gulf' had opened up 'between
Charles's determination to govern, and his opponents' determination to bypass him... . This was the issue on which it became necessary to fight.'[117] For Morrill, the key issue was religion. In his telling,
the gulf that developed was between those who were content to free
the church from popery and Laudian innovations and those who insisted on proceeding further to establish a more fully reformed
church. 'It was this which made civil war necessary.'[118] Although
there is a difference of emphasis in the interpretations of Russell

and Morrill, their views are not mutually exclusive. Indeed, else-where Russell virtually adopted Morrill's viewpoint.[119] More import-antly, both authors agree that the heart of the problem was Charles. As Morrill described it, religion put the 'fire in the belly' of men who were willing to resort to force against the king, but it was the king who brought matters to this pass. Thus constitutional alarms and re-ligious zeal combined to produce rebellion. 'The civil war was fought [both] to restrain an untrustworthy king and to release the forces of reformation.'[120]

The First Civil War

Henrietta Maria once scolded Charles for referring to his enemies as 'Parliament', and it was a point well taken.[121] It is customary to refer to the king's English opponents as 'Parliament' or the 'Parliamentarians', and the whole war is often simplistically ex-pressed in terms of king versus Parliament. This crude nomencla-ture is inescapable, but it obscures the important fact that many of the original members of the Long Parliament fought on the king's side against the so-called parliamentary side. At least two-fifths of the House of Commons and the overwhelming majority of the House of Lords sided with Charles, not Parliament.[122] It is astounding how few textbooks bother to make this basic distinction. None, of course, calls the king's enemies rebels, though that in fact is what they were. Just as it dignifies the rebels in Scotland to call them the Covenanters, so does it dignify the rebels in England to call them Parliamentarians. Despite the queen's admonition, no one appreci-ated this fact more than Charles. If war broke out, he warned just two months before that eventuality, 'We must not look upon it as an Act of Our Parliament, but as a Rebellion against Us and the Law'.[123]

Although a great many works have been published on the Civil War (or war of the three kingdoms), none has focused on King Charles during this period as intensely as authors like Cust, Reeve, and Sharpe have done for earlier periods. The great scholarly controversies surrounding the Civil War – about alle-giances, Presbyterians *versus* Independents, the significance of the Levellers, the impact of the New Model Army, and so forth – are not essentially controversies about Charles. In 1983 John Morrill

observed that an 'enormous amount could be learnt from a study
that looked at the 1640s from Charles's point of view, that set out
not to show why he failed, but what options were open to him at particular junctures and how his positive acts required responses from
his enemies'.[124] Ronald Hutton's *The Royalist War Effort 1642–1646* is
of some help in this respect. Yet Maurice Ashley could still observe
with justice in 1992: 'No entirely satisfactory biography of King
Charles I or analysis of his military strategy has yet been published –
a remarkable fact.'[125]

This is not the place to fight all the major battles of the First Civil
War again, but we do need to assess Charles's performance as a war
leader. When Charles raised his standard at Nottingham in August
1642, a small number of men had rallied to his cause. When he
fought the first major battle of the Civil War just two months later at
Edgehill, he had an army under his command of about 24,000 men.
The recruitment of this army was no mean feat, but how was it accomplished? According to Joyce Malcolm, the king's lack of popularity was a serious handicap and his initial recruiting efforts were 'worse
than disappointing'. It was only through the coercive power of a few
key landowners and the active enlistment of Catholics that Charles
managed to raise a respectable army.[126] M. D. G. Wanklyn, Peter
Young, P. R. Newman, and Ronald Hutton were less cynical.[127] As
Hutton portrayed him, Charles worked feverishly to win allies and
raise an army on the march southward. The king extended his personal efforts into northeastern Wales and hit upon the idea of
sending his oldest son Charles, the Prince of Wales, to represent his
cause in other areas of Wales. In Hutton's opinion this was a 'brilliant scheme', and overall 'Charles's achievement had been spectacu-
lar'.[128] Forming a party of supporters and raising an army of men who
would fight on his behalf required Charles to justify his actions,
appeal for help, issue manifestos, make speeches, woo supporters,
and court popularity – functions for which he had previously shown
little aptitude but which he now performed with surprising ability. In
Charles Carlton's opinion, the king was still too rigid and remote to
inspire the rank-and-file and cultivate their personal affection, but
there is no doubt that he displayed physical courage.[129] Moreover,
there is reason to believe that war did transform the shy, stuttering
king known for his curt speeches into an effective orator who moved
among his troops and stirred them to fight.[130] As Kevin Sharpe observed, 'Charles perforce became a rhetorician, a writer, in some ways
a politician.'[131] In some respects at least, Charles rose to the occasion.

In other respects, Charles's quality of leadership is more debatable. Some have criticised the command structure he established. In the beginning he gave overall command of his army to the Earl of Lindsey. At the same time, however, he appointed his nephew Prince Rupert to command the cavalry. Since Rupert enjoyed a privileged relationship with the king and was allowed to deal directly with him, this bypassed and undermined Lindsey's authority. The conflict between Lindsey and Rupert did not last long, however. When the two men argued over tactics before the Battle of Edgehill and Charles sided with his nephew, Lindsey resigned his command and was subsequently mortally wounded in the battle. Charles appointed another overall commander, the Earl of Forth, who was in fact much better qualified; but the man really in charge of operations all along was Charles himself. There was also a Council of War, and Charles listened to their advice; but he reserved the right to ignore it, which was not always wise. Meanwhile there was dissension within the Council of War, and Rupert carried on a running feud with one of its members, Lord Digby. There was also tension between the moderates and hardliners among the king's advisers, and the latter group tended to prevail in their desire for total victory. It would be unreasonable to expect unanimity of opinion, however, and we should be careful not to exaggerate the significance of these divided counsels.[132] The Parliamentarian camp was much more deeply and bitterly divided than the royalist camp. How we judge Charles depends to some extent on how we judge Rupert to whom he entrusted a great deal of power. Rupert, one of the younger sons of Charles's sister Elizabeth, came over to England expressly to help his uncle. He had acquired a small amount of military experience on the continent, but he was a volatile and impulsive young man in his early twenties. Nevertheless, the king's trust in Rupert can be justified by the results. As we shall see, Rupert made mistakes, but generally speaking his appearance on the scene was a stroke of good fortune for Charles. Rupert's charging cavalry became one of the royalists' chief military assets, and his personal skill and courage made him a terror to his enemies. Not the least of his contributions to the royalist cause was the way in which he strengthened the will and buoyed the spirits of his uncle. By contrast, the first commander on the parliamentary side, the Earl of Essex, was a great disappointment.

Command of the countryside was almost as important as command of the army. Generally speaking, Parliament gained the upper hand in the east and southeast of England. The midlands were hotly disputed territory. And the royalists enjoyed a considerable presence in the north, west, and southwest, plus Wales. To establish control over this far-flung territory and tap its resources, Charles appointed six lieutenant-generals. Because of his sense of hierarchy and perhaps because he thought the populace would respond better to their natural leaders, Charles initially appointed leading noblemen to these positions. In time, however, Charles, who had previously shown little capacity to learn from experience, did realise that he would have to employ individuals who had more military experience and were willing to do whatever was necessary to raise and maintain an army (men like Rupert and his younger brother Prince Maurice).[133] After studying this administrative structure and its adaptations over time, Hutton concluded that it was more effective and resilient than had been thought, though in the end still inadequate to the task. Royalist forces were spread out over a vast expanse, much of it relatively poor, peppered with parliamentary strongholds, and ravaged by battles; whereas the Parliamentarians enjoyed the wealth and security of most of the cities, particularly London, which provided a constant source of money and remained unscarred by battle. Both sides experienced tremendous local resistance in their fight off the battlefield for men and money. In this latter fight for resources, however, sheer circumstances placed the king at a great disadvantage. 'In the last analysis', Hutton concluded, 'it was the local community, not Parliament, which defeated Charles I, not from hatred of his cause but from hatred of the war itself.'[134]

None the less, the bloody, life-and-death struggle on the real battlefields was decisive, if only because local interests tended to respect and support whoever was winning the war on the battlefield at any particular time. Charles cannot escape responsibility for the strategic and tactical decisions he made about where and how to engage the enemy. In the beginning Charles, like most other people, probably expected the war to be won by one great battle, but no clear winner emerged from the Battle of Edgehill. Charles could claim to have won the battle because he stayed in position prepared to resume fighting the next day; it was the parliamentary forces under Essex that withdrew. After Edgehill, Charles briefly adopted the strategy of trying a direct assault on London, but he was thwarted by a larger parliamentary force at Turnham Green. Thereafter Charles established his base of operations at Oxford. Perhaps he continued to hope that eventually he would be able to draw in his armies from the north, west, and south to encircle London, but he was never again strong enough to act upon such a strategy.[135] More and more, his strategy became simply to cope with the annual assault of the parliamentary forces which came looking for him. Totally lacking in military experience, Charles was not an especially good tactician, but he had his moments and probably does not deserve as much scorn as historians like S. R. Gardiner heaped upon him. Gardiner wrote, for example, that the king's personal direction at Edgehill was a 'fatal disadvantage' for the royalists.[136] Yet the major tactical error on the royalist side at Edgehill was made by Rupert's cavalry when it pursued the enemy off the battlefield, and even Gardiner conceded that credit should be given to Charles for moving among the troops, exposing himself to danger, and continuing the fight until his cavalry returned to the field. It is routine to accuse Charles of being indecisive or vacillating, but he stood his ground at Edgehill and it was Essex who retreated. J. P. Kenyon provided a more judicious account of Edgehill but joined in the speculation as to whether Charles 'muffed his one chance of finishing the war quickly' by failing to strike at the heart of the Parliamentarian cause in London.[137] The fact is, however, Charles faced an army twice the size of his own at Turnham Green; even Rupert cautioned against attacking this superior force. When Charles retired to Oxford for the winter, it was true both that he had missed his best chance for a quick win and that he had conducted the war reasonably well so far.

The years 1643 and 1644 were more a mixed bag for Charles. In 1643 the royalist effort in general fared quite well until reversals at the end of the campaigning season, and Charles was directly involved in those reversals. After Rupert achieved a major victory by capturing the valuable seaport of Bristol, Charles tried to capture the town of Gloucester. Overruling Rupert's advice for a direct assault because it would have cost lives, Charles chose instead to lay siege to the town until Essex raced to its rescue at the head of a larger army. Faced with this superior force, it was prudent for Charles to make a tactical retreat, but this only accentuated the fact that he had wasted five weeks in a siege with nothing in the end to show for it. On the other hand, Essex was now overextended, and Charles had the opportunity to intercept him on his return march to London. Charles did intercept Essex at the Battle of Newbury but failed to defeat him. The failure at Newbury might have been a victory if Charles had not again overruled Rupert's tactical advice and if he had not run low on gunpowder, much of which had been wasted at Gloucester. Thus the season which had seen many royalist victories under other commanders, ended with two notable failures presided over by Charles.[138] There was one great personal consolation for Charles, however, because Henrietta Maria had returned to England. The queen brought valuable military supplies and boosted the king's morale, but she hurt his cause too by intensifying animosities at the Oxford court. She was particularly instrumental in rebuffing three peers who tried to come over to the royalist side. Charles was slightly more forgiving, but together the royal couple gave the damaging impression that defectors from the parliamentary side would find little welcome or magnanimity in the king's camp.[139] Charles and Henrietta Maria spent this one last year together, during which time their final child was conceived and born, before the queen sailed for France, never to see her husband again.

Both Charles and his adversaries were looking for an infusion of new blood that might tip the balance in their favour. Charles got his from Ireland. He arranged a 'cessation' or truce in Ireland, which freed up troops who were fighting there to join his army in England. Historians are not sure how many reinforcements Charles acquired from Ireland and who exactly they were. Probably half or more were English Protestants who had gone to Ireland to suppress the rebellion; but many must also have been Irish, and many of these must have been Catholics. In sheer numbers, Charles apparently gained somewhere between 17,000 and 22,000 soldiers, which would have been a considerable augmentation of his forces if they did in fact fight for the king after their arrival. Since these men did not appear on the scene as one large army but arrived in a trickle and were dispersed throughout the existing royalist forces, it is impossible to know how many actually fought and what impact they had. Whatever the military benefit of these troops, they came with a very high political cost. Whatever the reality was, the public impression was that Charles was employing Irish Catholics, or at the very least abandoning the fight against Irish Catholics, in order to strengthen his hand in England.[140] At the same time Charles obtained help from Ireland, Parliament obtained help from Scotland. The Scottish army came with a price tag too – the establishment of Presbyterianism in England – but this of course was not as repugnant to most English as the spectre of Roman Catholicism. The First Civil War was increasingly becoming a war of three kingdoms and a war of religion. John Pym died at the end of 1643 after securing the alliance with the Scots. It is usually described as his final service to the state, but it could just as well be considered his final disservice to the king.[141]

Parliament's alliance with the Scots drastically altered the military situation in 1644. In January a large Scottish army crossed the border into England. Up to this point the royalists had been doing very well in the north under the leadership of the Marquis of Newcastle, but he was no match for the Scots. Charles despatched Rupert to assist in repelling the Scots, but the result was the famous royalist defeat at Marston Moor. It is sometimes suggested that Charles was responsible for this defeat because he sent Rupert ambiguous orders that induced him to throw his forces into battle against the far larger combined forces of Parliament and the Scots, but Rupert hardly needed the king's letter to make such a bold move. At most perhaps both men were to blame for believing that Rupert could perform one more miracle.[142] If there were any miracles left on the royalist side in the summer of 1644, it was amazingly Charles who produced them. With Rupert drawn off to the north, it fell to Charles to evade and counter the parliamentary armies ranging around Oxford. Ronald Hutton described what happened at this juncture: 'One of the strangest episodes of the war now occurred; Charles and his advisers, who had hitherto responded to the Parliamentarian offensive with no imagination or daring, suddenly began to display both.'[143] Charles presided over two surprising victories: he got the best of an army under the command of Sir William Waller at the Battle of Cropredy Bridge, and he at last won a stunning victory over the Earl of Essex at Lostwithiel in Cornwall. Essex ignominiously escaped in a boat, leaving his soldiers behind to deal with Charles who treated them with exceptional leniency. Charles took no prisoners of war. The cavalry already having escaped under the cover of night, he allowed the infantry to march away after they laid down their weapons. Historians like Gardiner deplored this 'misplaced leniency', but it was merciful of Charles and it confirms what Clarendon said about him: 'He had a tenderness and compassion of nature, which restrained him from ever doing a hard-hearted thing'. Interestingly, it was Clarendon's opinion that if Charles 'had been of a rougher and more imperious nature, he would have found more respect and duty; and his not applying some severe cures to approaching evils proceeded from the lenity of his nature and the tenderness of his conscience, which in all cases of blood made him choose the softer way'.[144]

Charles showed renewed determination at the beginning of 1645, reorganising his high command, putting Rupert in overall charge, and winning back parts of the midlands and the west. Then came the crushing defeat in June at the Battle of Naseby. In Hutton's words, 'the royal army committed suicide at Naseby'. It is easy to see in retrospect that Charles should have avoided engaging the enemy at Naseby. He had made the fateful decision earlier to divide his army, sending a large contingent to the west, so the army actually under his command was not at full strength. As the parliamentary forces bore down on him, many of his advisers, including even Rupert, urged him to run. This was not necessarily the best course to take because the parliamentary army might still have caught up with him, attacked from the rear, and inflicted heavy casualties. This at least is the best defence that can be given for the king's decision to stand and fight. Perhaps the victories of 1644 had made him overly confident, or perhaps he was just impatient for a final victory.[145] It is not entirely inconceivable that the royalist army could have won at Naseby, and critical errors by others contributed to its defeat, but Charles must bear the principal responsibility.[146] The defeat was made even worse for Charles because his correspondence was captured, and it revealed his dealings with Ireland, France, the Pope, and anyone else he thought might be able to help him. Parliament, recognising the propaganda value in these letters, published the most incriminating under the title of *The King's Cabinet Opened*. Charles professed to be unashamed of these papers. He wrote to Henrietta Maria that 'I will neither deny that those things are mine ... nor, as a good Protestant or honest man, blush for any of those papers'.[147] The righteous indignation of the king's contemporaries has rubbed off on modern historians who, though they do not share Parliament's alarm about the popish plot, are appalled by the king's willingness to pursue any conceivable alliance and to lie about what he was up to. We should not forget, however, that these practices are commonplace in diplomacy and Charles was, after all, engaged in a war.

After Naseby it was only a matter of time before Charles was defeated altogether. In September one of his few remaining assets was lost when Rupert failed to save the city of Bristol. Furious at Rupert's surrender of Bristol, the king angrily lashed out against his nephew and stripped him of his command. Although Charles also expressed the hope that someday he would be able to reward Rupert for his services and a few weeks later formally absolved him of blame, the breach was irreparable and the charge of ingratitude which historians make against the king in this case seems more than warranted.[148] Virtually alone and with no army left to fight on his behalf, Charles surrendered in May 1646 to the Scots who turned him over to the English Parliament in early 1647.

Negotiations and the Second Civil War

After the king's surrender, mortal combat gave way to negotiating. To put it mildly, this was not Charles's strong suit. Negotiations had been carried on sporadically from the outset of the war, usually during the winter lull between campaigning seasons. Although nothing had come of these negotiations, it was not entirely the king's fault. Parliament consistently made him offers he could well afford to resist, especially at the beginning of the war when he still had a good chance of winning on the battlefield. The stronger Parliament's military position became, the more extreme their demands became and the more enemies they wished to exclude from any royal pardon or amnesty. The propositions of Oxford escalated into the propositions of Uxbridge, and after the king's surrender these escalated into the propositions of Newcastle.[149] At this point Parliament and the army began to fall out. The army took custody of Charles and tried to arrive at their own settlement with him embodied in the 'Heads of the Proposals'. This was an eminently sensible document that could have secured the objectives many people thought they had been fighting for. Ironically, it showed much more careful concern to establish a workable constitutional monarchy than Parliament's own Newcastle propositions did, and it took a far more conciliatory approach on divisive issues such as the future of the church and control of the military. Whereas Parliament insisted on a uniform Presbyterianism, the army would have allowed a nominal episcopacy to remain; and instead of taking the king's command of the military away for twenty years, it would have done so for only ten years. Charles professed to be pleased with the 'Heads of the Proposals', which he told Parliament were 'much more conducive to the satisfaction of all interests, and ... a fitter foundation for a lasting peace' than their own propositions.[150] Of course he could have been saying this merely to exacerbate tensions between the army and Parliament, but it agrees with what he said in private correspondence to the effect that the overtures of the army's leadership were 'much more frank and satisfactory to what I desire of this army than ever was offered me by the Presbyterians'.[151]

Based on the failure of all these talks and the king's eventual resort to renewed force, it is easy to assume that he was insincere about negotiating. In his formal responses and personal correspondence, however, there are indications that he was truly trying to negotiate, alien as that process was to him. For example, he contemplated conceding control of the military for seven years and allowing Presbyterianism for three years while a representative committee worked out a permanent solution. The influence of moderate advisers like Hyde is evident here, of course, but Charles seemed quite proud of himself for thinking of the latter compromise.[152] On the other hand, these bargaining positions were quintessentially Charles. They entailed merely temporary tactical concessions – be it for three years or seven years – in the hope of recouping everything in the long run. Charles was not entirely incapable of making permanent concessions; he made several in the first year of the Long Parliament. But there was considerable reason to suspect that he would find some way to wriggle out of any concession that was not made absolutely irreversible from the outset. Moreover, in his own mind Charles had already identified three issues which were in effect non-negotiable. 'I resolve, by the Grace of God', he declared, [1] 'never to yield up this church to the government of Papists, Presbyterians, or Independents, [2] nor to injure my successors, by lessening the crown of that ecclesiastical and military power which my predecessors left me, [3] nor forsake my friends.'[153]

The king's determination to stand by his friends was hardened by the haunting memory of Strafford, what Charles himself called 'that base, unworthy concession'.[154] Having failed that one friend, Charles explained, 'I am resolved that no consideration whatever shall ever make me do the like'.[155] Looking to the future, he exhorted his son in the same vein 'never to abandon the protection of your friends upon any pretence whatsoever'.[156] Parliament had identified 57 people they wanted to exclude from any general pardon, but Charles thought it would undermine a lasting peace and be a 'perpetual dishonour' if he were to 'abandon so many persons'.[157] Concerning control of the military, Charles wrote, 'my resolution is fixed never to part with the least tittle of right to the militia'.[158] A king without control of the military was no king in Charles's mind. Turning this control over to Parliament 'dethrones the king', leaving him with 'little more than the name and shadow' of monarchy.[159] It was on the question of the church, however, that Charles was most adamant. To abandon episcopacy and accept Presbyterianism, he thought, would jeopardise not only salvation but also order and authority. It would be a 'sin', he told his wife, asking her if she would give up Roman Catholicism as readily as she wished him to give up episcopacy merely for worldly gain. The chief duty of a king was to maintain the true religion, and religion in turn was the best prop for monarchy. 'For where was there ever obedience where religion did not teach it?', Charles asked. In his view, people were 'governed by the pulpit more than the sword', but Presbyterianism was perverse in this respect. It fostered anarchy and 'the doctrine of rebellion'. It would use the power of the pulpit 'to dethrone me at their pleasure, at least to keep me in subjection'.[160] It would 'make me but a titulary king', for 'they will introduce that doctrine which teaches rebellion to be lawful, and that the supreme power is in the people, to whom kings (as they say) ought to give an account, and be corrected if they do amiss'.[161] King James was famous for having said 'No bishop/No king', and his son entirely agreed. The way Charles came to view it, the First Civil War practically amounted to a Third Bishops' War, and this was not an unreasonable interpretation of events. On the other hand, the manner in which Charles magnified the importance of religion and in effect staked his crown on it suggests that something more was at work in his mind. Perhaps he was trying to deflect attention away from himself as the cause of war, or deny to himself that he had been to blame, or fix upon a higher purpose that would vindicate his past actions and give him courage to face what he might yet have to do.

In these efforts by Charles to explain and justify his negotiating position, we can see that his underlying concern was to avoid negotiating away monarchy itself or, as he put it, not 'to destroy the essence of monarchy'.[162] He had already relinquished many of the instruments of prerogative rule and he said that he would call frequent Parliaments in the future, but he could not comprehend giving up control over the church and the military. To go that far, he thought, would undermine all sense of hierarchy and result in anarchy. From our modern vantage point, it is easy to say that he could safely have made these further concessions without bringing ruin upon his heirs and chaos to his kingdoms, but he had no way of knowing that. Given his place in history, it was reasonable for him to believe that he could not afford to surrender the Crown's control over the church and the military.

Nor was Charles wrong to think that he might still avoid total capitulation. His bargaining position was stronger than it may appear to us in retrospect. His greatest bargaining chip was the simple fact that he was king. 'If we beat the king ninety and nine times', the Earl of Manchester had complained, 'yet he is king still.'[163] Unless his adversaries wished to do away with monarchy – and most of them still had no such intention – they had no choice but to strike a deal with Charles. Furthermore, those adversaries were far from united, and Charles could hope to exploit their differences. Many shared the king's view that monarchy needed to be maintained as a bulwark against the disintegration of the social order, and royalist propaganda played upon this fear to win support for the king's cause. Rule by Parliament or the army was beginning to look much more alarming than the familiar and traditional rule by the king. Meanwhile there was a resurgence of public affection for the monarchy, which may actually have emboldened Charles to overplay his hand. All these factors strengthened the king's bargaining position.

If it turned out that nothing but total capitulation would satisfy his captors, Charles was still prepared to refuse. The king's willingness to put his life on the line was the final factor that strengthened his bargaining position. He had already contemplated the possibility that if he would not yield he might have to die. At the outset of the war in December 1642, he had written that he was 'resolved that no extremity or misfortune shall make me yield; for I will either be a glorious king or a patient martyr'.[164] A few weeks before turning himself over to the Scots, he resumed this theme, stating that 'if I cannot live as a King, I shall die like a gentleman, without doing that which may make honest men blush for me'.[165] Charles found consolation in the fact that his wife and eldest son, the heir to the throne, were out of harm's way. As for himself, he professed, 'I have already cast up what I am like to suffer, which I shall meet (by the Grace of God) with that constancy that befits me.'[166] Because he would not back down, his adversaries would have to back down unless they were willing to eliminate him. Even toward the end when Charles had nothing else much to bargain with, this awful prospect still kept his cause alive until the few men who were willing to take such a drastic step did so.

The period between the king's surrender to the Scots in 1646 and his execution in 1649 witnessed a tangled web of negotiations, political realignments, and jockeying for power. The best guide to this period is Robert Ashton's detailed study entitled *Counter-Revolution*.[167] During this period Charles did precisely what we would expect of him. He did negotiate, but as we have already seen, he considered certain key issues non-negotiable. His offers to make concessions for a mere three years or seven years rang hollow. He never had any serious intention of settling for half a loaf because he never despaired of getting a whole loaf. Under these circumstances, negotiations dragged on but could not reach closure. Charles was also stalling for time, but his strategy was not as rational as that phrase suggests. He had no clear idea what to do with the time he gained; he was vaguely hoping something would develop. During this period he also continued his accustomed policy of negotiating with one party behind the back of another and playing one side off against another. These practices were no more inherently reprehensible in this context than they had been in the foreign affairs of the 1630s, but they carried the same high costs too: they reinforced the king's reputation for deviousness and made all parties less disposed to trust him. Far worse was Charles's continued yearning for a quick-fix, a bold resort to force that would suddenly end the irksome negotiating and miraculously deliver him from his predicament.

There is an eerie quality surrounding the course of events in this period, and Charles is the chief source of this impression. He looks like a trapped animal, wanting to free himself, making ineffectual efforts toward that goal, and yet at the same time doomed to repeat the behaviour that had brought him to this juncture and resistant to the very moves that might still have rescued him. In the summer of 1647, when the army's 'Heads of the Proposals' gave him a wonderful opportunity to strike a bargain, he tried to use this offer instead to play the army off against Parliament and extract even better terms. In the autumn when he was comfortably ensconced at Hampton Court, negotiating with Parliament again and the centre of attention, he made a hare-brained escape. With no certain destination in mind and no ship provided which might have carried him to the continent, Charles eventually turned himself over to the governor of the Isle of Wight. All he had gained by this inept break for freedom was a less commodious arrest in a more remote location, and at great cost to what little was left of his reputation. Up to this point Charles seemed confused and unsure what action to take. At the end of 1647 he made a more decisive move, entering into an 'Engagement' with a faction of the Scots by which he promised to establish Presbyterianism in England for at least three years.

Considering how irrevocably he was opposed to Presbyterianism, he must have viewed this as a merely temporary concession to draw the Scots over to his side against his English foes. Emboldened by his secret dealings with the Scots, Charles rejected Parliament's current demands known as the 'Four Bills'. Parliament in disgust voted to make no more overtures to the king, thereby leaving him in a sort of diplomatic limbo.

During 1648 Charles made further bumbling attempts at escape which got him nowhere. He also watched hopefully from the sidelines as the Second Civil War materialised. There were scattered uprisings in England, and the splinter-group of Scots who had allied with Charles invaded on his behalf. But these forces were not sufficiently strong or coordinated to win in the end. Even while the army was fighting this Second Civil War, Parliament resumed talking with Charles, and they kept on talking to the bitter end. Put simply, they were desperate to reach an accommodation with Charles before their own more radical members and the army gained the upper hand and dictated a more extreme settlement. These negotiations at Newport on the Isle of Wight looked promising for a while. Although Charles still balked at the number of his supporters Parliament wanted to punish (reduced now to 37) and the abolition of episcopacy, he made many other significant concessions. From his private correspondence it is clear, however, that he had no intention of honouring these concessions because they would make him 'no King' and reduce him to the state of 'a perpetual prisoner'. Distraught at this prospect, still trying to elude the logical consequence of his position, he continued to entertain dreams of escape. Referring to the greatest of his concessions, Charles explained that it 'was made merely in order to my escape, of which if I had not hope, I would not have done'.[168] At this point in early December the army intervened to take custody of the king and put him out of his misery. If Charles had only to deal with the politicians, his intransigence might still have paid off. Parliament wanted to continue talking, but the army was in charge of events now and their wrath could not so easily be appeased. The Second Civil War had been shorter but more ferocious than the first, and it proved to many in the army who were forced to risk their lives again that Charles could never be trusted. In their view he was a treacherous 'Man of Blood' who had to be stopped before he shed more innocent blood.[169]

First the weak-kneed politicians had to be cleared out of the way, and this was accomplished by forcibly excluding anyone from the

House of Commons who might object. Pride's Purge (named for Colonel Pride who carried it out) was no small event. David Underdown estimated that the army expelled at least 186 members from the House of Commons, and 45 of these were further placed under arrest for short periods of time.[170] Excluded and imprisoned members like William Prynne had good reason to ponder whether the king's rule had been as highhanded as the army's rule might be. Even among the members who were allowed to remain in the House, many, including John Selden, chose to absent themselves voluntarily in protest against the army's interference. What remained of the House, therefore, was a very small rump of perhaps no more than 60 men who carried through the plan to put the king on trial.

Trial and Execution

No peers were forcibly excluded from taking their seats in the House of Lords, but only a handful were still meeting at the beginning of January 1649 when the Commons asked for their vote in favour of the king's trial. Most in this small remnant of peers had fought against the king in the Civil War, but they knew the peerage depended on the monarchy, and they were genuinely offended by the illegality of the course now being taken. They refused to cooperate, whereupon the rump House of Commons asserted that they alone represented the will of the people and unilaterally created 'a High Court of Justice for the Trying and Judging of Charles Stuart'. Although 135 people were named to this tribunal, far fewer actually served. At the end of the trial 67 voted for the death sentence, but only 59 signed the death warrant.[171] Thus the king's death was demanded by a small minority of iron-willed extremists, nowhere near a majority of the British people, only about one-tenth of the legitimate membership of the Commons, not even a majority of the people appointed to the special tribunal.

Although these proceedings are conventionally referred to as a trial, it was more a case of judicial murder. The people who were now determined to do away with the king could have shot him, staged a suicide or accidental death, or announced his mysterious disappearance, but they were so convinced of the righteousness of their cause and so desirous to cloak their action in the mantle of legality that they insisted on a public trial. There was never any genuine intention to test the king's guilt or innocence. The act creating the tribunal made token references to the weighing of evidence and the ideal of impartiality, but it began by declaring it was 'notorious' that Charles had hatched 'a wicked design totally to subvert the ancient and fundamental laws and liberties of this nation, and in their place to introduce an arbitrary and tyrannical government, and ... he hath prosecuted it with fire and sword'.[172] In effect, the king was presumed guilty, and the purpose of the trial was to demonstrate his guilt to the world in order to justify his execution. As the prosecutor said during the trial, the king's guilt was 'as clear as crystal, and as the sun that shines at noon-day'.[173]

Rare as it is for historians to agree, they do agree that nothing became King Charles so much in life as his departing from it. Nor is this simply a matter of charity or pity for a doomed human being. Charles earned this respect because for once he did not disappoint. This time the king who had a knack for making matters worse and playing into the hands of his enemies actually made the best of a situation and denied his accusers an easy victory. Of course Charles was powerless to change the verdict of the court, but in a broader sense he could profoundly affect the outcome of the trial. He did not cower with fear, make lame excuses, or try to weasel out. Instead, he defended himself with trenchant arguments and genuine eloquence, and when these were of no further avail, he faced death with dignity and courage. His devoted followers were inspired by his example and compared him to Christ; a more mundane and contemporary comparison would be Sir John Eliot. Charles could not prevail in the face of this extraordinary tribunal any more than Eliot had been able to prevail against the power of the Crown. But, like Eliot, by his fortitude and principled resistance he transformed his death into an honourable martyrdom.

The king's trial began on 20 January 1649 and lasted about a week.[174] He made a very lonely figure, sitting by himself in a chair looking up at the judges who sat at a symbolically higher level on a raised platform. On four different days he was summoned before the court to answer the charge against him, and on the last of these the verdict and sentence were announced.[175] What happened on these occasions bore little resemblance to normal judicial procedure. Charles had no legal counsel. He was forced to defend himself, and the strategy he took was basically to refuse to play the game. There is a remote possibility that if he had appeared remorseful, he might yet have escaped with his life; but the only act for which Charles felt truly remorseful was his sacrifice of Strafford. Instead of defending himself against the formal charge, he vigorously questioned the source of the court's authority. How could the House of Commons which was no court of law create a court of law? How could it do so when it was well known that most of its members were absent or forcibly excluded? How could this rump claim to act on behalf of the people when the people had not been consulted? How could it act in this business without the concurrence of the House of Lords? How could the king in whose name impeachments were prosecuted be himself impeached? How could the king be expected to acquiesce in the court's illegal proceedings when to do so would actually violate his duty to uphold the laws? The king's refusal to cooperate exasperated the court, and on each occasion they ended by removing him.

Charles took the position that if he could be convinced by rational argument of the court's legitimacy, then he would attempt to answer the charge against him. This may seem like an artful dodge, but it was in fact an important point with consequences that extended far beyond the fate of just one man. 'For the Charge', said Charles, 'I value it not a rush.' Far more important was the basic issue of the rule of law. If this illegal tribunal were allowed to operate with impunity against the king, then no one was safe. The court stood for arbitrary power, said Charles; 'it is the liberty of the people of England that I stand for'. Thus Charles claimed to be protesting against the court's blatant exercise of raw power, not just for himself, but for everyone. In his own words, 'if power without law may make laws, may alter the fundamental laws of the kingdom, I do not know what subject he is in England, that can be sure of his life, or anything that he calls his own'. Using the very line of reasoning that his critics had so often used against him, Charles claimed to be defending liberty and property. 'I do plead for the liberties of the people of England more than you do', he told the tribunal.[176]

The arguments and overall posture of the king threw the judges off balance, and there appears to have been some temporary wavering among them. However, on 27 January they closed ranks and pronounced the king guilty of forming 'a wicked design to erect and uphold in himself an unlimited and tyrannical Power', guilty of waging war against Parliament, 'guilty of High Treason, and of the Murders, Rapines, Burnings, Spoils, Desolations, Damage, and Mischief to this Nation acted and committed in the said War'. In short, Charles was 'a Tyrant, Traitor, Murderer, and public Enemy to the good people of this Nation'.[177] The sentence was death by decapitation. The king tried vainly to speak out against this verdict, but he was once more silenced and removed. If the king could be prevented from speaking, Charles observed as he was being taken away, 'expect what justice other people will have'.[178]

Charles's performance at his trial almost makes us wonder whether he was a reformed man. He spoke so eloquently on behalf of his subjects' liberties and property that we are almost tempted to believe that he could have been trusted to protect these at least as well as the army and the rump. But when we remember his conduct between his surrender and trial, the verdict seems more just. When he was convinced of the rightness of his own position, which was most of the time, he adamantly refused to alter his course or bend to political reality. He acted as if political reality should bend to him. This habit of a lifetime was a prescription for trouble or, as it proved in 1649, for martyrdom. The king's resolute refusal to bend to political reality redounded to his benefit at his trial because here for once he had right on his side. What he did not have any longer on his side was might; we sympathise with him all the more for that very reason. It is worth remembering, however, that on previous occasions when he had the might, he had not shown much capacity to question the rightness of his own actions. Of course the arguments he and his spokesmen employed to defend cases like those involving arbitrary imprisonment and unparliamentary taxation were more solidly grounded than any that could be adduced for the outrageously illegal tribunal of 1649, but they were differences more of degree than kind. In the future Charles would have continued to find rationalisations for his actions, to reject criticism, and to stigmatise his critics. And even if he had cravenly promised to do better, his judges knew that he could not be trusted to keep his promise. Charles struck a heroic pose at his trial, but the court's presiding officer cut him down to size: 'How great a friend you have been to the laws and liberties of the people, let all England and the world judge.'[179]

Charles was executed on 30 January. He made a brief speech attesting to his faith, forgiving his enemies, and explaining his actions. He insisted that Parliament, not he, had started the Civil War (just as he had begun his reign insisting that Parliament had urged him into war on the continent). In the same vein, he identified control of the military as the central issue that had caused the breach between himself and Parliament. Charles was paying a high price for his determination to be *Rex Bellicosus*. Perhaps the most interesting statements Charles made at his execution concerned his view of government. The special tribunal that conducted his trial claimed that their authority derived from the people through Parliament. They described the king as accountable not only to God but to his people. At one point the prosecutor even referred to the king as 'elected', a slip which Charles was quick to point out.[180] This was a radically ascending view of authority.[181] All his life Charles had taken an equally extreme descending view of authority. This should not surprise us in a king. 'A subject and a sovereign are clean different things', Charles declared at his execution. Drawing the people into the actual government of the state, he believed, would ultimately undermine not only the powers of the king but the welfare of the people themselves. For the people, as he saw it, liberty and freedom consisted only in having a settled government and established laws. It did not consist in 'having [a] share in government', which 'is nothing pertaining to them'.[182] Such views are likely to offend modern sensibilities, but they were not unreasonable in their historical context. Charles foresaw that the men who had brought about his trial and execution in the name of the people were cutting Britain loose from its traditional moorings, and their rule might easily prove to be more oppressive than his own had been. Charles feared rule by the people or, to be more precise, rule by a body claiming to speak for the people. This was the fear that had coloured his perception of parliamentary politics from the outset of his reign. This was the fear that had made him resist any infringement on the royal prerogative. And now his greatest fear was coming to pass. Charles had never wished to be a tyrant, but he had an exceedingly traditional and hierarchical view of authority, and he feared that to compromise that authority was tantamount to jeopardising it. As he said so often in the 1640s, he would be no true king if he made the concessions being asked of him. He chose to die rather than compromise the powers of the monarchy, not merely because he wished to preserve his and his heirs' authority but also because he genuinely believed it was in the best interests of the people as well.

Although the arguments Charles made from the scaffold were not lost on his contemporaries, many of whom shared his concern for the preservation of tradition and hierarchy, what made a far more profound impression was the sheer manner of his dying. Charles faced death with courage and dignity. He dressed heavily so that he might not appear to be shivering from fear. He was accompanied by only one friend, Bishop Juxon. He spoke briefly, prayed, placed his head on the block, and then – as his final command – stretched out his hands signalling the executioner to wield the axe.[183] Charles had vowed, 'if I cannot live as a King, I shall die like a gentleman, without doing that which may make honest men blush for me'. For once he was true to his word.

CONCLUSION

G. R. Elton once said that British historians were the last in the western world still writing 'empirical' history.[1] While that is surely an exaggeration, it is true that political historians of the early Stuart period are noteworthy for the emphasis they continue to put on a close reading of manuscripts and the rather old-fashioned view they take of facts. Even the most iconoclastic revisionists of the 1970s and 1980s called for a return to the sources and challenged their critics to fight evidence with evidence.[2] When this challenge was taken up, however, when the documents were re-examined and sifted for the facts, these turned out to be very much what S. R. Gardiner had said they were 100 years ago. What we have shown in the present book is that the initial bold repudiation of Gardiner's views was followed by a gradual, though not always acknowledged, return to many of those same views.[3] It is an interesting question why historians have not more fully noticed or acknowledged that trend. Perhaps Gardiner has simply fallen victim to the youthful contempt for old age. Perhaps historians are so overwhelmed by the bulk of new work on Charles that they have no time to read through Gardiner's many old volumes. Perhaps the practical demands of the historical profession today make it too important to claim originality. Perhaps we have simply lost the habit of reading and acknowledging our distant predecessors. Whatever the reason, if recent historians had taken more trouble in their published works to engage in a dialogue with one another and with their predecessors, most especially to clarify their relationship to Gardiner, then there would have been less confusion about what in the end to think about Charles and less need for the present book.

It is true that Gardiner's dusty old volumes are marked by the biases of his age, an unctuous tone that at times is downright nauseating, and a flowery prose style uncongenial to modern tastes. Anyone who takes the trouble to read those volumes, however, will find that most of the opinions of King Charles I that are current

173

today were stated much earlier by Gardiner and often stated better. As we noted at the outset of the present book, Gardiner described Charles as unrealistic, untruthful, uncompromising, and unable to see things from anyone's point of view but his own. The way Charles reacted to criticism was especially unsettling because he was quick to divide people into friend and foe and to impute the worst possible motives to the latter. Of course more recent historians have made significant refinements to this picture. Kevin Sharpe contributed enormously to our understanding of the king's love of order and privacy. Richard Cust emphasised that Charles became obsessed about his subjects' loyalty. L. J. Reeve charged that he was an authoritarian personality with a penchant for political destruction because he was 'not, by inclination or equipment, a political man'.[4] Both Cust and Reeve thought the king's behaviour was practically paranoid. Historians like Nicholas Tyacke and Julian Davies refined our understanding of the king's religious convictions, revealing that he was not an innovator but an essentially conservative man who was attracted to the ceremony, formality, and centralised authority of the pre-Reformation church. Like all the rest of these historians, Peter Donald showed that it was difficult to give good counsel to Charles. According to Conrad Russell, the problem was that Charles tended to accept half counsel, which was worse than none at all. Russell also came to the realisation that Charles was a dangerous man who was quick to take offence and resort to force. The contributions of many other historians could be noted here (and have been in the pages above). Taken together, what all their researches have given us is a much more detailed and finely nuanced portrait of Charles than we had before, but still substantially the same flawed king that Gardiner described a century ago. For Charles Carlton writing in 1995, as for Gardiner writing in 1895, King Charles I 'failed because of his own personal defects', because, to put it more succinctly, 'character was destiny'.[5]

King Charles I's faults are so well known that we should for the sake of fairness take stock of his merits as well. Charles begins to look a lot better the minute we consider the competition. Unlike many other monarchs, he was not vicious, immoral, crude, lazy, irresponsible, extravagant, or stupid. Moreover he possessed several positive virtues which even his critics concede. 'High-minded, religiously devout and devoid of any form of carnal vice,' wrote Reeve, 'he was a loving husband, father and friend.' He was also a 'highly cultivated man' who understood, appreciated, and patronised the fine arts as well as anyone who ever occupied the British throne.[6] Charles did not have the talents of Queen Elizabeth, but in many ways he compares very favourably with other Tudor-Stuart monarchs. Charles loved order as much as Henry VII, but he was not as ruthless in pursuing it. Charles was far superior to Henry VIII, most conspicuously in his marital relations but in other ways too. Charles's court was a model of harmony and cooperation compared to the lethal competition at Henry's court; and Charles's efforts to protect unpopular servants like Buckingham and Strafford stand out in stark contrast to the brutality and ingratitude exhibited by Henry toward Wolsey and Cromwell. Charles was not as profligate as his father; and he was generally a model of virtue on the throne compared to his father and his oldest son, Charles II. In his affinity for Roman Catholicism, Charles most closely resembled Mary I and James II, but surely he ruled with a gentler and more enlightened hand than they did.

Furthermore, the very fact that Charles took his role as king so seriously tends to make us forget that he was also an ordinary human being handicapped by simple human inadequacies with which any of us should be able to sympathise. He was an ordinary human being expected to play an extraordinary role, and one gets the impression that he was out of his depth. He acted as if he was supremely confident, but some historians have sensed that this air of certitude masked a deeper insecurity. He surrounded himself with bigger-than-life portraits of himself on horseback, busts of Roman emperors, and masques that glorified his powers; but beneath it all he was a short, stuttering, ordinary man living in the shadow of his swaggering father (to whom he was always 'Baby Charles') and his illustrious brother whose shoes he could never fill. Perhaps this underlying self-doubt explains why Charles was attracted to strong people, like Buckingham, who bolstered his ego. Later in his reign, the people closest to Charles were the ones who shared his high opinion of the royal prerogative, reinforced his narrow views, and kept criticism at bay. He turned to people like this to shore up his regime at the end of the 1620s, to enforce his vision of order in the 1630s, and (most critically) to extricate him from his difficulties at the end of the personal rule. Ultimately these people (Portland, Strafford, Laud, Henrietta Maria) only got him into deeper trouble.

An even more important handicap of quite human proportions was Charles's glaring lack of interpersonal skills. Society prizes extroverts, but Charles unfortunately was an introvert. He was painfully uncomfortable in public settings. His speeches to Parliament were notoriously brief. His control, reserve, and self-discipline prevented other people from seeing any softer and more vulnerable side of his personality. To most people he merely appeared to be remote, aloof, imperious. By contrast it is touching to remember how Charles delighted in the company of the queen, how she managed to draw him out and even get him to participate in court masques. The queen wonderfully complemented Charles in this respect, but of course she also encouraged him to be more sympathetic toward Roman Catholicism, which carried a high political cost. Charles's love for Henrietta Maria thus made him a fuller human being and at the same time helped lead to his ruin. There is a real sadness in the fact that he could have such a loving relationship with his wife and fail so completely to establish any warm relationships outside his marriage. If he could have allowed others to see him the way she saw him, especially the way she must have seen him in his grief-stricken state in the summer of 1628 after Buckingham's assassination, then perhaps others would have empathised more with him. Of course this did happen belatedly during the Civil War when people at last saw him in more pitiable circumstances and admired him more for it. It was only in his suffering that other people witnessed his humanity. Through most of his reign, however, Charles succeeded too well in hiding his emotions.

Of course Charles did not hide all his emotions. People who dealt with him could see all too well the anger simmering beneath the surface. Charles was just plain scary. His barely concealed hostility was probably related to his obsession with order and control. Although historians appreciate how important order was to Charles, they have not gone very far in analysing how his behaviour was typical of a controlling personality. Charles exercised enormous self-control and tried to control his external surroundings with the same rigour. People who need control do best under conditions of routine and predictability. They like to make plans, and they want things to go according to those plans. They are not well equipped to handle unexpected changes or problems. That could help to explain why Charles was so quick to anger, so hard to advise, and why, as Glenn Burgess perceptively observed, he was so *impatient* with the political process, especially in the face of adversity.[7] Charles could not laugh in the face of adversity, shrug off his difficulties, and make light of the situation. There was a deadly earnestness about him; he had practically no sense of humour. He lacked flexibility and overreacted when things did not go his way. Given a bad situation, he usually managed to make it worse. This was not a matter of stupidity; it was a function of his temperament. Indeed, looked at this way it was actually smart of Charles to rule without Parliament for 11 years because it allowed him to enjoy maximum control and to avoid circumstances that were bound to bring out the worst in him.

Charles was a man of ordinary intelligence. He was not an intellectual like his father. He did not like dealing with contradictions and took no pleasure in debating (though he proved a good debater when forced into it). Part of the attraction of Arminianism or Laudianism for Charles must have been the comforting refuge of indisputable authority and routine ceremony it provided. As Charles saw it, people should prefer simple awesome authority – in church and state – over noisy and divisive controversy. Charles could not have comprehended the premise of modern liberal societies that somehow the product of free debate among the mass of people will amount to wisdom.

Charles genuinely longed for an incorruptible world of pure ideals. He had no taste for the nitty-gritty world where theories are tested by practice and even the best ideals must sometimes be compromised. Moments before he died he is supposed to have said, 'I go from a corruptible to an incorruptible Crown, where no disturbance can be, no disturbance in the world.'[8] Charles saw himself as a highly principled man (a view shared by Kevin Sharpe), but critics were more disturbed by the king's apparent inability to see how his own actions were incongruent with the high principles he claimed to respect. Recent historians of early Stuart politics have emphasised the extent to which there was a large body of widely shared assumptions among Charles and his contemporaries. The degree of this consensus can be (and has been) disputed, but Charles did certainly pay lip-service to many of the very same general ideals espoused by his critics. What he did not see – what his mentality was not prepared to grasp – was the relationship between word and deed. Too often Charles did not *act* as if he subscribed to the same body of widely shared assumptions, specifically where the limits of the royal prerogative were concerned. In these instances, his actions simply did not square with his reassuring professions. His speech at the end of the Short Parliament is an excellent example. For three weeks MPs bitterly complained about the exploitative revenue measures of the personal rule, but in his speech at the dissolution Charles continued to portray himself as the guardian of his subjects' property rights. Judged by what he said, he did not comprehend that his actions

were widely interpreted as having violated those very rights. Could
he have been that blind? Of course cynics would say that he knew
better but was simply striking a pose for political purposes. Charles's
constant denials struck many of his contemporaries and many
modern historians as little better than outright lies. It is possible,
however, that the real problem was he was lying to himself.

   There is widespread agreement that Charles peculiarly failed in
his capacity as king. In Reeve's words, Charles was 'fundamentally
unsuited to the task of kingship', and 'as a reigning monarch he was
woefully inadequate'.[9] In Russell's words, he was 'unfit to be a
king'.[10] Yet Charles brought a very high sense of purpose and dedica-
tion to the monarchy. He put great stock in being a king and tried
extremely hard to fulfil the role. What, then, made him peculiarly
unsuited or unfit? The problem seems to lie in his lack of political
aptitude. Charles was certainly no politician. On the other hand, the
kingship was not an elective office and political acumen was not a
prerequisite. Perhaps, then, the problem lay not so much with
Charles alone but with the fit between the monarchy and the people
at the time when he happened to come to the throne. For one thing,
Charles was far more tolerant of Roman Catholicism than his subjects were. The realisation that the Civil War was the last of Europe's
religious wars could have led to the conclusion that the problem lay
with the self-righteous zeal and ugly religious hatreds of Charles's
subjects, but the tendency instead has been to blame Charles
because he mismanaged these volatile forces. For another thing,
Charles and many of his subjects did not see political reality the
same way. Of course Charles was often unrealistic by anyone's standards, but it is worth remembering that reality is also mediated
through the minds of the people perceiving it. If Charles consistently failed to see political reality, perhaps it was because political
reality was changing. Many of Charles's subjects no longer operated
on the subservient, deferential, hierarchical assumptions that still informed the king's view of the political process. Historians sometimes
claim that Charles was heading toward continental absolutism. It
may be more instructive to think of him as clinging to the past. In his
view of the relationship between a king and his subjects, Charles had
a medieval mentality while increasing numbers of his subjects had
early modern mentalities. It is far more difficult to chart the history
of mentalities than to trace the financial fortunes of the gentry or
business affiliations in the City of London. Yet intellectual and cultural historians have had much to say about changes in mentality

during this period, and when political historians make more effort to incorporate this scholarship into their political narratives, they will better understand the incongruity that developed between Charles and his people.[11] It is true that Charles had serious deficiencies, but as Thomas Cogswell recently cautioned, 'it is worth considering whether the culprit was the declining quality of royal leadership or a rapidly changing political universe'.[12] When we know more about that broader political universe within which Charles operated, we will be in a better position to understand why people reacted to him the way they did. In other words, it is too easy to say that Charles was unsuited to be king. The more difficult question is why had his subjects become so unsuited to be subjects.

To put the question another way, was Charles wrong? Again and again he warned that monarchy was being undermined by a handful of extremists in the House of Commons and Puritans in the country at large. Historians respond by suggesting that Charles was paranoid. Considering the fact that he got his head chopped off, it is at least a little odd to accuse him of being paranoid. Surely those were not imaginary enemies who wielded the axe. Nor is it consistent for historians to scoff at the king's complaint that Parliament was being misled by a handful of malcontents in the 1620s when they themselves believe that Parliament was dominated in the 1640s by 'Pym's junto'. The usual way to reconcile the king's alleged paranoia in the earlier part of his reign with real rebellion and execution at the end is to say that the king's irrational fears had become a 'self-fulfilling prophecy'. It may also be, however, that Charles was more perceptive than the historians who write about him. Granted that he exaggerated the immediacy and extent of the threat, that he made matters worse by overreacting and drawing out the very philosophical differences he had most to fear, could he nevertheless have been right in his basic impression that monarchy was being undermined in the early Stuart period? It was once wisely said of the French Revolution that it was accomplished in the minds of people before they made it the work of their hands. Much recent work on British history rejects ideological explanations and assumes the contrary – that minds remained static in England until the Civil War forced people towards more revolutionary ideas. On the other hand, many other British historians – old Whig historians, scholars of Puritanism, and recent cultural historians – have discerned subversive and corrosive ideas ebbing into the minds of the British people before the Civil War. When we know who is right about this underlying question, we will then be in a better position to judge whether Charles's reading of the situation was paranoid or prescient.

To understand Charles, to give him credit for his virtues, and to take his ideas seriously is not the same as excusing him. In the end, his faults prevailed and the blame must be his. Two qualities in his nature were especially decisive. One was his combativeness. As Russell wrote, Charles was 'a king who invited resistance in all of his three kingdoms, and got what he was asking for'.[13] Charles was too eager to throw down the gauntlet, to convert simple arguments about limited issues into broader challenges against his authority. He bristled at dissent. When his will was thwarted, his goal was to force people into submission, not to reach a mutual accommodation. From beginning to end, he was *Rex Bellicosus*. The second decisive quality in Charles's nature was his untrustworthiness. For a person who tended to provoke fights, it was doubly unfortunate that he could not be trusted to honour the terms of reconciliation. People who extracted political concessions from him had good reason to doubt that he would honour those concessions and good reason to fear he would retaliate personally against them. Although Charles often invoked 'the word of a king', his subsequent actions made the phrase worthless. Time and again he tried to couch his concessions in ambiguous terms that could be evaded or misconstrued afterwards. Time and again he proved that he could not be trusted to respect any settlement he entered into if someday he became sufficiently powerful to renege. This was the fundamental, unforgivable defect in Charles's character that in the end made his execution necessary. It was truly his fatal flaw.

NOTES AND REFERENCES

Introduction

1. C. V. Wedgwood, *A Coffin for King Charles: The Trial and Execution of Charles I* (New York, 1964), pp. 128, 152, 181; S. R. Gardiner (ed.), *Constitutional Documents of the Puritan Revolution 1625–1660*, 3rd edn revised (Oxford, 1906), p. 380.
2. S. R. Gardiner, *History of England from the Accession of James I to the Outbreak of the Civil War, 1603–1642* (10 vols, London, 1883–4, 1894–6), V, 317–19, 379, 434; VI, 321, 328–9, 360, 376; VII, 352–3; X, 129, 136; *History of the Great Civil War* (4 vols, London, 1901–4, revised edn), IV, 326–8.
3. Christopher Hill, *The English Revolution 1640*, 3rd edn (London, 1985), p. 11. See also pp. 65–7.
4. See, for example, 'Recent Interpretations of the Civil War', in Christopher Hill, *Puritanism and Revolution: The English Revolution of the 17th Century* (New York, 1964), pp. 3–31. See also pp. VII–VIII.
5. Christopher Hill, *The Century of Revolution 1603–1714*, 2nd edn (New York, 1980), pp. 61–2.
6. Tim Harris and Christopher Husbands, 'Talking with Christopher Hill: Part II', in Geoff Eley and William Hunt (eds), *Reviving the English Revolution: Reflections and Elaborations on the Work of Christopher Hill* (London, 1988), p. 344.
7. Lawrence Stone, *The Causes of the English Revolution 1529–1642* (New York, 1972), pp. 48, 56, 71–2, 133, 137, 138. A new chapter entitled 'Second Thoughts in 1985' was added to the 1986 editon. See page 171. Stone has also written, 'Hill and I are thus now in agreement that the English Revolution was not caused by a clear conflict between feudal and bourgeois ideologies and classes'. 'The Bourgeois Revolution of Seventeenth-Century England Revisited', in Eley and Hunt, *Reviving the English Revolution*, p. 287. One of Stone's students, Robert Brenner, has recently breathed new life into the socio-economic explanation with *Merchants and Revolution: Commercial Change, Political Conflict, and London's Overseas Traders, 1550–1650* (Princeton, NJ, 1993).
8. Alan Everitt, 'The County Community' in E. W. Ives (ed.), *The English Revolution* (London, 1968), pp. 48, 62. See also his *The Community of Kent and the Great Rebellion 1640–1660* (Leicester, 1966), pp. 56–69.
9. Thomas Barnes, *Somerset 1625–1640: A County's Government During the 'Personal Rule'* (Cambridge, MA, 1961), p. 143.
10. For other examples, see J. T. Cliffe, *The Yorkshire Gentry from the Reformation to the Civil War* (London, 1969), pp. 282–335 and Anthony Fletcher, *A County Community in Peace and War: Sussex 1600–1660* (London, 1975). Fletcher especially goes out of his way to avoid criticising Charles, preferring instead to blame an amorphous 'Caroline government' or 'the Council' for the unrealistic and insensitive demands made on local governors. John Morrill, *The Revolt of the Provinces: Conservatives and Radicals in the English Civil War 1630–1650* (London, 1976), pp. 24–31.

11. For a recent survey and analysis of the movement, see Glenn Burgess, 'On Revisionism: An Analysis of Early Stuart Historiography in the 1970s and 1980s', *Historical Journal*, 33, no. 3 (1990), 609–27. For a spirited denial that there has been any revisionist movement, see Mark Kishlansky, 'Symposium: Revolution and Revisionism', *Parliamentary History*, 7, pt. 2 (1988), 330–2.

12. Glenn Burgess claimed that revisionism 'began as a reaction against Marxist, structural and sociological attempts to write the social history of politics'. This is a common but, I think, mistaken impression. The Marxist-sociological approach to early Stuart politics had failed so abysmally before the 1970s that it hardly needed to be revised. The only sociological approach that revisionists explicitly attacked was Perez Zagorin's version of the court versus the country. It is true that revisionists shifted the emphasis from long-term to short-term causes of the English Civil War, but here I think their concern was not to counter Marxist or sociological interpretations as much as to counter the Whig tradition that interpreted the whole early Stuart period as an escalating series of constitutional conflicts, marked by milestones along the way like the Petition of Right, and culminating in the Civil War. If one looks at what revisionists actually said, it was this Whig interpretation, not Marxist or other socio-economic interpretations, that they were chiefly concerned to refute. Revisionists could have dispelled much of this confusion if they had been more precise about which of their predecessors were allegedly at fault or which prior accounts they wished to revise. Often they referred simply to the 'Whig tradition' or 'what every schoolboy knows'. In any case, it is this kind of revisionism (what Burgess calls 'revisionism as a form of anti-whig history') that had most bearing on the reputation of King Charles and is therefore of most concern to us. Burgess, 'On Revisionism', pp. 612, 614.

13. Three of Elton's seminal essays were 'Studying the History of Parliament', 'The Stuart Century', and 'A High Road to Civil War?' These have been printed together in volume II of *Studies in Tudor and Stuart Politics and Government: Papers and Reviews 1946–1972* (2 vols, Cambridge, 1974). My quotations come from 'The Stuart Century', pp. 160–1. 'Studying the History of Parliament' provoked an exchange with J. H. Hexter in *British Studies Monitor*, 3, no. 1 (Fall 1972), 4–22.

14. Conrad Russell, 'Parliamentary History in Perspective, 1604–1629', *History*, 61 (1976), 25, 14, 6, 17, 26. Russell said Parliament was 'heading for extinction' (p. 6). Compare Thomas Cogswell, 'A Low Road to Extinction? Supply and Redress of Grievances in the Parliaments of the 1620s', *Historical Journal*, 33, no. 2 (1990), 283–303.

15. Conrad Russell, *Parliaments and English Politics 1621–1629* (Oxford, 1979), p. 423. In an earlier work Russell had emphasised the difficult circumstances faced by Charles, especially the inadequate financial resources of the Crown, but he took a dimmer view of Charles. Conrad Russell (ed.), *The Origins of the English Civil War* (London, 1973). See Russell's introduction, pp. 1–34, and the chapter he contributed to this volume entitled 'Parliament and the King's Finances', pp. 91–118.

16. J. N. Ball, 'Sir John Eliot and Parliament, 1624-1629', in Kevin Sharpe (ed.), *Faction and Parliament: Essays on Early Stuart History* (Oxford, 1978), p. 204.

17. Anthony Fletcher, *The Outbreak of the English Civil War* (New York, 1981), pp. xxx, 408. For Pym in the 1620s see Conrad Russell, 'The Parliamentary Career of John Pym, 1621-9', in Peter Clark, Alan G. R. Smith, and Nicholas Tyacke (eds), *The English Commonwealth 1547–1640: Essays in Politics and Society Presented to Joel Hurstfield* (Leicester, 1979), pp. 147–165. While Fletcher and Russell emphasised Pym's obsession with religious issues, Perez Zagorin has argued that he was no less concerned with political and constitutional issues. Zagorin, 'The Political Beliefs of John Pym to 1629', *English Historical Review*, 109, no. 433 (Sept. 1994), 867–90. See also John Morrill, 'The Unweariableness of Mr Pym: Influence and

Eloquence in the Long Parliament', in Susan Amussen and Mark Kishlansky (eds), *Political Culture and Cultural Politics in Early Modern England: Essays Presented to David Underdown* (Manchester, 1995), pp. 19–54.

18. The most elaborate exposition of this position was in the opening chapter of Russell's *Parliaments*. Derek Hirst summarised the literature on this issue and attempted to rebut it in 'The Place of Principle', *Past and Present*, 92 (August 1981), 79–99. J. H. Hexter saw the elimination of principle and constitutional issues as the 'Namierization' of seventeenth-century politics. He charged that 'the current reflex among English historians is to shrink from anything that looks like a big idea'. *Times Literary Supplement*, 21 January 1983, pp. 51–4. For a defiantly heroic treatment of one MP under Charles, see Robert Zaller, 'Edward Alford and the Making of Country Radicalism', *Journal of British Studies*, 22 (Spring 1983), 59–79.

19. Kevin Sharpe, 'Faction at the Early Stuart Court', *History Today*, 33 (Oct. 1983), 43; Kevin Sharpe, 'Crown, Parliament and Locality: Government and Communication in Early Stuart England', *English Historical Review*, 101 (April 1986), 321–50; Linda Peck, '"For a King not to be bountiful were a fault": Perspectives on Court Patronage in Early Stuart England', *Journal of British Studies*, 25 (Jan. 1986), 51–8.

20. These themes were repeatedly emphasised by Russell. On the alleged localism of the country gentry, see Sharpe, 'Crown, Parliament and Locality'; Clive Holmes, 'The County Community in Stuart Historiography', *Journal of British Studies*, 19 (1980), 54–73; and Anthony Fletcher, 'National and Local Awareness in the County Communities', in Howard Tomlinson (ed.), *Before the English Civil War: Essays on Early Stuart Politics and Government* (London, 1983), 151–74.

21. Russell, *Parliaments*, p. 414.

22. Sharpe, *Faction and Parliament*, p. 42.

23. J. P. Kenyon, *Stuart England* (Harmondsworth, 1978), pp. 44–6, 84–5, 97, 107. Referring to the earlier 'Addled Parliament' of James I's reign, Kenyon called it 'childish, hysterical, and downright vicious'. In his later, revised edition of documentary sources for the Stuart period, Kenyon continued these themes. Parliament behaved with 'customary foolishness and narrow-mindedness at times', and the king's imprisonment of Eliot 'was not so outrageous as all that'. J. P. Kenyon, *The Stuart Constitution 1603–1688: Documents and Commentary*, 2nd edn (Cambridge, 1986), pp. 22, 24.

24. *Times Literary Supplement*, 16 September 1983, p. 990.

25. Russell pioneered this theme in his article on 'Parliamentary History in Perspective'. The most formidable contributions on this point came from Mark Kishlansky, first in his article 'The Emergence of Adversary Politics in the Long Parliament', *Journal of Modern History*, 49 (Dec. 1977), 617–40, and later in his book *Parliamentary Selection: Social and Political Choice in Early Modern England* (Cambridge, 1986).

26. Russell, 'Parliamentary History in Perspective', pp. 3–4, 18–22; *Parliaments and English Politics*, pp. 4–26.

27. The most ambitious statement of this theory is Perez Zagorin, *The Court and the Country: The Beginnings of the English Revolution* (New York, 1971). For a review of the controversy, see Dwight D. Brautigam, '*The Court and the Country* Revisited', in *Court, Country and Culture: Essays on Early Modern British History in Honor of Perez Zagorin*, ed. Bonnelyn Young Kunze and Dwight D. Brautigam (Rochester, NY, 1992), pp. 55–64. See also Morrill, *Revolt of the Provinces*, pp. 14–22; Kevin Sharpe, *Criticism and Compliment: The Politics of Literature in the England of Charles I* (Cambridge, 1987), pp. 11–22; P. W. Thomas, 'Two Cultures? Court and Country Under Charles I', in Russell, *Origins*, pp. 168–93; Derek Hirst, 'Court, Country, and Politics before 1629', in *Faction and Parliament: Essays on Early Stuart History* ed. Kevin Sharpe (Oxford, 1978), pp. 105–38.

28. Russell, 'Parliamentary History in Perspective', p. 4; Russell, *Parliaments and English Politics*, pp. 6, 427. But see also Perez Zagorin, 'Did Strafford Change Sides?' *English Historical Review*, 101 (January 1986), 149–63.

29. Russell, *Parliaments and English Politics*, pp. 22–3.

30. Roger Lockyer, *Buckingham: The Life and Political Career of George Villiers, First Duke of Buckingham 1592–1628* (London, 1981), pp. 269, 474. For an alternative view, see Michael B. Young, 'Buckingham, War, and Parliament: Revisionism Gone Too Far', *Parliamentary History Yearbook*, 4 (1985), 45–69.

31. Roy Strong, *Van Dyck: Charles I on Horseback* (New York, 1972); Stephen Orgel, *The Illusion of Power* (Berkeley, CA, 1975); R. Malcolm Smuts, *Court Culture and the Origins of a Royalist Tradition in Early Stuart England* (Philadephia, 1987).

32. Martin J. Havran, 'The Character and Principles of an English King: The Case of Charles I', *The Catholic Historical Review*, 69 (April 1983), 169–208.

33. Kevin Sharpe, 'The Personal Rule of Charles I', in Tomlinson, *Before the English Civil War*, pp. 53–78 and 'The Image of Virtue: the Court and Household of Charles I, 1625–1642', in David Starkey (ed.), *The English Court from the Wars of the Roses to the Civil War*, pp. 226–60. Both these essays are now available in a collection of Sharpe's works entitled *Politics and Ideas in Early Stuart England* (London, 1989). I discuss Sharpe's book below.

34. William Hunt, *The Puritan Moment: The Coming of Revolution in an English County* (Cambridge, MA, 1983) and Ann Hughes, *Politics, Society and Civil War: Warwickshire 1620–1660* (Cambridge, 1987).

35. Richard Cust, *The Forced Loan and English Politics* (Oxford, 1987).

36. L. J. Reeve, *Charles I and the Road to Personal Rule* (Cambridge, 1989).

37. Richard Cust and Ann Hughes (eds), *Conflict in Early Stuart England: Studies in Religion and Politics 1603–1642* (London, 1989).

38. Ibid., p. 187.

39. Caroline Hibbard, *Charles I and the Popish Plot* (Chapel Hill, NC, 1983); Nicholas Tyacke, *Anti-Calvinists: The Rise of English Arminianism c.1590–1640* (Oxford, 1987); Julian Davies, *The Caroline Captivity of the Church* (Oxford, 1992).

40. Allan I. Macinnes, *Charles I and the Making of the Covenanting Movement 1625–1641* (Edinburgh, 1991), pp. 1, 129.

41. Peter Donald, *An Uncounselled King: Charles I and the Scottish Troubles, 1637–41* (Cambridge, 1990), p. 322. See also David Stevenson, *The Scottish Revolution 1637–1644: The Triumph of the Covenanters* (New York, 1973) and Maurice Lee, Jr, *The Road to Revolution: Scotland Under Charles I, 1625–37* (Urbana, IL, 1985).

42. J. P. Sommerville, *Politics and Ideology in England 1603–1640* (London, 1986), pp. 140 and especially 231–8.

43. John Morrill, 'What Was the English Revolution?' *History Today*, 34 (March 1984), 12. See also Morrill's collected essays in *The Nature of the English Revolution* (London, 1993).

44. Conrad Russell, 'Why Did Charles I Call the Long Parliament?' *History*, 69, no. 227 (Oct. 1984), 375–83; 'Why Did Charles I Fight the Civil War?' *History Today*, 34 (June 1984), 31–4; 'The British Problem and the English Civil War' *History*, 72 (1987), 395–415; 'The First Army Plot of 1641', *Transactions of the Royal Historical Society*, fifth series, 38 (1988), 85–106. Russell took a more favourable view of Charles in 'Charles I's Financial Estimates for 1642', *Bulletin of the Institute for Historical Research*, 58, no. 137 (May 1985), 109–20 and 'The British Background to the Irish Rebellion of 1641', *Historical Research*, 61, no. 145 (June 1988), 166–82. Most of these articles have been reprinted in *Unrevolutionary England, 1603–1642* (London, 1990).

45. Conrad Russell, *The Causes of the English Civil War* (Oxford, 1990) and *The Fall of the British Monarchies* (Oxford, 1991). We shall, of course, examine Russell's portrait of Charles in these works in detail later. The reader can find Russell's views on Charles summarised in chapter 8 of *Causes*.

46. Russell, *Causes*, pp. 11–25, 211.
47. Kevin Sharpe, *The Personal Rule of Charles I* (New Haven, CT, 1992), p. 954.
48. There are two solid and readable modern biographies of Charles: Pauline Gregg, *King Charles I* (Berkeley, CA, 1981) and Charles Carlton, *Charles I: The Personal Monarch* (London, 1983). The second edition of Carlton's biography, published in 1995, has a new preface briefly summarising recent scholarship.

1 Prior Committments

1. Kevin Sharpe, 'The Image of Virtue: The Court and Household of Charles I, 1625–1642', in David Starkey (ed.), *The English Court from the Wars of the Roses to the Civil War* (London, 1987), p. 227; Thomas Cogswell, *The Blessed Revolution: English Politics and the Coming of War, 1621–1624* (Cambridge, 1989), p. 62.
2. Maurice Ashley, *The House of Stuart: Its Rise and Fall* (London, 1980), p. 116. Similarly, see David Willson, *King James VI and I* (Oxford, 1956), p. 95. A welcome corrective to this standard view is provided by Leeds Barroll, 'The Court of the First Stuart Queen', in *The Mental World of the Jacobean Court*, ed. Linda Levy Peck (Cambridge, 1991), pp. 191–208.
3. This is one of the points emphasised by David M. Bergeron, who examines the royal family with insight and sympathy, though traditional historians have been unimpressed. See his *Shakespeare's Romances and the Royal Family* (Lawrence, KA, 1985) and *Royal Family, Royal Lovers: King James of England and Scotland* (Columbia, MO, 1991).
4. Roy Strong, *Henry, Prince of Wales and England's Lost Renaissance* (New York, 1986), p. 14.
5. Philip Yorke, second Earl of Hardwicke (ed.), *Miscellaneous State Papers from 1501 to 1726* (London, 1778), I, 461–2.
6. Ibid., I, 460.
7. Carlton further speculated that Charles 'employed a substitute elder brother to resolve an oedipal conflict'. Carlton, *Royal Childhoods* (London, 1986), pp. 82, 90; Carlton, *Charles I: The Personal Monarch*, 2nd edn (London, 1995), pp. 12, 14, 29.
8. Kevin Sharpe, *The Personal Rule of Charles I* (New Haven, CT, 1992), p. 5.
9. Roger Lockyer, *Buckingham: The Life and Political Career of George Villiers, First Duke of Buckingham 1592–1628* (London, 1981), p. 34.
10. Carlton, *Royal Childhoods*, p. 78, citing William Laud, *Works*, ed. W. Scot and J. Bliss (Oxford, 1847–60), III, 147.
11. L. J. Reeve, *Charles I and the Road to Personal Rule* (Cambridge, 1989), p. 103.
12. Cogswell, *Blessed Revolution*, p. 63, citing Godfrey Goodman, *The Court of King James the First* (London, 1839), I, 382.
13. Maija Jansson and William B. Bidwell (eds), *Proceedings in Parliament 1625* (New Haven, CT, 1987), p. 219.
14. Charles Petrie (ed.), *The Letters, Speeches, and Proclamations of King Charles I* (London, 1968), p. 6. The questionable dating of this letter makes it impossible to know for certain which events in the Commons were referred to by Charles. See Robert E. Ruigh, *The Parliament of 1624* (Cambridge, MA, 1971), p. 12 n. 18 and Conrad Russell, *Parliaments and English Politics, 1621–1629* (Oxford, 1979), p. 137 n. 2. Charles was one of the less forgiving persons in the House of Lords regarding the Commons' conduct in the case of Edward Floyd. Robert Zaller, *The Parliament of 1621: A Study in Constitutional Conflict* (Berkeley, CA, 1971), p. 112.
15. Petrie, *Letters*, p. 6.

16. Lockyer, *Buckingham*, p. 168.
17. Cogswell, *Blessed Revolution*, pp. 66–76.
18. In Simon Adams's words: 'Hostilities with Spain and a new bride for Charles were, therefore, essential; only when war was declared and Charles married would he be really safe.' Simon Adams, 'Foreign Policy and the Parliaments of 1621 and 1624', in *Faction and Parliament: Essays on Early Stuart History*, ed. Kevin Sharpe (Oxford, 1978), p. 155.
19. *Cabala Sive Scrinia Sacra* (London, 1654), I, 289. I have modernised spelling.
20. Allen B. Hinds (ed.), *Calendar of State Papers and Manuscripts, Relating to English Affairs, Existing in the Archives and Collections of Venice* (London, 1912), XVIII, 115. Hereafter *CSPV*.
21. S. R. Gardiner, *History of England from the Accession of James I to the Outbreak of the Civil War, 1603–1642* (10 vols, London, 1883–4, 1894–6), V, 130, 180, 194; Lockyer, *Buckingham*, p. 192. When a fleet was despatched to assault Spain in late 1625, one contemporary wrote that Buckingham sent it 'as revenge to Olivares who put a trick upon him when he was in Spain'. Anonymous diary, MS. 0.7.3, fol. 3v, Trinity College, Cambridge.
22. *CSPV*, XVIII, 134.
23. Gardiner, *History*, V, 173.
24. Ruigh, *The Parliament of 1624*, p. 14.
25. Simon Adams, 'Spain or the Netherlands? Dilemmas of Early Stuart Foreign Policy', in Howard Tomlinson (ed.), *Before the English Civil War: Essays in Early Stuart Politics and Government* (London, 1983), p. 97.
26. Kevin Sharpe, 'The Personal Rule of Charles I', in Tomlinson, *Before the English Civil War*, pp. 54–5.
27. Tomlinson, *Before the English Civil War*, p. 2.
28. John Morrill, 'The Stuarts (1603–1688)', in Kenneth O. Morgan (ed.), *The Oxford History of Britain* (Oxford, 1988), p. 354.
29. The enthusiasm of the Lords for war can be seen running throughout S. R. Gardiner (ed.), *Notes of the Debates in the House of Lords ... 1624 and 1626* (London, 1879).
30. Russell, *Parliaments*, pp. 164, 172, 174, 190, 78, 82.
31. Cogswell, *Blessed Revolution*, pp. 137, 146–7, 188, 207, 225, 266, 310–12.
32. Russell made a brief rebuttal to Cogswell in 'Issues in the House of Commons, 1621–1629: Predictors of Civil War Allegiance', *Albion*, 23 (Spring 1991), 31–4. Other treatments of the Parliament of 1624 are Robert E. Ruigh's *Parliament of 1624*, cited above, and Mark E. Kennedy, 'Legislation, Foreign Policy, and the "Proper Business" of the Parliament of 1624', *Albion*, 23 (Spring 1991), 41–60.
33. Robert Zaller, 'Edward Alford and the Making of Country Radicalism', *Journal of British Studies*, 22, no. 2 (Spring 1983), 63.
34. My quotations from the parliamentary diaries of 1624 are taken from the transcripts at the Yale Center for Parliamentary History. This quote comes from the Nicholas diary, fol. 69v. When these diaries are eventually published, readers will be in a better position to judge for themselves whether Russell or Cogswell has interpreted them more correctly.
35. Norman McClure (ed.), *The Letters of John Chamberlain* (Philadelphia, 1939), II, 548–9.
36. Cogswell, *Blessed Revolution*, p. 191. Cogswell observes that 'Sandys's volte-face was almost total'.
37. *Journals of the House of Commons* [*CJ*], I, 682, 733; Spring diary, p. 144.
38. Spring diary, p. 88.
39. *Journals of the House of Lords* [*LJ*], III, 275.
40. Cogswell, 'War and the Liberties of the Subject', in J. H. Hexter (ed.), *Parliament and Liberty from the Reign of Elizabeth to the English Civil War* (Stanford, CA, 1992), pp. 233–4; Cogswell, *Blessed Revolution*, pp. 222–5, 311.

41. London, Public Record Office, State Papers Domestic, Charles I, SP 16/1/58. Thomas Rymer, *Foedera*, 3rd edn (10 vols, London, 1737–45), VIII, pt. 1, pp. 18–19.
42. Spring diary, p. 142.
43. The text of the subsidy act is readily accessible in J. P. Kenyon, *The Stuart Constitution 1603–1688: Documents and Commentary*, 2nd edn (Cambridge, 1986), pp. 64–7. The four points were framed by Sir Benjamin Rudyerd. Since he was one of the most ardent advocates of war in the Commons, he presumably construed them as a mandate for war; and he did indeed tell later Parliaments that they were obligated to finance the Crown's military enterprises because of the promise in the 1624 Subsidy Act. However, Rudyerd conveniently ignored all the surrounding language regarding the contingency of war. In later Parliaments, Rudyerd found himself in a quickly shrinking minority. Most other MPs who sat in later Parliaments did not think they had voted for what they got. Historians do not agree on whether Rudyerd was part of the coalition put together by Charles and Buckingham. Compare Cogswell, *Blessed Revolution*, pp. 154–6; Russell, 'Parliamentary History in Perspective, 1604–1629', *History*, 61 (1977), 8; and Adams, 'Foreign Policy', pp. 143, 156, 165–6.
44. Russell belittles the constitutional significance of this concession. Cogswell supports the traditional view that this was a significant constitutional innovation. On this point Cogswell is right. Russell, *Parliaments*, pp. 177–8; Cogswell, *Blessed Revolution*, pp. 221–2.
45. *LJ*, III, 283.
46. Earle diary, fol. 95v.
47. Adams, 'Spain or the Netherlands? p. 99.
48. Pym diary, fol. 34. Seymour's speech apparently touched a responsive chord with the parliamentary diarists of the time, nearly everyone of whom recorded it. Earle diary, fol. 95v: 'His Majesty hath told us plainly that it is the Palatinate the war shall be for, which if it be so, the difficulties will be so great as it will not be unworthy the consideration of this House.' Nicholas diary, fol. 91v: 'He would be glad to know where and with whom the war shall be. That he thinketh a war in the Palatinate is not worthy our consideration.' Spring diary, p. 128: 'War is spoken of and an army, but where and against whom is fit to be known; if in the Palatinate (as the King seems to imply) the charge is too great, and it hath been far from our thoughts, but we must leave that to the King.'
49. Spring diary, p. 141.
50. *LJ*, III, 283.
51. Earle diary, fols. 184–184v.
52. London, Public Record Office, State Papers Domestic, James I. SP 14/164/91, 92; 14/167/10.
53. Gardiner, *History*, V, 235. John Chamberlain similarly recorded at the close of Parliament: 'The parting were with no more contentment than needed on either side.' Thomas Birch (ed.), *The Court and Times of James the First* (London, 1849), II, 457; McClure, *Chamberlain Letters*, II, 561.
54. Lockyer, *Buckingham*, p. 183.
55. Adams, 'Foreign Policy', pp. 157–9. Adams does allow that the French alliance and marriage may have been insisted upon by James. In another work, Adams was more inclined to excuse Buckingham and attribute this policy to James. See Adams, 'Spain or the Netherlands?', pp. 97–8. It is debatable whether Mansfeld's army was an improper use of the subsidy money. I agree with Simon Adams that it was. See Michael B.Young, 'Revisionism and the Council of War, 1624-1626', *Parliamentary History*, 8, pt. 1 (1989), 1–27. Cogswell disagrees. See his *Blessed Revolution*, p. 223.
56. Cogswell, *Blessed Revolution*, pp. 69–76.
57. Russell, *Parliaments*, p. 422.

58. Most of this fascinating correspondence among the Harleian MSS in the British Library was printed in Hardwicke, *Miscellaneous State Papers*, I, 399–472 and James Orchard Halliwell (ed.), *Letters of the Kings of England* (London, 1848), II, 162–229.

59. *Ibid.*, I, 410.

60. *Ibid.*, I, 420.

61. See, for example, Cogswell, *Blessed Revolution*, pp. 148, 194, 197–8.

62. Earle diary, fol. 33v.

63. Birch, *Court and Times*, II, 450, 453; McClure, *Chamberlain Letters*, II, 546, 550.

64. Earle's diary, fol. 43v. In the words of the *Commons Journal* (1:725), Charles 'bid him [James] think no more of him (for he lost) but desire him to reflect his Royal Thoughts on his Sister, and her Children'. See also SP 14/160/33.

65. Nicholas diary, fols. 72–72v.

66. Edward Hyde, Earl of Clarendon, *The History of the Rebellion and Civil Wars in England*, ed. W. Dunn Macray (Oxford, 1888), I, 28.

67. Historical Manuscripts Commission, *Supplementary Report on the Manuscripts of the Earl of Mar & Kellie* (London, 1930), pp. 200–3. I have modernised the spelling.

68. Lockyer, *Buckingham*, p. 188.

69. Birch, *Court and Times*, II, 464, 482–3; McClure, *Chamberlain Letters*, II, 568, 584.

2   A Bad Start, 1625–1629

1. Blair Worden, 'Revising the Revolution', *The New York Review of Books*, 17 January 1991, p. 40.

2. G. A. Harrison, 'Innovation and Precedent: A Procedural Reappraisal of the 1625 Parliament', *English Historical Review*, 102, no. 402 (Jan. 1987), 58. In Harrison's view, 'Charles largely created, he did not inherit, his major problems' (p. 59).

3. Kevin Sharpe, 'Introduction: Parliamentary History 1603–1629: In or out of Perspective?' in Sharpe (ed.), *Faction and Parliament: Essays on Early Stuart History* (Oxford, 1978), pp. 38–9, 42.

4. Kevin Sharpe, 'Crown, Parliament and Locality: Government and Communication in Early Stuart England', *English Historical Review*, 101, no. 394 (April 1986), 339–40.

5. Conrad Russell, *Parliaments and English Politics, 1621–1629* (Oxford, 1979), pp. 64, 423. This latter sentence is an especially good example of Russell's rhetorical style. Even before war occurred, Russell tells us, the administration was in a state of functional breakdown, and then war was imposed, not by Charles but by the Duke of Buckingham, and this in turn increased friction between the centre and the localities, and that is what finally brought relations between king and Parliament to the point of collapse. Charles, relegated to the end of this sentence and referred to only impersonally, appears to be one of the effects rather than a cause of what went wrong.

6. Russell, *Parliaments*, pp. 237, 259, 422–3.

7. Conrad Russell, 'Monarchies, Wars, and Estates in England, France, and Spain, c.1580–1640', *Legislative Studies Quarterly*, 7, no. 2 (May 1982), 205–20.

8. *Ibid.*, pp. 214, 211. Russell does not explain how Charles's unprovoked assaults against Spain and France amounted to an urgent necessity of defence. Indeed, elsewhere Russell had observed that for England to become engaged in war simultaneously with Spain and France, far from being a necessity, was as absurd

'as if Britain should today find itself at war with Russia and the United States simultaneously'. Conrad Russell, 'Parliament and the King's Finances', in Russell (ed.), *The Origins of the English Civil War* (London, 1973), p. 104.

9. Russell, 'Monarchies', p. 211.
10. Russell, *Parliaments*, pp. 78, 172, 190. As noted in chapter 1, of course, Thomas Cogswell disputes Russell's interpretation of the 1624 Parliament.
11. There are several accounts of the 1625 Parliament to choose from. Russell's account in chapter 4 of *Parliaments* is full of insights but coloured by his determination to downplay constitutional issues and upset traditional assumptions. Christopher Thompson provides a useful corrective in 'Court Politics and Parliamentary Conflict in 1625', in Richard Cust and Ann Hughes (eds), *Conflict in Early Stuart England: Studies in Religion and Politics 1603–1642* (London, 1989), pp. 168–92. S. R. Gardiner's account holds up well. See his *History of England from the Accession of James I to the Outbreak of the Civil War, 1603–1642* (10 vols, London, 1883–4, 1894–6), V, 337–74, 397–435. To simplify the narrative, I have not distinguished between the two separate meetings of the 1625 Parliament. On this point see Harrison's 'Innovation and Precedent' cited above.
12. Russell wrote: 'This thesis, that Parliament was "engaged" to support the war, appears to have been Charles's real conviction, and was repeated by him with increasing exasperation as the decade continued.' *Parliaments*, p. 219.
13. Maija Jansson and William B. Bidwell (eds), *Proceedings in Parliament 1625* (New Haven, CT, 1987), pp. 28–30, 190–3, 492–3, 647–8.
14. Ibid., pp 161, 435.
15. Roger Lockyer, *Buckingham: The Life and Political Career of George Villiers, First Duke of Buckingham 1592–1628* (London, 1981), pp. 267, 315–16.
16. Kevin Sharpe, 'The Personal Rule of Charles I', in H. Tomlinson (ed.), *Before the English Civil War: Essays on Early Stuart Politics and Government* (London, 1983), p. 55. Tomlinson also faults Parliament for its 'reluctance to finance a war which it had advocated' (p. 2).
17. *1625 Proceedings*, pp. 28–9.
18. *Journals of the House of Lords*, III, 275.
19. J. P. Kenyon, *The Stuart Constitution: Documents and Commentary*, 2nd edn (Cambridge, 1986), p. 64.
20. *1625 Proceedings*, pp. 403, 658–9.
21. Robert Ruigh, *The Parliament of 1624* (Cambridge, MA, 1971), p. 383. Simon Adams likewise wrote: 'The war Charles and Buckingham had entered into was not that intended by parliament in 1624.' Simon Adams, 'Spain or the Netherlands? The Dilemmas of Early Stuart Foreign Policy', in Tomlinson, *Before the English Civil War*, p. 99.
22. See Michael B. Young, 'Revisionism and the Council of War', *Parliamentary History*, 8, no. 1 (1989), 1–27.
23. *1625 Proceedings*, pp. 190, 492.
24. Ibid., p. 278. For similar views from Sir Francis Seymour, Sir Simon Weston, Sir Edward Coke, and Sir Nathaniel Rich, see pp. 394, 393, 399, 413.
25. Ibid., pp. 166, 438.
26. Ibid., p. 407. For this debate over the alleged engagement, see also Sir John Eliot's *Negotium Posterorum* in ibid., pp. 546–8.
27. The cost of the fleet was not always reported correctly at the time, and Conrad Russell was led into a rare error on this point (*Parliaments*, p. 236). Sir John Coke's drafts of his speech to Parliament on this subject clearly show that the additional cost of the fleet was expected to be £293,000. SP 16/4/23, 24, 25. See also Michael B. Young, *Servility and Service: The Life and Work of Sir John Coke* (London, 1986), p. 142.
28. S. R. Gardiner (ed.), *Debates in the House of Commons in 1625* (London, 1873), p. vi.

29. Sir John Eliot and Sir Clement Throckmorton called it a 'pretended necessity'. Sir Robert Phelips observed that necessity was a perennial argument 'and one of those things which can never be satisfied'. Sir Francis Seymour was even more sceptical, suggesting that the 'causes of this necessity are more fit to be opened than the necessity itself'. Christopher Sherland charged that the necessity had 'come into the King's estate by a postern gate, and to have avoided it, those which gave this counsel might have spared their works of magnificence'. *1625 Proceedings*, pp. 416, 448, 450, 465, 474.

30. Ibid., pp. 133, 386, 389, 534.

31. The Earl of Kellie summed up debate on the issue this way: 'It was moved in the Parlament that noe man culd see to what good purpose this navye was keeped soe long and not sete furthe, and that their was lytill hope of doing onye good with it, the tyme of yeare being soe farr spent, and mutche more to this effekt.' Historical Manuscripts Commission, *Supplementary Report on the Manuscripts of the Earl of Mar & Kellie* (London, 1930), p. 232.

32. *1625 Proceedings*, p. 449.

33. Kevin Sharpe, *The Personal Rule of Charles I* (New Haven, CT, 1992), p. 8.

34. The seriousness of the piracy problem is easy to underestimate. For a good corrective, see David Hebb, *Piracy and the English Government 1616–1642* (Aldershot, 1994).

35. *1625 Proceedings*, p. 396.

36. Ibid., p. 156.

37. Against the background of these events, the Earl of Kellie observed, 'you can not beleive the alteratione that is in the opinione of the world tuiching his Majestie'. HMC, *Earl of Mar and Kellie*, p. 231.

38. For the prejudice against Roman Catholicism, see Robin Clifton, 'Fear of Popery', in Conrad Russell (ed.), *The Origins of the English Civil War* (London, 1973), pp. 144–67 and Peter Lake, 'Anti-popery: the Structure of a Prejudice', in Cust and Hughes, *Conflict*, pp. 72–106. For an appreciative appraisal of Charles on this score, see Martin J. Havran, 'The Character and Principles of an English King: The Case of Charles I', *Catholic Historical Review*, 69, no. 2 (April 1983), pp. 169–208.

39. *1625 Proceedings*, pp. 330 n. 3, 359, 379, 381–2.

40. For Buckingham's monopoly of patronage, see Linda Levy Peck, '"For a King not to be bountiful were a fault": Perspectives on Court Patronage in Early Stuart England', *Journal of British Studies*, 25 (Jan. 1986), 51–8.

41. *1625 Proceedings*, p. 403.

42. Ibid., p. 460.

43. Ibid., pp. 397, 449.

44. The Earl of Kellie reported the popular impression that Charles dissolved the Parliament of 1625 'out of a violent course he did find sattilled in their mynd for the overthrow of my Lord Bukkinghame, and that noe thing wold content them but that bye violence thaye warre resolved to pull him out of his Majesties breeste, and that he culd not endure.' HMC, *Earl of Mar and Kellie*, p. 232.

45. Sir John Eliot was probably not as alienated yet as these others. As J. N. Ball has written, however, his 'decision to move into open opposition certainly came before parliament met again in February 1626'. 'Sir John Eliot and Parliament' in Sharpe, *Faction and Parliament*, p. 178. For Williams see Gardiner, *History*, VI, 30–2.

46. Russell, *Parliaments*, p. 259.

47. Thompson, 'Court Politics', pp. 186–9.

48. *1625 Proceedings*, pp. 190–1, 493–4, 648, 653. The Lord Keeper continued, 'His Majesty puts his fame, his reputation (which is all he has of a king) upon us ... as soon as he shall be known for a valiant prince, you shall be esteemed a faithful people'.

49. Gardiner, *History*, VI, 10–23.
50. James Orchard Halliwell (ed.), *Letters of the Kings of England* (London, 1848), II, 261; Charles Petrie (ed.), *The Letters, Speeches, and Proclamations of King Charles I* (London, 1968), p. 40.
51. Russell, *Parliaments*, pp. 209–10, 239–40.
52. Thomas Cogswell, 'Prelude to Rhé: The Anglo-French Struggle Over La Rochelle, 1624–1627', *History*, 71, no. 231 (1986), 1–21; 'Foreign Policy and Parliament: the case of La Rochelle, 1625–1626', *English Historical Review*, 99, no. 391 (April 1984), 241–67. See also Lockyer, *Buckingham*, pp. 252–4, 290–5; Russell, *Parliaments*, pp. 209–11. Historians do not agree on whether the loan was initially the work of Buckingham or King James. The story gets much more complicated. As Cogswell explains, Charles and Buckingham might have thought the prospect of a French war could work to their advantage. The best way to deflect criticism over the ignominious affair of the loan ships might be to ask Parliament to finance a crusade to rescue the ships and the Huguenots. Unfortunately for this strategy, just before the Parliament of 1626 met, the French government appeared willing to return the ships and settle with the Huguenots. Suddenly Charles and Buckingham, instead of leading the expression of outrage against the French, now had to refrain from criticism in the hope of composing their differences with the French and salvaging an alliance after all.
53. William B. Bidwell and Maija Jansson, *Proceedings in Parliament 1626* (New Haven, CT, 1992), II, 350; SP 16/521/181.
54. Ibid., II, 351, 380.
55. Their final word on the subject was 'remove this person from access to your sacred person'. Ibid., III, 441.
56. Ibid., II, 249–50, 376. Sir John Eliot made the same point: 'If our monies which we shall give be so expended as has been formerly, we shall have little reason to give hereafter.' See also III, 441.
57. What Charles wanted, Buckingham just as stubbornly agreed, was simply 'that you that were the abbetters and counselors of this war would take a greater part of the burden to yourselves'. Ibid., II, 395, 405.
58. Gardiner, *History*, VI, 33, 71–2, 92–7, 115, 123. See also Kevin Sharpe, 'The Earl of Arundel, His Circle and the Opposition to the Duke of Buckingham, 1618–1628' in *Faction and Parliament*, pp. 209–44.
59. The six were Alford, Coke, Phelips, Seymour, Wentworth, and Sir Guy Palmes. Russell, *Parliaments*, p. 268. Charles was reported to have said that one reason for dissolving the Parliament of 1625 was 'the prolixity of a few bad ones'. Allen B. Hinds (ed.), *Calendar of State Papers and Manuscripts Relating to English Affairs, Existing in the Archives and Collections of Venice* (London, 1913), XIX, 147. [Hereafter *CSPV*].
60. *1626 Proceedings*, II, 250.
61. Sir Robert Harley pointed this out to his fellow members, but they refused to agree with him. Ibid., II, 378–9.
62. SP 16/22/51.
63. See Young, 'Revisionism and the Council of War', pp. 13–18.
64. *1626 Proceedings*, II, 285, 294. See also the proclamation Charles issued after dissolving this Parliament. James F. Larkin (ed.), *Stuart Royal Proclamations*, vol. II, *Royal Proclamations of King Charles I 1625–1646* (Oxford, 1983), 94. The proclamation declared, 'through the sides of a Peere of this Realme, they wound the honour of their Soveraignes'.
65. Ibid., II, 250, 285. See also p. 395.
66. Ibid., I, 398.
67. Thomas Birch (ed.), *The Court and Times of Charles I* (London, 1849), I, 101; James Orchard Halliwell (ed.), *The Autobiography and Correspondence of Sir Simonds D'Ewes* (London, 1845), II, 186.

68. For the dissolution of this Parliament, compare Russell, *Parliaments*, pp. 309–22 and Jess Stoddart Flemion, 'The Dissolution of Parliament in 1626: a Revaluation', *English Historical Review*, 88, no. 345 (Oct. 1972), 784–90.
69. *1626 Proceedings*, III, 429.
70. Ibid., III, 350–65.
71. Lockyer, *Buckingham*, p. 329. Lockyer does acknowledge another essential truth however: 'He was the King's chief minister, yet he did not have the trust of Parliament or the nation at large. His continuance in office and favour made impossible the achievement of that harmony between king and people which alone could give England the chance of unity at home and success abroad.' Documents relative to five of the charges were assembled by S. R. Gardiner in *Documents Illustrating the Impeachment of the Duke of Buckingham in 1626* (London, 1889). See also Gardiner (ed.), *Constitutional Documents of the Puritan Revolution 1625–1660*, 3rd edn revised (Oxford, 1906), pp. 3–44 and chapter 7 of Colin G. C. Tite, *Impeachment and Parliamentary Judicature in Early Stuart England* (London, 1974).
72. *CSPV*, XIX, 462.
73. Russell speculates about one possible effort at compromise, but, as he concedes, there is no direct evidence for it. *Parliaments*, pp. 294–9.
74. *1626 Proceedings*, III, 36.
75. Ibid., II, 395. For the subject of 'new counsels' see III, 31, 36, 237, 241–2, 350–65, 439–40. On the subject of new counsels, see also Russell, *Parliaments*, pp. 301, 306.
76. Birch, *Court and Times*, I, 104.
77. Cust, 'Charles I, the Privy Council, and the Forced Loan', *Journal of British Studies*, 24, no. 2 (April 1985), 234; Cust, *The Forced Loan and English Politics* (Oxford, 1987), p. 88.
78. Gardiner, *History*, VI, 149; W. R. Prest (ed.), *The Diary of Sir Richard Hutton 1614–1639* (London, 1991), pp. xxx–xxxi, 63–6.
79. Cust, *Forced Loan*, p. 56.
80. Ibid., p. 106.
81. Ibid., p. 320.
82. These were the words of the Lord Keeper in a speech given to both Houses in the presence of the King after Charles himself had spoken. *1626 Proceedings*, II, 391.
83. 'A Declaration of the true causes which moved his Majestie to assemble and after inforced him to dissolve the two last meetings in Parliament' (1626), printed in *The Parliamentary or Constitutional History of England* (London, 1763), VII, 300–9. See also Larkin, *Stuart Royal Proclamations*, II, 93–5.
84. This point was also made by Christopher Hill in 'Parliament and People in Seventeenth-Century England', *Past and Present*, 92 (August 1981), p. 110.
85. Cust, *Forced Loan*, p. 328.
86. Ibid., pp. 12, 328.
87. Cust, 'News and Politics in Early Seventeenth-Century England', *Past and Present*, 112 (1986), 60–90. See also Cust's 'Politics and the Electorate in the 1620s', in Cust and Hughes, *Conflict*, pp. 134–67 and 'Parliamentary Elections in the 1620s: The Case of Great Yarmouth', *Parliamentary History*, 11, pt. 2 (1992), 179–91. One diarist wrote 'Turnecoate' beside the name of Thomas Wentworth, who accepted royal office after having been a leading critic of the Crown in Parliament. On the subject of Wentworth, see also Perez Zagorin, 'Did Strafford Change Sides?' *English Historical Review*, 101, no. 398 (Jan. 1986), 149–63.
88. Cust, 'News', pp. 87, 90. See also Thomas Cogswell, 'The Politics of Propaganda: Charles I and the People in the 1620s', *Journal of British Studies*, 29 (July 1990), 187–215.
89. Cust, *Forced Loan*, p. 337.
90. Ibid., pp. 40–2.

91. Ibid., p. 88.
92. Ibid., p. 185. On this point, see all of Cust's chapter 3.
93. J. A. Guy, 'The Origins of the Petition of Right Reconsidered', *Historical Journal*, 25, no. 2 (1982), 289–312.
94. Sharpe, *Personal Rule*, p. 662; *1628 Proceedings*, V, 203; VI, 36–41.
95. Russell, 'Monarchies', pp. 211, 214.
96. Lockyer, *Buckingham*, p. 344.
97. For the background to the French war, see Cogswell's 'Prelude to Ré' and 'Foreign Policy and Parliament'.
98. L. J. Reeve, *Charles I and the Road to Personal Rule* (Cambridge, 1989), p. 15.
99. Halliwell, *Letters of the Kings of England*, II, 270; Petrie, *Letters*, p. 45.
100. As reported by the Venetian ambassador, quoted in Gardiner, *History*, VI, 221.
101. J. R. Jones wrote that engaging in war against France when war was already under way against Spain 'can only be described as lunatic'. *Britain and Europe in the Seventeenth Century* (New York, 1967), p. 21.
102. Lockyer, *Buckingham*, pp. 378–408. The House of Commons estimated the losses at 6000 or 7000 men. Robert C. Johnson, Maija Jansson Cole, Mary Frear Keeler, and William B. Bidwell (eds), *Commons Debates 1628* (5 vols, New Haven, CT, 1977), IV, 315. Buckingham fought bravely at Rhé, but that was beside the point. As S. R. Gardiner long ago observed, 'the charge which history has to bring against Buckingham is not so much that he failed in the expedition to Rhé, as that there was an expedition to Rhé at all'. Gardiner, *History*, VI, 200.
103. Gardiner, *History*, VI, 158.
104. Cust, *Forced Loan*, p. 92.
105. SP 16/79/2.
106. Halliwell, *Letters of the Kings of England*, II, 280–2; Petrie, *Letters*, p. 57.
107. *1628 Debates*, II, 3.
108. Gardiner, *History*, VI, 231.
109. *1628 Debates*, II, 7.
110. Gardiner, *History*, VI, 225. The names of the MPs are listed in *1628 Debates*, I, 63–6.
111. *1628 Debates*, II, 102. Compare the version of this speech at II, 111.
112. Ibid., II, 122. Four days earlier (II, 61) Phelips had said: 'I more fear the violation of public rights at home than a foreign enemy.'
113. Ibid., II, 60, 99, 103. The quoted words belong to Sir Nathaniel Rich.
114. Ibid., II, 57, 67.
115. Ibid., II, 66. Phelips compared Englishmen to Roman slaves (II, 61). Henry Sherfield argued that kings must rule within the law, for if they can arbitrarily take away a subject's property, then 'there is no difference between a subject and a bondman'; and if they can arbitrarily imprison a subject, then 'that is a thraldom' (II, 189).
116. Ibid., III, 98.
117. On the 'crisis of the common law' precipitated by Charles, see chapter 7 of Glenn Burgess, *The Politics of the Ancient Constitution: An Introduction to English Political Thought 1603–1642* (University Park, PA, 1992).
118. *1628 Debates*, II, 297.
119. Ibid., III, 125.
120. Ibid., III, 189.
121. J. A. Guy, 'The Origins of the Petition of Right Reconsidered', p. 306.
122. *1628 Debates*, III, 213. This was his message of 2 May delivered through Secretary Coke. On 5 May, Charles was present in person when Lord Keeper Coventry explained that the king would only accept a bill confirming existing laws 'without additions, paraphrases, or explanations' (III, 254).
123. Ibid., III, 270.
124. Ibid., III, 563–5. Emphasis mine.

125. Reeve, *Charles I*, pp. 14–15, 22; Cust, *Forced Loan*, pp. 102, 170–5; Gardiner, *History*, VI, 232.
126. Conrad Russell called it 'the key event of 1628'. *Parliaments*, p. 374.
127. *1628 Debates*, IV, 86.
128. Ibid., IV, 113–15.
129. L. J. Reeve, 'The Legal Status of the Petition of Right', *Historical Journal*, 29, no. 2 (1986), 257–77.
130. *1628 Debates*, IV, 182.
131. Ibid., IV, 204 n. 39. Elizabeth Read Foster, 'Printing the Petition of Right', *Huntington Library Quarterly* , 38 (Nov. 1974), 81–3.
132. Charles Carlton, *Charles I: The Personal Monarch*, 2nd edn (London, 1995), pp. 101, 159, in the latter instance citing John Hacket, *Scrinia Reserata* (London, 1693), II, 8.
133. Derek Hirst, *Authority and Conflict: England 1603–1658* (Cambridge, MA, 1986), p. 138.
134. Richard Cust, 'Charles I, the Privy Council and the Parliament of 1628', *Transactions of the Royal Historical Society*, sixth series, 2 (London, 1992), 25–50.
135. *1628 Debates*, IV, 352.
136. Gardiner, *History*, VI, 351; Russell, *The Crisis of Parliaments: English History 1509–1660* (Oxford, 1971), p. 308.
137. Reeve, *Charles I*, p. 36; Sharpe, *Personal Rule*, pp. 48–9.
138. W. Dunn Macray, *The History of the Rebellion and Civil Wars in England* (6 vols, Oxford, 1888), I, 38.
139. Gardiner, *History*, VI, 351, 356–7.
140. Ibid., VI, 370.
141. For the diplomacy of this period, see Reeve, *Charles I*, pp. 40–57.
142. The standard work on the growth of Arminianism in this period is Nicholas Tyacke, *Anti-Calvinists: The Rise of English Arminianism c.1590–1640* (Oxford, 1987). For an excellent concise explanation of the subject, see Reeve, *Charles* I, pp. 64–71.
143. Cust, *Forced Loan*, pp. 62–7; J. P. Sommerville, *Politics and Ideology in England 1603–1640* (London, 1986), pp. 127–31; Burgess, *Politics of the Ancient Constitution*, pp. 173–8.
144. *1628 Debates*, IV, 313.
145. Gardiner, *History*, VI, 330; VII, 8–9. For Neile and Montagu, see chapters 5 and 6 of Tyacke's *Anti-Calvinists*.
146. Russell, *Parliaments*, p. 396.
147. William R. Stacy, 'Parliamentary Judicature under the Early Stuarts', *Parliamentary History* 11, part 1 (1992), 54.
148. Larkin, *Stuart Royal Proclamations*, II, 218–20.
149. Julian Davies, *The Caroline Captivity of the Church: Charles I and the Remoulding of Anglicanism* (Oxford, 1992). See especially chapter 3.
150. For the 1629 session, see chapter 67 of Gardiner's *History*, chapter 7 of Russell's *Parliaments*, chapter 3 in Reeve's *Charles I*, and Christopher Thompson, 'The Divided Leadership of the House of Commons in 1629', in Sharpe's *Faction and Parliament*. The sources are printed in one handy volume: Wallace Notestein and Helen Relf (eds), *Commons Debates for 1629* (Minneapolis, 1921).
151. *1629 Debates*, pp. 11, 245.
152. Ibid., pp. 8–9, 245–6.
153. Ibid., pp. 12–13.
154. Ibid., p. 15.
155. Ibid., p. 16.
156. Thompson, 'The Divided Leadership of the House of Commons', referred to above. Thompson sees Pym and Rich as more concerned with religion, Eliot and

Selden more concerned with political issues. Reeve and Russell agree. Reeve, *Charles I*, pp. 71–5, 94; Russell, *Parliaments*, p. 404. Russell assigned paramount importance to religion in John Pym's career. But Perez Zagorin has questioned this distinction and re-emphasised Pym's constitutional concerns. Russell, 'The Parliamentary Career of John Pym, 1621–9', in Peter Clark, Alan G. R. Smith, and Nicholas Tyacke (eds), *The English Commonwealth 1547–1640: Essays in Politics and Society Presented to Joel Hurstfield* (Leicester, 1979), pp. 147–65. Zagorin, 'The Political Beliefs of John Pym to 1629', *English Historical Review*, 109, no. 433 (Sept. 1994), 867–90.

157. *1629 Debates*, p. 19.
158. Linda Popofsky, 'The Crisis Over Tonnage and Poundage in Parliament in 1629', *Past and Present*, 126 (Feb. 1990), 61, 71, 74.
159. *1629 Debates*, p. 94.
160. Thompson, 'Divided Leadership', p. 283.
161. There is still no better account of this episode than Gardiner, *History*, VII, 67–76.
162. The resolutions are printed in a number of places – for example, *1629 Debates*, pp. 101–2; Gardiner, *Constitutional Documents*, pp. 82–3; Kenyon, *Stuart Constitution*, p. 71.
163. John Reeve, 'The Arguments in King's Bench in 1629 Concerning the Imprisonment of John Selden and Other Members of the House of Commons', *Journal of British Studies*, 25, no. 3 (July 1986), 264–87.
164. Reeve, *Charles I*, pp. 3, 24, 172–80, 296. See also pp. 29, 103–4.
165. Ibid., pp. 94–7, 102–6. Richard Cust also speaks of conspiracy theories which were the 'mirror-image' of one another. 'Charles I and a draft Declaration for the 1628 Parliament', *Historical Research*, 63, no. 151 (June 1990), 155. Peter Lake likewise refers to 'two structurally similar but mutually exclusive conspiracy theories'. 'Anti-popery', p. 91.
166. Ball, 'Sir John Eliot and Parliament', pp. 173–207.
167. Thompson, 'Divided Leadership', pp. 276–7.
168. *1629 Debates*, p. 155. See also Eliot's speech on pp. 24–8.
169. For a dissenting view, see Sommerville, *Politics and Ideology*, p. 158.
170. 'The King's Declaration Showing the Causes of the Late Dissolution', printed in Gardiner, *Constitutional Documents*, pp. 83–99. 'There was truth, as well as paranoia, in all this', as L. J. Reeve has observed. *Charles I*, p. 105. See also Richard Cust's 'Charles I and a draft Declaration', cited above. Charles used similar language regarding 'the disobedient and seditious carriage of those said ill affected persons' in the proclamation he issued upon dissolving the Parliament. Larkin, *Stuart Royal Proclamations*, II, 223–4.
171. *1628 Debates*, I, 19; IV, 66 n. 42, 70. David Harris Willson, *The Privy Councillors in the House of Commons 1604–1629* (Minneapolis, 1940), pp. 203–4.
172. Margaret Judson, *The Crisis of the Constitution: An Essay in Constitutional and Political Thought, 1603–45* (New Brunswick, NJ, 1949).
173. David L. Smith, 'The Impact on Government', in John Morrill (ed.), *The Impact of the English Civil War* (London, 1991), pp. 32–3.
174. Sharpe made this concession in the brief essay entitled ' "Revisionism" Revisited', which was printed at the beginning of the paperback edition of *Faction and Parliament* in 1985, p. xi.
175. *Journal of British Studies*, 30, no. 3 (July 1991), 332–3.
176. Russell, *Parliaments*, p. 423.
177. Sommerville, *Politics and Ideology*, pp. 140, 182, 231–6. See also Clive Holmes, 'The County Community in Stuart Historiography', *Journal of British Studies*, 19, no. 2 (Spring 1980), 54–73 and Derek Hirst, 'The Place of Principle', *Past and Present*, no. 92 (August 1981), 79–99.
178. Burgess, *Politics of the Ancient Constitution*, pp. 173–224. See also Reeve, 'Legal Status', pp. 275–7.

3 The Personal Rule I

1. This label was not used by S. R. Gardiner. In fact, Gardiner wrote that Charles 'had no wish to erect a despotism, to do injustice, or to heap up wealth at the expense of his subjects'. Elsewhere he wrote: 'His was a government not of fierce tyranny, but of petty annoyance.' *History of England from the Accession of James I to the Outbreak of the Civil War, 1603–1642* (10 vols, London, 1883–4, 1894–6), VIII, 299, 222–3. Compare H. Kearney, *The Eleven Years' Tyranny of Charles I* (London, 1962).

2. Morrill wrote that there is a 'formidable *prima facie* case of legal tyranny' against Charles for what he did in the period 1626–9 and 'very palpable' evidence for the period 1639–42. 'Charles I, Tyranny and the English Civil War', in *The Nature of the English Revolution: Essays by John Morrill* (London, 1993), pp. 291–2.

3. Edward Hyde, Earl of Clarendon, *The History of the Rebellion and Civil Wars in England*, ed. W. Dunn Macray (Oxford, 1888), I, 28.

4. James F. Larkin (ed.), *Stuart Royal Proclamations*, vol. II, *Royal Proclamations of King Charles I 1625–1646* (Oxford, 1983), pp. 226–8.

5. Charles Carlton, *Charles I: The Personal Monarch*, 2nd edn (London, 1995), p. 155.

6. *CSPV*, 1636–39, p. 124.

7. Charles Petrie (ed.), *The Letters, Speeches, and Proclamations of King Charles I* (London, 1968), pp. 95–6; James Orchard Halliwell (ed.), *Letters of the Kings of England* (London, 1848), II, 287, 290–1.

8. Kevin Sharpe, *The Personal Rule of Charles I* (New Haven, CT, 1992), p. 210.

9. Ibid., p. 220.

10. Ibid., p. 209.

11. L. J. Reeve, *Charles I and the Road to Personal Rule* (Cambridge, 1989), p. 296. See also p. 179.

12. For an earlier and more traditional view of the personal rule, see Esther Cope, *Politics Without Parliaments 1629–1640* (London, 1987).

13. Sharpe, *Personal Rule*, pp. 44, 60.

14. Ibid., pp. 65–6.

15. As Conrad Russell expressed it, the Parliaments of the 1620s resisted the king's 'attempts to put the administration on a war footing'. *Parliaments and English Politics, 1621–1629* (Oxford, 1979), p. 77.

16. For Weston, see Michael Van Cleave Alexander, *Charles I's Lord Treasurer: Sir Richard Weston, Earl of Portland* (London, 1975). For Laud, see H. R. Trevor-Roper, *Archbishop Laud, 1573–1645* (London, 1940) and the other works cited below in our discussion of Laudianism.

17. Reeve, *Charles I*, pp. 90, 188. See also pp. 82–90, 114–17, 133, 180–8.

18. Ibid., pp. 123–4. For Reeve's full account of these proceedings, see pp. 118–56 and 'The Arguments in King's Bench in 1629 concerning the Imprisonment of John Selden and Other Members of the House of Commons', *Journal of British Studies*, 25, no. 3 (July 1986), 264–87.

19. Reeve, *Charles I*, p. 127.

20. Ibid., pp. 146–56; G. E. Aylmer, *The King's Servants: The Civil Service of Charles I 1625–1642* (London, 1961), pp. 111–12. For Charles's intimidation of the judges see also W. R. Prest (ed.), *The Diary of Sir Richard Hutton 1614–1639* (London, 1991), pp. xxxi, 77–8.

21. Reeve, *Charles I*, pp. 146–7, 158–61; Gardiner, *History*, VII, 140–1.

22. Sharpe, *Personal Rule*, pp. 655–8.

23. Chambers's case is described in Reeve, *Personal Rule*, p. 164; Gardiner, *History*, VII, 3–5, 84–6, 114; and *DNB*, IV, 21.

24. Gardiner, *History*, VII, 84.

25. Ibid., VII, 85.

26. Reeve, *Charles I*, pp. 164–5; Gardiner, *History*, VII, 143–51; *DNB*, XI, 880–1.
27. Sharpe, *Personal Rule*, pp. 659–83.
28. S. R. Gardiner (ed.), *Constitutional Documents of the Puritan Revolution 1625–1660*, 3rd edn revised (Oxford, 1906), pp. 209–10.
29. L. J. Reeve, 'Sir Robert Heath's Advice for Charles I in 1629', *Bulletin of the Institute of Historical Research*, 59 (1986), 221–2, 224; Reeve, *Charles I*, p. 191; Sharpe, *Personal Rule*, p. 660; Paul E. Kopperman, *Sir Robert Heath 1575–1649: Window on an Age* (London, 1989), pp. 231–46.
30. A. J. Loomie, 'The Spanish Faction at the Court of Charles I, 1630–8', *Bulletin of the Institute of Historical Research*, 59, no. 139 (May 1986), 37–49.
31. For Cottington, see Martin Havran, *Caroline Courtier: The Life of Lord Cottington* (London, 1973).
32. R. Malcolm Smuts, 'The Puritan Followers of Henrietta Maria in the 1630s', *English Historical Review*, 93 (Jan. 1978), 26–45.
33. For Holland, see Barbara Donagan, 'A Courtier's Progress: Greed and Consistency in the Life of the Earl of Holland', *Historical Journal*, 19 (1976), 317–53.
34. Sharpe, *Personal Rule*, pp. 173–9.
35. Gardiner, *History*, VII, 218.
36. Ibid., VII, 355–6.
37. Sharpe, *Personal Rule*, pp. 537–41, 825, 837–42. Writing about faction in October 1636, the Earl of Dorset observed, 'wee have too much of itt in Court'. David L. Smith, 'The Fourth Earl of Dorset and the Personal Rule of Charles I', *Journal of British Studies*, 30, no. 3 (July 1991), 278.
38. Ann Hughes, *Politics, Society and Civil War in Warwickshire, 1620–1660* (Cambridge, 1987), p. 111. On the subjects of the queen's faction and isolation, see also Caroline Hibbard, 'The Role of a Queen Consort: The Household and Court of Henrietta Maria, 1625–42', in Ronald G. Asch and Adolf M. Birke (eds), *Princes, Patronage, and the Nobility: The Court at the Beginning of the Modern Age c.1450–1650* (Oxford, 1991), pp. 393–414.
39. Larkin, *Stuart Royal Proclamations*, II, 34–8.
40. Sharpe, *Personal Rule*, pp. 215–16.
41. Kevin Sharpe, 'The Image of Virtue: the Court and Household of Charles I, 1625–42', in David Starkey (ed.), *The English Court: from the Wars of the Roses to the Civil War* (London, 1987), pp. 226–60. *CSPV*, 1625–6, p. 21 quoted in ibid., p. 228.
42. Sharpe, 'Image', p. 229.
43. For this whole subject, see also Sharpe, *Personal Rule*, pp. 209–17.
44. Warwick's *Memoirs*, pp. 65–6 cited in Richard Ollard, *The Image of the King: Charles I and Charles II* (New York, 1979), p. 28.
45. Sharpe, 'Image', p. 230.
46. Ibid., p. 228.
47. Warwick's *Memoirs*, pp. 64–5 cited in Ollard, *Image*, p. 30.
48. Sharpe, *Personal Rule*, p. 190.
49. Ibid., pp. 183, 193–4.
50. For the efforts to control corruption, see Sharpe, *Personal Rule*, pp. 235–9 and G. E. Aylmer, 'Attempts at Administrative Reform, 1625–40', *English Historical Review*, 72, no. 283 (April 1957), 246–59.
51. Sharpe, 'Image', p. 236.
52. Ibid., p. 213.
53. Gardiner, *History*, VIII, 22.
54. Roy Strong, *Van Dyck: Charles I on Horseback* (New York, 1972), p. 70.
55. Ibid., pp. 59–63; C. V. Wedgwood, *A Coffin for King Charles* (New York, 1966), p. 181.
56. Strong, *Van Dyck*, pp. 25, 63.

57. See J. S. A. Adamson, 'Chivalry and Political Culture in Caroline England', in Kevin Sharpe and Peter Lake (eds), *Culture and Politics in Early Stuart England* (Stanford, CA, 1993), pp. 161–97. Adamson generally follows Strong's analysis but relates it much better to the actual politics of Charles's reign.

58. Strong, *Van Dyck*, pp. 92–3.

59. Stephen Orgel, *The Illusion of Power: Political Theater in the English Renaissance* (Berkeley, CA, 1975), p. 43.

60. Ibid., pp. 49–52, 87–9.

61. Peter W. Thomas, 'Charles I of England: The Tragedy of Absolutism', in A. G. Dickens (ed.), *The Courts of Europe: Politics, Patronage and Royalty, 1400–1800* (London, 1977), pp. 191–211; Graham Parry, *The Golden Age Restor'd: The Culture of the Stuart Court, 1603–42* (Manchester, 1981).

62. Thomas, 'Charles I', pp. 209, 211.

63. R. Malcolm Smuts, *Court Culture and the Origins of a Royalist Tradition in Early Stuart England* (Philadelphia, 1987), p. 254.

64. Ibid., p. 168.

65. Ibid., p. 171.

66. Ibid., pp. 120–33.

67. Ibid., pp. 192–8.

68. Ibid., pp. 247–53.

69. Ibid., pp. 252–62.

70. Albert H. Triconi, *Anticourt Drama in England 1603–1642* (Charlottesville, VA, 1989), chapter 17, especially pp. 172–3, 187–8.

71. Martin Butler, *Theatre and Crisis 1632–1642* (Cambridge, 1984), pp. 1, 280–1, 284–5.

72. Martin Butler, 'Reform or Reverence? The Politics of the Caroline Masque', in J. R. Mulryne and Margaret Shewring (eds), *Theatre and Government Under the Early Stuarts* (Cambridge, 1993), pp. 149–53.

73. See Sharpe's *Criticism and Compliment: The Politics of Literature in the England of Charles I* (Cambridge, 1987); *Politics and Ideas in Early Stuart England: Essays and Studies* (London, 1989); and Sharpe and Lake, *Culture and Politics in Early Stuart England*.

74. Sharpe, *Personal Rule*, pp. 219–35.

75. Ibid., pp. 180–1.

76. Ibid., p. 223.

77. Judith Richards, '"His Nowe Majestie" and the English Monarchy: The Kingship of Charles I Before 1640', *Past and Present*, no. 113 (Nov. 1986), 70, 74–5.

78. Ibid., pp. 83–93.

79. Sharpe, *Personal Rule*, p. 180 and 'Image', p. 244.

80. P. W. Thomas, 'Two Cultures? Court and Country under Charles I', in Conrad Russell (ed.), *The Origins of the English Civil War* (London, 1973), pp. 168–93, quoting p. 175.

81. Smuts, *Court Culture*, pp. 177, 227.

82. David Delison Hebb, *Piracy and the English Government, 1616–1642* (Aldershot, 1994), pp. 222–6.

83. Reeve, *Charles I*, pp. 186, 256, 265.

84. Ibid., pp. 262–91. Quotations are from pp. 281, 290, and 291. Gardiner came to the same conclusion but expressed it more dramatically: 'Perish Europe if only England may fiddle in safety!' Gardiner was wiser to reflect in another place: 'It might be a question whether Charles was able to interfere at all with profit on the Continent.' *History*, VII, 98, 208.

85. In his eagerness to portray Charles as a king who did have a foreign policy and could have made a difference in the Thirty Years War, Kevin Sharpe does not vindicate Charles as much in his dealings with Sweden as he could have. What Sharpe does emphasise is that Gustavus Adolphus drove a hard bargain and

would not have been as obliging an ally as English Protestants assumed. See Sharpe, *Personal Rule*, pp. 78–82.

86. G. M. D. Howat, *Stuart and Cromwellian Foreign Policy* (New York, 1974), p. 46.

87. Gardiner, *History*, VII, 169–70, 352.

88. J. R. Jones, *Britain and Europe in the Seventeenth Century* (New York, 1967), pp. 22–4.

89. I am simplifying here. The situation was complicated by the division of the Palatinate into Upper and Lower. The Upper Palatinate was a special problem because the Emperor had conferred it and the electoral status on Maximilian of Bavaria, who had further strengthened his position by marrying the Emperor's daughter. Caroline Hibbard, *Charles I and the Popish Plot* (Chapel Hill, NC, 1983), pp. 26–9.

90. Simon Adams, 'Spain or the Netherlands? The Dilemmas of Early Stuart Foreign Policy', in Howard Tomlinson (ed.), *Before the English Civil War: Essays on Early Stuart Politics and Government* (London, 1983), pp. 79–101. Adams explains (p. 101): 'James and Charles may have preferred to ally with the leading dynasty of Europe rather than with republicans and Calvinist incendiaries, but too many of their subjects preferred the company of the godly to that of the adherents of antichrist.'

91. Harland Taylor, 'Trade, Neutrality, and the "English Road", 1603–1648' and J. S. Kepler, 'Fiscal Aspects of the English Carrying Trade during the Thirty Years War', *Economic History Review*, 2nd series, 25 (May 1972), 236–83.

92. Although the conventional wisdom is that Charles respected the concept of balance of power, it might be argued that he actually went where the power was, courting whichever nation was strongest at the time. This policy might not appeal to advocates of the balance of power, but it is not without merit.

93. The most thorough re-evaluation of Charles's foreign relations in print is Sharpe's *Personal Rule*. For his general approach to the subject see pp. 86–97. Another major effort, especially emphasising Charles's concern for the preservation of Flanders, is Patricia Haskell's unpublished PhD dissertation, 'Sir Francis Windebank and the Personal Rule of Charles I' (Southampton University, 1978). See also Hibbard, *Charles I and the Popish Plot*, chapter 4, and Hebb, *Piracy and the English Government*, chapter 10.

94. Loomie, 'The Spanish Faction', pp. 16–7.

95. Sharpe, *Personal Rule*, 513, 524.

96. Smith, 'The Fourth Earl of Dorset', p. 272. I have modernised the spelling.

97. There is an excellent summary of the negotiations with France in the introduction to Historical Manuscripts Commission, *De'Lisle and Dudley MSS*, vol. 6 (London, 1966).

98. Gardiner, *History*, VIII, 213.

99. Petrie, *Letters*, 99; Halliwell, *Letters*, II, 295.

100. Sharpe, *Personal Rule*, pp. 533, 826.

101. HMC, *De'Lisle and Dudley MSS.*, VI, 77, 101. I have modernised the spelling.

102. Edward Hyde, Earl of Clarendon, *State Papers Collected by Edward, Earl of Clarendon, Commencing from the Year 1621*, quarto edn (Oxford, 1767–86), II, 2–3.

103. *CSPV*, 1636–39, p. 108.

104. Reeve, *Charles I*, p. 260.

105. Sharpe, *Personal Rule*, pp. 155–6.

106. Michael B. Young, *Servility and Service: The Life and Work of Sir John Coke* (London, 1986), pp. 229–52. I stand corrected, however, on the subject of Coke's speech to the Privy Council advocating ship money in 1634. For that subject see Kenneth R. Andrews, *Ships, Money and Politics: Seafaring and Naval Enterprise in the Reign of Charles I* (Cambridge, 1991), pp. 134–5. An earlier historian of the Secretary's office, Florence M. Grier Evans, concluded: 'Jealousy and rivalry were the

inevitable results of such a system.' *The Principal Secretary of State: A Survey of the Office from 1558–1680* (London, 1923), p. 95.

107. Young, *Servility and Service*, p. 274.

108. Aylmer, *King's Servants*, pp. 62–3.

109. Ibid., pp. 63, 369–71.

110. Ibid., p. 371; Kevin Sharpe, 'Thomas Witherings and the Reform of the Foreign Posts, 1632–40', *Bulletin of the Institute of Historical Research*, 57, no. 136 (Nov. 1984), 59.

111. Aylmer, *King's Servants*, pp. 349–51; Aylmer, 'Attempts at Administrative Reform', pp. 244, 252–3.

112. Gardiner, *History*, VIII, 89–91; Alexander, *Charles I's Lord Treasurer*, pp. 199–200; Historical Manuscripts Commission, *The Manuscripts of the Earl Cowper* (London, 1888), 12th report, appendix, II, 163–4, 166.

113. Paul Slack, 'Books of Orders: the making of English social policy, 1577–1631', *Transactions of the Royal Historical Society*, 5th series, 30 (1981), 1–22; Brian W. Quintrell, 'The Making of Charles I's Book of Orders', *English Historical Review*, 95, no. 376 (July 1980), 553–72; Sharpe, *Personal Rule*, pp. 456–63, 485–7.

114. On the other hand, the Privy Council's whole centralised, top-down approach to local government may have reduced the opportunities for participation in governance at the local level and aggravated the feeling of alienation from the centre. See Cynthia Herrup, 'The Counties and the Country: Some Thoughts on Seventeenth-Century Historiography', in Geoff Eley and William Hunt (eds), *Reviving the English Revolution: Reflections and Elaborations on the Work of Christopher Hill* (London, 1988), pp. 289–304.

115. Quintrell, 'The Making of Charles I's Book of Orders', pp. 559–60, 570.

116. Sharpe, *Personal Rule*, pp. 407, 455, 557.

117. Ibid., pp. 425–8.

118. Ibid., pp. 414–15.

119. See Cogswell's review in *Albion*, 25, no. 4 (Winter 1993), 690.

120. For example, James required noblemen and gentry to remain in the countryside 'out of our Princely care of the common good', and in the proclamation establishing a monopoly over the manufacture of gold and silver thread he averred that 'in all Our Actions and proceedings [we] have Our eye of grace rather upon the flourishing estate of Our Kingdomes, and the comfort of Our people, then upon Our profit'. James F. Larkin and Paul L. Hughes (eds), *Stuart Royal Proclamations* (Oxford, 1973), I, 357, 386.

121. Clarendon, *History of the Rebellion*, I, 85.

122. Gardiner, *History*, VIII, 71–7, 284; Sharpe, *Personal Rule*, pp. 122–3, 259–62.

123. Valerie Pearl, *London and the Outbreak of the Puritan Revolution: City Government and National Politics, 1625–43* (Oxford, 1961); Robert Ashton, *The City and the Court 1603–1643* (Cambridge, 1979); Robert Brenner, *Merchants and Revolution: Commercial Change, Political Conflict, and London's Overseas Traders, 1550–1650* (Princeton, NJ, 1993).

124. Aylmer, 'Attempts at Administrative Reform', pp. 232–3.

125. Larkin, *Stuart Royal Proclamations*, II, 673–6.

126. Gardiner, *History*, VIII, 223.

127. Mark E. Kennedy, 'Charles I and Local Government: The Draining of the East and West Fens', *Albion*, 15, no. 1 (Spring 1983), 23, 27–8, 31.

128. PRO, SO 1/2, fos. 5v–6, quoted in ibid., p. 24.

129. Sharpe, *Personal Rule*, p. 255.

130. Gardiner, *History*, VIII, 295–8.

131. Keith Lindley, *Fenland Riots and the English Revolution* (London, 1982), pp. 12–22.

132. Ibid., pp. 1, 49, 107. Court connections figured prominently in other money-making schemes of the personal rule. See Ronald G. Asch, 'The Revival of Monopolies: Court and Patronage during the Personal Rule of

Charles I, 1629–1640', in Asch and Birke, *Princes, Patronage, and the Nobility*, pp. 377–8.

133. Kennedy, 'Charles I and Local Government', p. 31.
134. Frederick C. Dietz, *English Public Finance 1558–1641*, 2nd edn (London, 1964), pp. 269–72; Aylmer, *King's Servants*, pp. 64–7; Sharpe, *Personal Rule*, pp. 126–30; David Thomas, 'Financial and Administrative Developments', in Tomlinson, *Before the English Civil War*, pp. 118–22. Useful tables of data can be found in Gardiner, *History*, X, 222–3.
135. Dietz, *English Public Finance*, p. 263 and n. 24.
136. Andrew Thrush, 'Naval Finance and the Origins and Development of Ship Money', in Mark Charles Fissel (ed.), *War and Government in Britain, 1598–1650* (Manchester, 1991), pp. 133–62.
137. For Sharpe's whole discussion of ship money see *Personal Rule*, pp. 545–98. For the amounts assessed and collected see pp. 583–95.
138. Ibid., p. 558. On page 585, Sharpe similarly wrote that ship money 'must qualify as one of the most successful taxes, indeed governmental enterprises, in early modern history'.
139. The official justification was spelled out in the ship money writs, one of which is readily available in Gardiner, *Constitutional Documents*, pp. 105–7.
140. The expedition against the pirates of Sallee in 1637 is a notable exception. See Michael Oppenheim, *A History of the Administration of the Royal Navy and of Merchant Shipping in Relation to the Navy* (London, 1896), pp. 277–8 n. 3; Hebb, *Piracy*, chapter 11; Andrews, *Ships, Money and Politics*, chapter 7.
141. Gardiner, *History*, VIII, 223. See also VII, 390; VIII, 84, 270.
142. Sharpe, *Personal Rule*, pp. 102–4; Andrews, *Ships, Money and Politics*, chapter 6; Hebb, *Piracy*, chapter 10; and Thrush's chapter on 'Naval Finance' cited above.
143. HMC, *Cowper MSS*, II, 95. Sir Kenelm Digby wrote these words in closing a letter to Sir John Coke, his patron and a fond advocate of sea power, so they should not necessarily be taken at face value.
144. Gardiner, *History*, IX, 61. Gardiner's account is still the most detailed.
145. Sharpe, *Personal Rule*, p. 832.
146. B. W. Quintrell, 'Charles I and the Navy in the 1630s', *Seventeenth Century*, 3 (1988), 159–79. The data which follow are taken from Oppenheim, *Royal Navy*, pp. 260–2.
147. Andrews, *Ships, Money and Politics*, p. 158.
148. Oppenheim, *Royal Navy*, p. 240.
149. Gardiner, *History*, VIII, 94.
150. Ibid., VIII, 206–8.
151. Sharpe, *Personal Rule*, pp. 721, 723, 725.
152. An extract of Oliver St John's argument is printed in Gardiner, *Constitutional Documents*, pp. 109–15. Hampden's other counsel, Robert Holborne, made the more radical argument against the king's right to determine the existence of an emergency. Gardiner, *History*, VIII, 272–5. My discussion of the case here is necessarily very abbreviated. For a thorough examination see D. L. Keir, 'The Case of Ship-money', *Law Quarterly Review*, 52 (1936), 546–74. See also W. J. Jones, *Politics and the Bench: The Judges and the Origins of the English Civil War* (London, 1971), pp. 123–31 and Conrad Russell, 'The Ship Money Judgements of Bramston and Davenport', *English Historical Review*, 77 (1962), 312–18.
153. This same fear had been expressed about the forced loan, and Charles issued a proclamation to dispel this rumour spread by 'malevolous persons'. Larkin, *Stuart Royal Proclamations*, II, 110–12.
154. Gardiner, *Constitutional Documents*, pp. 121–3.
155. Jones, *Politics and the Bench*, pp. 141–3, 211, 214.
156. Hughes, *Politics, Society and Civil War in Warwickshire*, pp. 99–100. For ship money see also pp. 108–10.

157. S. P. Salt, 'Sir Simonds D'Ewes and the Levying of Ship Money, 1635–40', *Historical Journal*, 37, no. 2 (June 1994), 285.
158. Clarendon, *History of the Rebellion*, I, 136.

4   The Personal Rule II

1. *Calendar of State Papers Venetian* [*CSPV*], 1636–39, pp. 296–7, 308.
2. S. R. Gardiner, *History of England from the Accession of James I to the Outbreak of the Civil War, 1603–1642* (10 vols, London, 1883–4, 1894–6), VIII, 229. For records of the case, see S. R. Gardiner (ed.), *Documents Relating to the Proceedings Against William Prynne in 1634 and 1637* (London, 1877). See also Susan Dwyer Amussen, 'Punishment, Discipline, and Power: The Social Meanings of Violence in Early Modern England', *Journal of British Studies*, 34, no. 1 (January 1995), 7–12.
3. Kenneth Fincham and Peter Lake, 'The Ecclesiastical Policies of James I and Charles I', in Kenneth Fincham (ed.), *The Early Stuart Church* (Stanford, CA, 1993), pp. 45–6.
4. For the altar controversy see Julian Davies, *The Caroline Captivity of the Church: Charles I and the Remoulding of Anglicanism 1625–1641* (Oxford, 1992), chapter 6 and Kevin Sharpe, *The Personal Rule of Charles I* (New Haven, CT, 1992), pp. 333–44.
5. Sharpe, *Personal Rule*, pp. 275–402. See also Sharpe's 'Archbishop William Laud and the University of Oxford', in his collected works entitled *Politics and Ideas in Early Stuart England: Essays and Studies* (London, 1989), pp. 123–46.
6. Davies, *Caroline Captivity*, p. 303.
7. Ibid., chapter 5. Compare Sharpe, *Personal Rule*, pp. 351–9.
8. Davies, *Caroline Captivity*, pp. 73–9. Compare Sharpe, *Personal Rule*, pp. 322–7. Charles Carlton wrote that 'this project took up more of Charles's time and energy than any other matter pertaining to the church', and there 'can be no question' he was behind the campaign. *Charles I: The Personal Monarch*, 2nd edn (London, 1995), pp. 164–5.
9. Andrew Foster, 'Church Policies of the 1630s', in Richard Cust and Ann Hughes (eds), *Conflict in Early Stuart England: Studies in Religion and Politics 1603–1642* (London, 1989), pp. 193, 212.
10. Davies, *Caroline Captivity*, pp. 3, 10, 13–14, 290–2. See also Richard Cust, 'Anti-puritanism and Urban Politics: Charles I and Great Yarmouth', *Historical Journal*, 35, no. 1 (March 1992), 1–26.
11. Davies, *Caroline Captivity*, pp. 1–21, 288–305.
12. Charles Carlton and Kevin Sharpe both believe that a manuscript in the Bodleian Library is Charles's testament of faith. See Sharpe, *Personal Rule*, p. 280 n. 26, pp. 278–84 and Carlton, *Charles I*, pp. 62–3, 138–40.
13. As Davies put it, 'his ideological baggage was light'. *Caroline Captivity*, p. 12.
14. James F. Larkin (ed.), *Stuart Royal Proclamations*, vol. II, *Royal Proclamations of King Charles I 1625–1646* (Oxford, 1983), II, 90–3.
15. Ibid., II, 218–20.
16. Sharpe, *Personal Rule*, pp. 374–82, 758–65, 665–82.
17. Gardiner, *History*, VII, 248–50.
18. James S. Hart, *Justice Upon Petition: The House of Lords and the Reformation of Justice 1621–1675* (London, 1991), p. 65. See also pp. 4, 8, 65–85, 98.
19. This was the conclusion of H. E. Phillips in his 1939 University of London MA thesis on the Court of Star Chamber and 'The Last Years of the Court of Star

Chamber, 1630–41', *Transactions of the Royal Historical Society*, 4th series, 21 (1939), 103–31.

20. Sharpe, *Personal Rule*, chapter 12 and pp. 842–7, 934–9.

21. Davies, *Caroline Captivity*, pp. 290–318. Quotations come from pp. 290, 295, and 305.

22. Michael Finlayson's *Historians, Puritanism, and the English Revolution: The Religious Factor in English Politics before and after the Interregnum* (Toronto, 1983) so skilfully dissected the old rise of Puritanism that it should have cautioned anyone against positing a comparable rise of Arminianism.

23. Nicholas Tyacke, 'Puritanism, Arminianism and Counter-Revolution', in Conrad Russell (ed.), *The Origins of the English Civil War* (London, 1973), pp. 119–43 and *Anti-Calvinists: The Rise of English Arminianism c.1590–1640* (Oxford, 1987). Major contributions to the controversy include Peter White 'The Rise of Arminianism Reconsidered', *Past and Present*, 101 (1983), 34–54; White, 'A Rejoinder', *Past and Present*, 115 (1987), 201–29; White, *Predestination, Policy and Polemic: Conflict and Consensus in the English Church from the Reformation to the Civil War* (Cambridge, 1992); Peter Lake, 'Calvinism and the English Church 1570–1635', *Past and Present*, 114 (1987), 32–76; Kenneth Parker, *The English Sabbath: A Study of Doctrine and Discipline from the Reformation to the Civil War* (Cambridge, 1988); and two works already cited – Davies, *Caroline Captivity* and Fincham, *The Early Stuart Church*.

24. For a discussion of terminology, see the introduction to Fincham, *The Early Stuart Church*. Peter Lake may take the more prudent course by continuing to emphasise Laudianism. See his 'The Laudian Style: Order, Uniformity and the Pursuit of the Beauty of Holiness in the 1630s' in ibid., pp. 161–85 and 'The Laudians and the Argument from Authority', in Bonnelyn Young Kunze and Dwight D. Brautigam (eds), *Court, Country and Culture: Essays on Early Modern British History in Honor of Perez Zagorin* (Rochester, NY, 1992), pp. 149–75.

25. In addition to the temperamental and aesthetic preferences of the king, Davies connects the church policies of the 1630s with a revival of Patristic studies and Aristotle. He writes, 'we do not need the rise of Arminianism (even if Arminianism needed to rise) to explain Laudianism'. *Caroline Captivity*, pp. 50–61.

26. Ibid., p. 90. Examine, for example, the Root and Branch Petition, the Ten Propositions, and the Grand Remonstrance in S. R. Gardiner (ed.), *Constitutional Documents of the Puritan Revolution 1625–1660*, 3rd edn revised (Oxford, 1906), pp. 137–44, 163–6, 202–32.

27. Caroline Hibbard, *Charles I and the Popish Plot* (Chapel Hill, NC, 1983). See also Robin Clifton, 'Fear of Popery', in Russell, *Origins*, pp. 144–67 and Peter Lake, 'Anti-popery: the Structure of a Prejudice', in Cust and Hughes, *Conflict in Early Stuart England*, pp. 72–106.

28. Hibbard, *Charles I and the Popish Plot*, pp. 44, 49.

29. Ibid., pp. 16, 24.

30. Ibid., pp. 44–57, 71, 83–9. See also Hibbard's 'The Role of a Queen Consort: The Household and Court of Henrietta Maria, 1625–42', in Ronald G. Asch and Adolf M. Birke (eds), *Princes, Patronage, and the Nobility: The Court at the Beginning of the Modern Age c.1450–1650* (Oxford, 1991).

31. Andrew Foster, 'The Clerical Estate Revitalised', in Fincham, *Early Stuart Church*, pp. 141, 152–3.

32. Hibbard, *Charles I and the Popish Plot*, p. 13.

33. Sharpe, *Personal Rule*, chapter 12, especially pp. 739, 750.

34. See Judith Maltby, ' "By this Book": Parishioners, the Prayer Book and the Established Church', in Fincham, *The Early Stuart Church*, pp. 115–37.

35. John Morrill, *The Nature of the English Revolution: Essays by John Morrill* (London, 1993), pp. 15, 270.

36. Sharpe, *Personal Rule*, pp. 774–92.
37. Maurice Lee, Jr, *The Road to Revolution: Scotland under Charles I, 1625–37* (Urbana, IL, 1985).
38. Peter Donald, *An Uncounselled King: Charles I and the Scottish Troubles 1637–1641* (Cambridge, 1990).
39. Allan I. Macinnes, *Charles I and the Making of the Covenanting Movement 1625–1641* (Edinburgh, 1991).
40. Keith M. Brown, 'Aristocratic Finances and the Origins of the Scottish Revolution', *English Historical Review*, 104, no. 410 (Jan. 1989), 84; Brown, *Kingdom or Province? Scotland and the Regal Union, 1603–1715* (New York, 1992), p. 118.
41. A good example of this is page 115 of Brown's *Kingdom or Province?* The page begins with the assertion that 'Charles refused to compromise and decided on war'. Later on the same page Brown notes that 'Charles revoked the canons and prayer book, dismantled the court of high commission and suspended the five articles'.
42. David Stevenson, *The Scottish Revolution 1637–1644: The Triumph of the Covenanters* (New York, 1973). See especially his warning against Whig teleological assumptions on p. 48.
43. Compare the censorious tone in Macinnes, *Charles I and the Making of the Covenanting Movement*, p. 2 with Conrad Russell's explanation in *The Fall of the British Monarchies 1637–1642* (Oxford, 1991), p. 30.
44. Lee, *Road to Revolution*, p. 33.
45. Sharpe, *Personal Rule*, p. 776. Similarly, regarding the introduction of the new canons and prayer book, Sharpe wrote, 'Charles, *as always*, acted precipitately.' Ibid., p. 783. In both quotations italics are mine. Macinnes, *Charles I and the Making of the Covenanting Movement*, pp. 52, 72. Compare Stevenson, *The Scottish Revolution*, p. 34.
46. John Morrill, 'The Scottish National Covenant of 1638 in its British Context', in *The Nature of the English Revolution*, p. 95; Macinnes, *Charles I and the Making of the Covenanting Movement*, pp. 86–9, 97. For other accounts of the coronation visit see Lee, *Road to Revolution*, pp. 128–36; Sharpe, *Personal Rule*, pp. 778–83; Donald, *An Uncounselled King*, pp. 29–31.
47. Macinnes, *Charles I and the Making of the Covenanting Movement*, p. 128.
48. Stevenson, *Scottish Revolution*, p. 44.
49. Lee, *Road to Revolution*, p. 162.
50. Macinnes, *Charles I and the Making of the Covenanting Movement*, pp. 138, 141.
51. Conrad Russell, 'The British Problem and the English Civil War', *History*, 72 (1987), 395–415; Morrill, 'Scottish National Covenant', p. 101 and 'A British Patriarchy? Ecclesiastical Imperialism under the Early Stuarts', in Anthony Fletcher and Peter Roberts (eds), *Religion, Culture and Society in Early Modern Britain* (Cambridge, 1994), pp. 209–10, 222–37. See also chapter 5 of Russell's *The Causes of the English Civil War* (Oxford, 1990).
52. Russell, *Fall*, pp. 44, 529; 'British Problem', p. 399.
53. For the details of events in this paragraph see Donald, *An Uncounselled King*, pp. 40–118.
54. Ibid., p. 41.
55. Russell, *Causes*, pp. 60, 117, 201.
56. Charles Petrie (ed.), *The Letters, Speeches, and Proclamations of King Charles I* (London, 1968), pp. 106–10; James Orchard Halliwell (ed.), *Letters of the Kings of England* (London, 1848), II, 298–306.
57. Larkin, *Stuart Royal Proclamations*, II, 663, 665.
58. See chapter 5 of Hibbard's *Charles I and the Popish Plot*. Quotations in this paragraph are from p. 108.
59. Donald, *An Uncounselled King*, pp. 55, 71.

60. Gardiner, *History*, VIII, 321.
61. Donald, *An Uncounselled King*, p. 119.
62. Mark Charles Fissel, *The Bishops' Wars: Charles I's campaigns against Scotland, 1638–40* (Cambridge, 1994). For the negotiations at Berwick see also Donald, *An Uncounselled King*, pp. 152–61 and Stevenson, *Scottish Revolution*, pp. 151–61.
63. Fissel, *The Bishops' Wars*, pp. 19–33, 290; Marc L. Schwarz, 'Viscount Saye and Sele, Lord Brooke, and Aristocratic Protest to the First Bishops' War', *Canadian Journal of History*, 7, no. 1 (April 1972), 17–36.
64. Petrie, *Letters*, 104; Halliwell, *Letters*, II, 318–19.
65. Halliwell, *Letters*, II, 322–5; Stevenson, *Scottish Revolution*, pp. 162–75; Donald, *An Uncounselled King*, pp. 157–71; Gardiner, *History*, IX, 47–53, 93–4.

5   A Matter of Trust, 1640–1649

1. An excellent recent summary is Ann Hughes, *The Causes of the English Civil War* (New York, 1991).
2. Anthony Fletcher, *The Outbreak of the English Civil War* (New York, 1981). See especially pp. 33–4, 413–14.
3. John Morrill, *The Nature of the English Revolution* (London, 1993), pp. 6, 9, 69.
4. John Morrill, 'The English Civil Wars 1642–1649', *History Today*, 32 (Sept. 1982), 52. See also Morrill, *Reactions to the English Civil War, 1642–1649* (New York, 1983), pp. 2–4.
5. Conrad Russell, *Parliaments and English Politics 1621–1629* (Oxford, 1979), p. 423. Russell said this was one of Charles's 'few catastrophic errors', but he did not specify any others.
6. Richard Cust and Ann Hughes (eds), *Conflict in Early Stuart England: Studies in Religion and Politics 1603–1642* (London, 1989), pp. 11–12.
7. Conrad Russell (ed.), *The Origins of the English Civil War* (London, 1973), pp. 1–2.
8. Russell's review of Reeve's *Charles I and the Road to Personal Rule* (Cambridge, 1989), in *Historical Journal*, 34, no. 1 (1991), 225.
9. Conrad Russell, *The Causes of the English Civil War* (Oxford, 1990), p. viii.
10. Conrad Russell, *The Fall of the British Monarchies* (Oxford, 1991), p. 497; *Causes*, chapter 7, especially p. 166.
11. *Causes*, chapters 2 and 5; *Fall*, pp. 27–31.
12. *Causes*, p. 213.
13. Ibid., 14, 18, 121, 129–30, 155; *Fall*, 99–107, 121, 153, 205, 351, 405, 409, 412, 414, 445, 448, 495, 500, 513, 529–31.
14. *Causes*, pp. 182–3.
15. *Fall*, p. 530.
16. *Causes*, pp. 191–4.
17. *Fall*, pp. vii–viii.
18. *Causes*, p. 207.
19. Ibid., pp. 116, 200. See also *Fall*, p. 51.
20. *Causes*, pp. 200, 208.
21. Ibid., p. 198. See also *Fall*, p. 228.
22. *Causes*, pp. 204–5.
23. Ibid., p. 188; *Fall*, p. 300.
24. Conrad Russell, 'Why Did Charles I Fight the Civil War?', *History Today*, 34 (June 1984), 32–4; Conrad Russell, 'The First Army Plot of 1641', *Transactions of the Royal Historical Society*, fifth series, 38 (1988), 101.

25. G. E. Aylmer, review of Russell's *Fall* in *English Historical Review*, 107 (April 1992), 401–3.
26. *Causes*, pp. 194–6. See also *Fall*, pp. 5, 90, 208.
27. *Fall*, p. 530.
28. Ibid., pp. 39, 44.
29. *Causes*, p. 117.
30. Russell, *Parliaments*, p. 423.
31. *Causes*, p. 203; *Fall*, pp. 92, 206.
32. *Fall*, p. 30.
33. *Causes*, p. 107.
34. Ibid., pp. 112, 186.
35. Ibid. p. 188.
36. *Fall*, p. 525. See also *Causes*, p. 11.
37. Conrad Russell, 'The British Problem and the English Civil War', *History*, 71 (1987), 412.
38. *Causes*, p. 24. See also pp. 185–6.
39. Ibid., p. 212.
40. Ibid., p. 217.
41. Russell, 'The British Problem', p. 408.
42. Sharpe, *Personal Rule*, chapter 12 and pp. 842–7, 934–9.
43. Morrill, *Nature of the English Revolution*, p. 261.
44. There are three standard accounts of the Short Parliament: Russell, *Fall*, pp. 90–123; Sharpe, *Personal Rule*, pp. 851–77; S. R. Gardiner, *History of England from the Accession of James I to the Outbreak of the Civil War, 1603–1642* (10 vols, London, 1883–4, 1894–6), IX, 96–118.
45. Esther S. Cope and Willson H. Coates (eds), *Proceedings of the Short Parliament of 1640*, Camden Society fourth series, vol. 19 (London, 1977), pp. 78, 135, 138; Judith D. Maltby (ed.), *The Short Parliament (1640) Diary of Sir Thomas Aston*, Camden Society fourth series, vol. 35 (London, 1988), pp. 3, 42.
46. Cope, *Proceedings*, pp. 141, 214, 252.
47. Ibid., p. 155.
48. Ibid., pp. 142, 215.
49. Ibid., p. 195.
50. Ibid., p. 146.
51. Kevin Sharpe, *The Personal Rule of Charles I* (New Haven, CT, 1992), p. 859.
52. Cope, *Proceedings*, pp. 70, 264.
53. See, for example, ibid., pp. 70–1, 73, 74, 81, 166, 171, 178; Maltby, *Aston Diary*, pp. 29, 36, 38, 42, 63, 65.
54. Cope, *Proceedings*, pp. 81, 121, 237.
55. Ibid., p. 178. Compare p. 221.
56. Russell, *Fall*, p. 100.
57. For comments on this latter speech by Finch see Cope, *Proceedings*, p. 100.
58. Mark Fissel, 'Scottish War and English Money: the Short Parliament of 1640', in Fissel (ed.), *War and Government in Britain, 1598–1650* (Manchester, 1991), p. 199.
59. Cope, *Proceedings*, p. 95.
60. See, for example, Finch's speech in ibid., p. 133.
61. Ibid., pp. 69–70, 264–5.
62. Ibid., pp. 81, 177; Maltby, *Aston Diary*, p. 64.
63. Gardiner, *History*, IX, 87.
64. Cope, *Proceedings*, pp. 82–3, 102.
65. Russell, *Fall*, p. 111.
66. Cope, *Proceedings*, pp. 173, 190, 192, 207; Maltby, *Aston Diary*, pp. 122–3.
67. Fissel, 'Scottish War and English Money', pp. 205–12.
68. Cope, *Proceedings*, pp. 193–7; Maltby, *Aston Diary*, pp. 128–44.

69. Maltby, *Aston Diary*, pp. 144-5; Cope, *Proceedings*, 198, 210.
70. Sharpe, *Personal Rule*, pp. 877-81.
71. Maltby, *Aston Diary*, pp. 30-4, 50-4, 61-2, 87-8.
72. Russell, *Fall*, p. 125.
73. J. P. Kenyon, *The Stuart Constitution 1603–1688: Documents and Commentary*, 2nd edn (Cambridge, 1986), pp. 433-4; Russell, *Parliaments*, pp. 125-9; Gardiner, *History*, IX, 119-29.
74. For the Second Bishops' War see Mark Charles Fissel, *The Bishops' Wars: Charles I's campaigns against Scotland, 1638–40* (Cambridge, 1994), pp. 39-61. Kevin Sharpe thought Charles might still have avoided total defeat if his commander had not surrendered the city of Newcastle. *Personal Rule*, pp. 894-5.
75. Conrad Russell, 'Why Did Charles I Call the Long Parliament?', *History*, 69, no. 227 (Oct. 1984), 380, 382.
76. James Orchard Halliwell (ed.), *Letters of the Kings of England* (London, 1848), II, 295; Charles Petric (ed.), *The Letters, Speeches, and Proclamations of King Charles I* (London, 1968), p. 98.
77. Gardiner, *History*, IX, 236, 243, 246-7, 289, 298.
78. Kenyon, *Stuart Constitution*, pp. 17-18.
79. For the events of this conciliatory phase see Gardiner, *History*, IX, 257-301, chapter 1 of Fletcher's *Outbreak*, and chapter 6 of Russell's *Fall*.
80. Halliwell, *Letters*, II, 327; Petrie, *Letters*, p. 115.
81. Gardiner, *History*, IX, 346.
82. Ibid., IX, 367.
83. Petrie, *Letters*, p. 116; Halliwell, *Letters*, II, 328-9.
84. On the subject of Charles's conscience in general and the decision regarding Strafford in particular, see Keith Thomas, 'Cases of Conscience in Seventeenth-Century England' and Patricia Crawford, 'Public Duty, Conscience, and Women in Early Modern England', in John Morrill and others (eds), *Public Duty and Private Conscience in Seventeenth-Century England: Essays Presented to G. E. Aylmer* (Oxford, 1993), pp. 33, 61.
85. Conrad Russell, 'The First Army Plot of 1641', *Transactions of the Royal Historical Society*, fifth series, 38 (1988), 85-106, quoting p. 100.
86. Russell, *Fall*, pp. 291-302, quoting p. 301.
87. The Ten Propositions are printed in Kenyon, *Stuart Constitution*, pp. 201-4 and S. R. Gardiner (ed.), *Constitutional Documents of the Puritan Revolution 1625-1660*, 3rd edn revised (Oxford, 1906), pp. 163-6.
88. In Russell's words, it had become essential 'that Charles should never recover the full power to govern'. *Fall*, p. 333. See also pp. 412, 414.
89. Russell, *Causes*, p. 118; Russell, *Fall*, p. 168.
90. Russell, *Fall*, p. 530.
91. Ibid., p. 405.
92. Ibid., p. 414.
93. Ibid., pp. 333, 529.
94. Russell, *Causes*, p. 160.
95. For a good critique of the narrow focus on elite or high politics, see Thomas Cogswell's 'Underground Verse and the Transformation of Early Stuart Political Culture', in Susan D. Amussen and Mark Kishlansky (eds), *Political Culture and Cultural Politics in Early Modern England: Essays Presented to David Underdown* (Manchester, 1995), pp. 277-95.
96. John Morrill, *Nature of the English Revolution*, p. 10. See also Morrill's 'The Religious Context of the English Civil War', 'The Attack on the Church of England in the Long Parliament', and 'The Causes of Britain's Civil Wars' in ibid., pp. 45-68, 69-90, 252-72.
97. Russell, *Fall*, p. 201 and chapter 8; Peter Donald, *An Uncounselled King: Charles I and the Scottish troubles 1637-1641* (Cambridge, 1990), pp. 308-19.

98. M. Perceval-Maxwell, *The Outbreak of the Irish Rebellion of 1641* (Montreal, 1994), p. 290. See also chapter 10 of Russell's *Fall* and his article, 'The British Background to the Irish Rebellion of 1641', *Historical Research*, 61, no. 145 (June 1988), 166–82.

99. In addition to the sources in the preceding note, see the exchange between Perceval-Maxwell and Jane H. Ohlmeyer in *Historical Journal*, 37, no. 2 (1994) and Ohlmeyer's *Civil War and Restoration in the Three Stuart Kingdoms: The Career of Randal MacDonnell, Marquis of Antrim, 1609–1683* (Cambridge, 1993).

100. Russell, *Fall*, p. 531.

101. Gardiner, *Constitutional Documents*, pp. 202–32, quoting p. 203.

102. 'His Majesty's Declaration to all His Loving Subjects, of the 12 of Aug. 1642', printed in *The Works of King Charles the Martyr*, 2nd edn (London, 1687), p. 295.

103. J. S. A. Adamson thinks the arrest of the bishops was the pivotal event for Charles. 'Parliamentary Management, Men-of-Business and the House of Lords, 1640–49', in Clyve Jones (ed.), *A Pillar of the Constitution: The House of Lords in British Politics, 1640–1784* (London, 1989), p. 28.

104. For a description and analysis of the atmosphere in London at this time see chapter 4 of Brian Manning's *The English People and the English Revolution 1640–1649* (London, 1976).

105. Russell, *Fall*, pp. 447–9. As Gardiner expressed it, 'they were guilty of treason at least as much as Strafford had been guilty'. *History*, X, 129.

106. In the proclamation Charles issued for the apprehension of the five members, he declared that there was 'in us no intention at all to use any force against them, or any of them, but to proceed against them in a legall, faire way'. James F. Larkin (ed.), *Stuart Royal Proclamations*, vol. II, *Royal Proclamations of King Charles I 1625–1646* (Oxford, 1983), p. 758.

107. Gardiner, *History*, IX, 134.

108. Fletcher, *Outbreak*, p. 181.

109. Charles Carlton, *Charles I: The Personal Monarch*, 2nd edn (London, 1995), pp. 232, 236.

110. Russell, *Fall*, p. 445.

111. Manning, *The English People*, p. 96.

112. Morrill, *Nature of the English Revolution*, p. 265; Carlton, *Charles I*, p. 234.

113. Edward Hyde, Earl of Clarendon, *The History of the Rebellion and Civil Wars in England*, ed. W. Dunn Macray (Oxford, 1888), I, 508.

114. Ibid., I, 590.

115. Morrill, *Nature of the English Revolution*, p. 62.

116. Kenyon, *Stuart Constitution*, p. 19.

117. *Causes*, p. 121. Compare chapters 13 and 14 of Russell's *Fall* and his 'Why Did Charles I Fight the Civil War?', *History Today*, 34 (June 1984), 31–4.

118. Morrill, *Nature of the English Revolution*, p. 85.

119. Conrad Russell, 'Issues in the House of Commons, 1621–1629: Predictors of Civil War Allegiance', *Albion*, 23, no. 1 (Spring 1991), 23–39. For a rejoinder see Wilfrid Prest, 'Civil War Allegiances: The Lawyer's Case Considered', *Albion*, 24, no. 2 (Summer 1992), 225–36.

120. Morrill, *Nature of the English Revolution*, p. 44. See also pp. 45–68.

121. Halliwell, *Letters*, II, 358.

122. Very controversial statistics have been available since the 1950s. See D. Brunton and D. H. Pennington, *Members of the Long Parliament* (London, 1954), pp. 1, 2, 16 and Mary Frear Keeler, *The Long Parliament, 1640–1641: A Biographical Study of its Members* (Philadelphia, 1954). Although the exact allegiances and statistical correlations proposed by these authors have been seriously criticised, it appears that no more than 302 out of slightly more than 500 original members of the Commons stayed behind to continue serving in the Long Parliament. An even

smaller proportion of the peers, somewhere between one-fifth and one-quarter, continued to function in the Lords.

123. 'His Majesty's Declaration', in *Works*, p. 314.
124. John Morrill (ed.), *Reactions to the English Civil War 1642–1649* (New York, 1983), p. 19.
125. Maurice Ashley, *The Battle of Naseby and the Fall of King Charles I* (New York, 1992), p. 158.
126. Joyce Malcolm, 'A King in Search of Soldiers: Charles I in 1642', *Historical Journal*, 21, no. 2 (1978), 251–73.
127. M. D. G. Wanklyn and P. Young, 'A King in Search of Soldiers: Charles I in 1642. A Rejoinder', *Historical Journal*, 24, no. 1 (1981), 147–54; P. R. Newman, 'The Royalist Officer Corps 1642–1660: Army Command as a Reflexion of the Social Structure', *Historical Journal*, 26, no. 4 (1983), 945–58; Ronald Hutton, *The Royalist War Effort 1642–1646* (London, 1982).
128. Hutton, *Royalist War Effort*, pp. 26, 31.
129. Charles Carlton, *Going to the Wars: The Experience of the British Civil Wars 1638–1651* (London, 1992), pp. 186–7.
130. See, for example, Philip Tennant, *Edgehill and Beyond: The People's War in the South Midlands 1642–1645* (Phoenix Mill, Stroud, Glos., 1992), pp. 62, 275–7.
131. Kevin Sharpe, 'The King's Writ: Royal Authors and Royal Authority in Early Modern England', in Kevin Sharpe and Peter Lake (eds), *Culture and Politics in Early Stuart England* (Stanford, CA, 1993), p. 135.
132. Robert Ashton, *The English Civil War: Conservatism and Revolution 1603–1649* (New York, 1979), pp. 206–14; Ian Roy, 'The Royalist Council of War, 1642–6', *Bulletin of the Institute of Historical Research*, 35 (1962), 150–68.
133. James Daly argued that Hutton exaggerated these polarities in 'The Implications of Royalist Politics, 1642–1646', *Historical Journal*, 27, no. 3 (1984), 745–55.
134. Hutton, *Royalist War Effort*, p. 203. See also Hutton, 'The Royalist War Effort', in Morrill, *Reactions*, pp. 51–66.
135. S. R. Gardiner, *History of the Great Civil War 1642–1649* (London, 1904), I, 67–8; II, 62–4; G. E. Aylmer, *Rebellion or Revolution? England from Civil War to Restoration* (Oxford, 1986), p. 51.
136. Gardiner, *Great Civil War*, I, 43.
137. J. P. Kenyon, *The Civil Wars of England* (New York, 1988), p. 60.
138. Ibid., pp. 81–4; Gardiner, *Great Civil War*, I, 197–218.
139. Gardiner, *Great Civil War*, I, 201–2, 246; Carlton, *Charles I*, p. 258–9.
140. Compare Kenyon, *Civil Wars*, pp. 90–1 with Joyce Lee Malcolm, 'All the King's Men: the Impact of the Crown's Irish Soldiers on the English Civil War', *Irish Historical Studies*, 22, no. 83 (March 1979), 239–64.
141. John Morrill has written a sensible re-evaluation of Pym. See 'The Unwearifulness of Mr Pym: Influence and Eloquence in the Long Parliament', in Amussen and Kishlansky, *Political Culture and Cultural Politics*, pp. 19–54.
142. Kenyon, *Civil Wars*, pp. 102–3.
143. Hutton, *Royalist War Effort*, p.146.
144. Gardiner, *Great Civil War*, I, 351, 362; II, 10–19; Clarendon, *History of the Rebellion*, IV, 489–90. See also Carlton, *Going to the Wars*, pp. 197, 243–4.
145. Hutton, 'Royalist War Effort', pp. 62–3 and *Royalist War Effort*, p. 178.
146. Ashley, *Battle of Naseby*, pp. 64–5, 77, 92–8.
147. Halliwell, *Letters*, II, 387.
148. Gardiner, *Great Civil War*, II, 316–18, 372–5; Petrie, *Letters*, 156–8; Halliwell, *Letters*, II, 391–5.
149. All these are printed in Gardiner, *Constitutional Documents*, pp. 262–7, 275–87, 290–306.
150. Ibid., pp. 316–27; Petrie, *Letters*, p. 230.

151. Halliwell, *Letters*, II, 442.
152. Petrie, *Letters*, pp. 172, 208–10, 216–17.
153. Halliwell, *Letters*, II, 389.
154. Ibid., II, 431.
155. Ibid., II, 336.
156. Petrie, *Letters*, p. 206.
157. The persons Parliament wanted to exclude were listed in the Propositions of Newcastle. Gardiner, *Constitutional Documents*, pp. 298–9; Petrie, *Letters*, p. 218.
158. Halliwell, *Letters*, II, 430.
159. Ibid., II, 430; Petrie, *Letters*, pp. 206, 217.
160. Petrie, *Letters*, pp. 174, 204–7.
161. Halliwell, *Letters*, II, 426.
162. Petrie, *Letters*, p. 204.
163. Gardiner, *Great Civil War*, II, 59.
164. Halliwell, *Letters*, II, 336.
165. Petrie, *Letters*, p. 176.
166. Ibid., p. 200.
167. Robert Ashton, *Counter-Revolution: The Second Civil War and its Origins, 1646–8* (New Haven, CT, 1994).
168. Gardiner, *Great Civil War*, IV, 220–5.
169. Patricia Crawford, ' "Charles Stuart, That Man of Blood"', *Journal of British Studies*, 16, no. 2 (Spring 1977), 41–61. See also 'The Man of Blood' in Christopher Hill, *The English Bible and the Seventeenth-Century Revolution* (London, 1993), pp. 324–31.
170. David Underdown, *Pride's Purge: Politics in the Puritan Revolution* (Oxford, 1971), pp. 210–13.
171. Samuel M. Koenigsberg, 'The Vote to Create the High Court of Justice: 26 to 20?' *Parliamentary History*, 12, no. 3 (1993), 281–6.
172. Gardiner, *Constitutional Documents*, p. 357.
173. Petrie, *Letters*, p. 252.
174. The classic account is C. V. Wedgwood, *A Coffin for King Charles: The Trial and Execution of Charles I* (New York, 1966).
175. The charge is printed in Gardiner, *Constitutional Documents*, pp. 371–4 and Petrie, *Letters*, pp. 241–3.
176. Petrie, *Letters*, pp. 248–9, 253–4; Roger Lockyer (ed.), *The Trial of Charles I* (London, 1959), pp. 88–9, 93. See also the king's explanation printed shortly after his execution. Gardiner, *Constitutional Documents*, pp. 374–6; Kenyon, *Stuart Constitution*, pp. 292–3; Petrie, *Letters*, pp. 259–61.
177. Lockyer, *Trial*, pp. 111–15.
178. Petrie, *Letters*, p. 258.
179. Ibid., p. 251.
180. Ibid., p. 245.
181. For the development of ascending and descending theories of authority during the Civil War, see John Sanderson, *'But the People's Creatures': The Philosophical Basis of the English Civil War* (Manchester, 1989).
182. Kenyon, *Stuart Constitution*, pp. 293–5.
183. The king's final thoughts were also represented in a letter he gave to Juxon to convey to the Prince of Wales (printed in Petrie, *Letters*, pp. 261–73). Almost simultaneously with his execution a book appeared which purported to be his personal memoir of the 1640s, though historians question its true authorship. Philip A. Knachel (ed.), *Eikon Basilike: The Portraiture of His Sacred Majesty in His Solitudes and Sufferings* (Ithaca, NY, 1966).

Conclusion

1. In remarks during an appearance at the University of Illinois in 1989. Of course see also his *The Practice of History* (New York, 1967).
2. Kevin Sharpe wrote: 'If the Old Guard is to stand, it will have to do more than rally around the flag. It will need to answer evidence with evidence.' Sharpe, 'An Unwanted Civil War?' *The New York Review of Books*, 2 Dec. 1982, p. 45. Conrad Russell wrote: 'If [American] scholars think most of the work done in England is wrong, it is always open to them to publish a detailed, factual refutation, from which a new dialogue might begin.' Russell, 'Communications' section of the *American Historical Review*, 88, no. 4 (Oct. 1983), 1141.
3. Of course favourable references to Gardiner can be found scattered throughout the literature, but they tend to be qualified and tepid. Richard Cust is exceptional in noting the trend back toward Gardiner's views and giving him due credit for having been right in the first place. See chapter 2 above.
4. L. J. Reeve, *Charles I and the Road to Personal Rule* (Cambridge, 1989), p. 4.
5. Charles Carlton, *Charles I: The Personal Monarch*, 2nd edn (London, 1995), pp. xiv and xviii.
6. Reeve, *Charles I*, p. 173.
7. Glenn Burgess, *The Politics of the Ancient Constitution: An Introduction to English Political Thought 1603–1642* (University Park, PA, 1992), p. 200.
8. C. V. Wedgwood, *A Coffin for King Charles: The Trial and Execution of Charles I* (New York, 1966), p. 180.
9. Reeve, *Charles I*, pp. 3, 173.
10. Conrad Russell, *The Causes of the English Civil War* (Oxford, 1990), p. 207.
11. As noted in the chapters above, Kevin Sharpe has made important contributions in this respect. Several good examples of this broader cultural approach can also be found in Susan D. Amussen and Mark Kishlansky (eds), *Political Culture and Cultural Politics in Early Modern England: Essays Presented to David Underdown* (Manchester, 1995). An older but valuable contribution from intellectual history is Stephen L. Collins, *From Divine Cosmos to Sovereign State: An Intellectual History of Consciousness and the Idea of Order in Renaissance England* (Oxford, 1989).
12. Thomas Cogswell, 'Underground Verse and the Transformation of Early Stuart Political Culture', in Amussen and Kishlansky, *Political Culture and Cultural Politics*, p. 295.
13. Conrad Russell, 'The British Problem and the English Civil War', *History*, 71 (1987), 412.

FURTHER READING

General

In view of the voluminous endnotes for the chapters above, we will list here only the most general and important works. For more specialised works refer to the appropriate endnotes.

There are two good modern biographies of King Charles I: Pauline Gregg's *King Charles I* (Berkeley, CA, 1981) and Charles Carlton's *Charles I: The Personal Monarch*, 2nd edn (London, 1995). Conrad Russell wrote a perceptive character sketch of Charles entitled 'That Man Charles Stuart', which is chapter 8 in *The Causes of the English Civil War* (Oxford, 1990). Other good short sketches can be found at the beginning of chapter 6 in L. J. Reeve's *Charles I and the Road to Personal Rule* (Cambridge, 1989) and the end of chapter 4 in Kevin Sharpe's *The Personal Rule of Charles I* (New Haven, CT, 1992). Despite all the recent work on Charles's reign, there is still nothing quite like S. R. Gardiner's encyclopaedic 10-volume *History of England from the Accession of James I to the Outbreak of the Civil War, 1603–1642* (London, 1883–4, 1894–6). It is a *tour de force* of organisation with sub-headings printed on every page, often helpfully accompanied by dates; just a quick look at the detailed index in volume 10 can answer many questions of fact.

A sampling of writings by Charles himself is available in Charles Petrie's edition of *The Letters, Speeches, and Proclamations of King Charles I* (London, 1968). An earlier collection can be found in volume 2 of James Orchard Halliwell's *Letters of the Kings of England* (London, 1848). Another valuable source is James F. Larkin's edition of the *Royal Proclamations of King Charles I 1625–1646* (Oxford, 1983). Other key documents for this period are handily available in S. R. Gardiner's *Constitutional Documents of the Puritan Revolution 1625–1660*, 3rd edn revised (Oxford, 1906) and J. P. Kenyon's *The Stuart Constitution 1603–1688: Documents and Commentary*, 2nd edn (Cambridge, 1986).

Prior Commitments

Two major works dominate this period, though both are also written with a strong bias: Conrad Russell's *Parliaments and English Politics, 1621–1629* (Oxford, 1979) and Roger Lockyer's *Buckingham: The Life and Political Career of George Villiers, First Duke of Buckingham 1592–1628* (London, 1981). For balance see the following other works. For the Parliament of 1624 there is Robert E. Ruigh's *The Parliament of 1624* (Cambridge, MA, 1971) and Thomas Cogswell's more recent *The Blessed Revolution: English Politics and the Coming of War, 1621–1624* (Cambridge, 1989). For the period in general see also the articles by Cogswell cited above in chapters 2 and 3 as well as his forthcoming book on Parliaments and war in the 1620s. Other provocative essays relative to this period can be found in Kevin Sharpe (ed.), *Faction and Parliament: Essasys on Early Stuart History* (Oxford, 1978) and Howard Tomlinson (ed.), *Before the English Civil War: Essays in Early Stuart Politics and Government* (London, 1983). For foreign policy see especially Simon Adams's 'Foreign Policy and the Parliaments of 1621 and 1624' in the former anthology and his 'Spain or the Netherlands? Dilemmas of Early Stuart Foreign Policy' in the latter anthology.

A Bad Start, 1625–1629

Russell's *Parliaments and English Politics* is still the central work for this period. Several of his articles have also been collected in one volume under the title of *Unrevolutionary England, 1603–1642* (London, 1990). The two most prominent alternative views of Charles I are Richard Cust's *The Forced Loan and English Politics* (Oxford, 1987) and L. J. Reeve's *Charles I and the Road to Personal Rule* (Cambridge, 1989). Also valuable are the several articles by Cust cited in chapter 2 above and the anthology he edited with Ann Hughes entitled *Conflict in Early Stuart England: Studies in Religion and Politics 1603–1642* (London, 1989). In this anthology see especially the introduction and Christopher Thompson's 'Court Politics and Parliamentary Conflict in 1625'. An influential article is J. A. Guy's 'The Origins of the Petition of Right Reconsidered', *Historical Journal*, 25 (1982). Several of the articles in Sharpe's *Faction and*

Parliament are relevant to this period, especially Derek Hirst's 'Court, Country, and Politics before 1629', J. N. Ball's 'Sir John Eliot and Parliament, 1624–1629', Kevin Sharpe's 'The Earl of Arundel, His Circle and the Opposition to the Duke of Buckingham, 1618–1628', and Christopher Thompson's 'The Divided Leadership of the House of Commons in 1629'. A controversial effort to resurrect the role of ideas in the politics of the period is J. P. Sommerville's *Politics and Ideology in England 1603–1640* (London, 1986). Along these same lines see Glenn Burgess's *The Politics of the Ancient Constitution: An Introduction to English Political Thought 1603–1642* (University Park, PA, 1992).

The parliamentary sources for this period are unusually rich and readily accessible in the magnificent volumes published through the Yale Center for Parliamentary History. Historians and students have barely begun to explore the possibilities in these: Maija Jansson and William B. Bidwell (eds), *Proceedings in Parliament 1625* (New Haven, CT, 1987); William B. Bidwell and Maija Jansson (eds), *Proceedings in Parliament 1626* (New Haven, CT, 1992); Robert C. Johnson, Maija Jansson Cole, Mary Frear Keeler, and William B. Bidwell (eds), *Commons Debates 1628* (New Haven, CT, 1977). For 1629 there is the earlier *Commons Debates for 1629* (Minneapolis, 1921), ed. Wallace Notestein and Helen Relf.

The Personal Rule I

The starting-point for the personal rule is Kevin Sharpe's mammoth *The Personal Rule of Charles I* (New Haven, CT, 1992). Much briefer and more traditional is Esther Cope's *Politics Without Parliaments 1629–1640* (London, 1987). For the origins of the personal rule compare Reeve's *Charles I and the Road to Personal Rule* and 'The Arguments in King's Bench in 1629 concerning the Imprisonment of John Selden and Other Members of the House of Commons', *Journal of British Studies*, 25, no. 3 (July 1986).

The culture of Charles's court is a burgeoning topic. A few of the major works are Roy Strong's *Van Dyck: Charles I on Horseback* (New York, 1972); Stephen Orgel's *The Illusion of Power: Political Theater in the English Renaissance* (Berkeley, CA, 1975); and R. Malcolm Smuts's *Court Culture and the Origins of a Royalist Tradition in Early Stuart*

England (Philadelphia, 1987). See also Sharpe's *Criticism and Compliment: The Politics of Literature in the England of Charles I* (Cambridge, 1987); the collection of his essays entitled *Politics and Ideas in Early Stuart England: Essays and Studies* (London, 1989); and the volume he edited with Peter Lake entitled *Culture and Politics in Early Stuart England* (Stanford, CA, 1993).

One almost has to go back to Gardiner to find anything like Sharpe's treatment of foreign policy in the 1630s. Two relevant and more recent articles are A. J. Loomie's 'The Spanish Faction at the Court of Charles I, 1630–8', *Bulletin of the Institute of Historical Research*, 59 (May 1986) and R. Malcolm Smuts's 'The Puritan Followers of Henrietta Maria in the 1630s', *English Historical Review*, 93 (Jan. 1978).

In the area of domestic policy, see G. E. Aylmer's *The King's Servants: The Civil Service of Charles I 1625–1642* (London, 1961) and 'Attempts at Administrative Reform, 1625–40', *English Historical Review*, 72 (April 1957). More recent and specialised are Kenneth R. Andrews, *Ships, Money and Politics: Seafaring and Naval Enterprise in the Reign of Charles I* (Cambridge, 1991) and Brian W. Quintrell, 'The Making of Charles I's Book of Orders', *English Historical Review*, 95 (July 1980). For the king's relations with the business community see Valerie Pearl's *London and the Outbreak of the Puritan Revolution: City Government and National Politics, 1625–43* (Oxford, 1961); Robert Ashton's *The City and the Court 1603–1643* (Cambridge, 1979); and Robert Brenner's *Merchants and Revolution: Commercial Change, Political Conflict, and London's Overseas Traders, 1550–1650* (Princeton, NJ, 1993).

The Personal Rule II

In the area of religion, Arminianism has received a great deal of attention beginning with Nicholas Tyacke's *Anti-Calvinists: The Rise of English Arminianism c.1590–1640* (Oxford, 1987). The chief rebuttals are Peter White's *Predestination, Policy and Polemic: Conflict and Consensus in the English Church from the Reformation to the Civil War* (Cambridge, 1992) and Julian Davies's *The Caroline Captivity of the Church: Charles I and the Remoulding of Anglicanism 1625–1641* (Oxford, 1992). A good introduction to the current state of the debate can be found in Kenneth Fincham (ed.), *The Early Stuart Church* (Stanford, CA, 1993). For anti-popery see Caroline Hibbard's *Charles I and the Popish Plot* (Chapel Hill, NC, 1983).

Three good readable introductions to the personal rule in Scotland are Maurice Lee Jr's *The Road to Revolution: Scotland Under Charles I, 1625–37* (Urbana, IL, 1985); Keith M. Brown's *Kingdom or Province? Scotland and the Regal Union, 1603–1715* (New York, 1992); and the first chapter of David Stevenson's *The Scottish Revolution 1637–1644* (New York, 1973). There is a good historiographical overview toward the end of Brown's 'Aristocratic Finances and the Origins of the Scottish Revolution', *English Historical Review*, 104 (Jan. 1989), although it was written before the appearance of Peter Donald's *An Uncounselled King: Charles I and the Scottish troubles 1637–1641* (Cambridge, 1990) and Allan I. Macinnes's *Charles I and the Making of the Covenanting Movement 1625–1641* (Edinburgh, 1991). These recent studies are important but far from perfect. For balance see chapter 13 of Sharpe's *Personal Rule* and chapter 1 of Conrad Russell's *The Fall of the British Monarchies 1637–1642* (Oxford, 1991). See also Russell's influential article, 'The British Problem and the English Civil War', *History*, 72 (1987), 395–415. For the Bishops' Wars, the authority now is Mark Charles Fissel, *The Bishops' Wars: Charles I's campaigns against Scotland 1638–1640* (Cambridge, 1994).

A Matter of Trust, 1640–1649

A highly readable and perceptive survey of this period is G. E. Aylmer's *Rebellion or Revolution? England from Civil War to Restoration* (Oxford, 1986). The best survey of the historiographical debate regarding the causes of the civil wars is Ann Hughes's *The Causes of the English Civil War* (New York, 1991). More advanced readers should tackle Conrad Russell's *Causes of the English Civil War* (Oxford, 1990). Several stimulating essays by John Morrill have been collected in a volume entitled *The Nature of the English Revolution* (London, 1993). For the actual course of events leading up to the outbreak of war see Conrad Russell's *Fall of the British Monarchies* (Oxford, 1991) and Anthony Fletcher's *The Outbreak of the English Civil War* (New York, 1981). For the Irish Rebellion see M. Perceval-Maxwell's *The Outbreak of the Irish Rebellion of 1641* (Montreal, 1994) and Jane Ohlmeyer's

Civil War and Restoration in the Three Stuart Kingdoms: The Career of Randal MacDonnell, Marquis of Antrim, 1609–1683 (Cambridge, 1993).

For anyone interested in the published sources of the Short Parliament, there are two excellent volumes: Esther S. Cope and Willson H. Coates (eds), *Proceedings of the Short Parliament of 1640*, Camden Society fourth series, vol. 19 (London, 1977) and Judith D. Maltby (ed.), *The Short Parliament (1640) Diary of Sir Thomas Aston*, Camden Society fourth series, vol. 35 (London, 1988). Although, as John Morrill has warned, it should be used with caution, Sir Simonds D'Ewes's diary of the Long Parliament has been published in three segments edited by Wallace Notestein (New Haven, CT, 1923), Willson Coates (New Haven, CT, 1942) and Vernon F. Snow and Anne Steele Young (New Haven, CT, 1992). Maija Jansson has also edited *Two Diaries of the Long Parliament* (New York, 1984).

On the subject of the civil wars two classics are still useful: the Earl of Clarendon's *History of the Rebellion and Civil Wars in England*, ed. W. Dunn Macray in six volumes (Oxford, 1888) and S. R. Gardiner's four-volume *History of the Great Civil War 1642–1649* (London, 1904). For a strictly military history see *The English Civil War: A Military History of the Three Civil Wars* (London, 1974) by Peter Young and Richard Holmes. A valuable study that focuses on the king and his armed forces is Ronald Hutton's *The Royalist War Effort 1642–1646* (London, 1982). We know much more about the politics of Westminster in this period than the politics of the king and his court-in-exile at Oxford, but Robert Ashton illuminates both in *The English Civil War: Conservatism and Revolution 1603–1649* (New York, 1979). For the Second Civil War the indispensable authority is now Robert Ashton's *Counter-Revolution: The Second Civil War and its Origins, 1646–8* (New Haven, CT, 1994). For the king's viewpoint at a critical juncture see J. Bruce (ed.), *Charles I in 1646: Letters of King Charles the First to Queen Henrietta Maria*, Camden Society, old series, 63 (London, 1856).

For the background to the king's trial and execution see David Underdown's *Pride's Purge: Politics in the Puritan Revolution* (Oxford, 1971). Roger Lockyer edited key sources for the trial in *The Trial of Charles I* (London, 1959), and C. V. Wedgwood provided a vivid account in *A Coffin for King Charles: The Trial and Execution of Charles I* (New York, 1966).

INDEX

218

Saw Palmetto